MORE PRAISE FOR THE NEW CHRISTIANS

"No one I know is better equipped than Tony Jones to write an insider's history of emergent churches. Tony brings to his work deep, intuitive, first-hand observations. His bright intellect and inherent goodness and fair-mindedness make him an especially appropriate advocate and critic. *The New Christians* is a joy to read. It both challenged and inspired me. It made me miss old friends and caused me to re-cherish Emergent's vision 'to follow God in the Way of Jesus.'"

—Todd Hunter, national director, Alpha USA, and former president, Vineyard Churches USA

"Tony Jones pulls no punches in calling for new ways of being church—and after reading this book I have a few bruises to show for it! But it was well worth the scuffle. This is a challenging and engaging call to think new thoughts about what it means to be faithful to the Gospel in our present context."

—Richard J. Mouw, president and professor of Christian philosophy, Fuller Theological Seminary

"This is an insider's journal of the journey called emergent Christianity, and it is the book I have been looking for. If you want to know what emergent Christianity is, buy this book, read it, talk about it and then give it to someone else. But don't leave it around—someone will swipe it!"

—Scot McKnight, Karl A. Olsson Professor in Religion Studies, North Park University, and author, *A Community Called Atonement*

"There is indeed new life arising from the compost of Christendom. Tony's book lets us see it, smell it, and touch it. The challenge with a book like this is neither to be overcome by the smell of the poop, nor stupefied by the beauty of a

flower—more than anything we must see this book as an invitation to get our hands dirty, break a sweat, get messy outside the air-conditioned walls of comfort, and not just read more books on gardening."
—Shane Clairborne, author, activist, and recovering sinner

"The emergent church, which Tony Jones describes for us in this book, must be taken seriously. Offering both hope and challenges for the rest of us, this postmodern version of Christianity will certainly change the face of the religious landscape."
—Tony Campolo, Eastern University, and coauthor, *The God of Intimacy and Action*

"There is simply no way to think about the future of the church without knowing of the emergent journey. Tony will give you an all-access tour from the inside."
—John Ortberg, author and pastor, Menlo Park Presbyterian Church

"Tony Jones relentlessly and rightly challenges us to examine what Christianity *means* in our historical context. The more you might have questions or possible disagreements with Tony or emergent ideas, the more you need to read *The New Christians*."
—Bruce Ellis Benson, professor of philosophy, Wheaton College

"Lots of people have questions about just what this emergent church thing is all about. Tony Jones has the answer for them here. A great starting point for understanding a significant movement."
—Christian Smith, William R. Kenan Jr. Professor of Sociology and Director of the Center for the Study of Religion and Society at the University of Notre Dame, and author, *Soul Searching: The Religious and Spiritual Lives of American Teenagers*

THE NEW CHRISTIANS

THE NEW CHRISTIANS

DISPATCHES FROM THE EMERGENT FRONTIER

TONY JONES

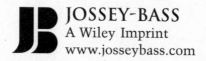
JOSSEY-BASS
A Wiley Imprint
www.josseybass.com

Published by Jossey-Bass
A Wiley Imprint
989 Market Street, San Francisco, CA 94103-1741   www.josseybass.com

Jossey-Bass books and products are available through most bookstores. To contact Jossey-Bass directly call our Customer Care Department within the U.S. at 800-956-7739, outside the U.S. at 317-572-3986, or fax 317-572-4002.

Jossey-Bass also publishes its books in a variety of electronic formats. Some content that appears in print may not be available in electronic books.

Library of Congress Cataloging-in-Publication Data

Jones, Tony, date
   The new Christians : dispatches from the emergent frontier / Tony
Jones. — 1st ed.
      p. cm.
   Includes bibliographical references and index.
   ISBN-13: 978-0-7879-9471-6 (cloth)
   ISBN-13: 978-0-4704-5539-5 (paperback)
   1. Christianity—21st century. 2. Emerging church movement. 3.
Postmodernism—Religious aspects—Christianity.   I.   Title.
   BR121.3.J665 2008
   270.8′3—dc22

                                                    2007038030

Printed in the United States of America
FIRST EDITION
HB Printing   10 9 8 7 6 5 4 3 2 1
PB Printing   10 9 8 7 6 5 4 3 2 1

A LIVING WAY
emergent visions

Soul Graffiti: Making a Life in the Way of Jesus by Mark Scandrette

The New Christians: Dispatches from the Emergent Frontier by Tony Jones

A Christianity Worth Believing: Hope-Filled, Open-Armed, Alive-and-Well Faith for the Left Out, Left Behind, and Let Down in Us All, by Doug Pagitt

Contents

"A LIVING WAY: Emergent Visions" Series Foreword   xiii

PREFACE   xv

INTRODUCTION: What Is "Emergent"?   xvii

CHAPTER 1 ~ Leaving the Old Country   1

4   "Church Is Dead"

5   Signs of Death—and Life

7   The Problem on the Left

10   A Case Study: Go Where I Send Thee

11   The Problem on the Right

13   A Case Study: Don't Ask Us About the Chickens

18   The *Real* Problem: Left Versus Right

21   Caught in the *Crossfire*

24   **Dispatch from the Blogosphere:** Musings of a Postmodern Negro

CHAPTER 2 ~ Dispatches from the Frontier of the American Church   31

31   An Allegory

33   An Alternative Ending

35   Geological Musings

37   What Exactly Is Emerging?

41   The Beginnings

43   "The Bible Is Propaganda"

49   The *New Kind of Christian* Effect

52   Meanwhile, Across the Pond

55   Then till Now

57   The Church's Choice

60   **Dispatch from the Rocky Mountains:** Katie and Kristen

CHAPTER 3 ~ Who Are the Emergent Christians?   67

68   Hunches and Intuitions

72   Influencing Culture or Influenced by Culture?

76   An "Envelope of Friendship"

80   An Emergent Voters' Guide

86   **Dispatch from I-35:** The Terrific Tale of Trucker Frank

CHAPTER 4 ~ The Theology, Stupid   95

96   Dartmouth Days

104   What, Exactly, Is Theology?

106   Theology on the Rise

111   Going Deep

115   Skiing the Slippery Slope

123   So, a Biblicist and a Relativist Walk into a Pastors' Conference . . .

130   The Expurgated Lectionary

134   **Dispatch from Seminary:** Legalisms of the Left

CHAPTER 5 ~ After Objectivity: Beautiful Truth   139

140   The Thrill of Interpretation

143   Reading the *Whole* Bible

148   "Sonny, It Ain't Nothing till I Call It"

152 Truth (a.k.a. God)

155 After Objectivity: Dialogue

157 Beautiful, Messy, Incarnational Truth

162 Paradoxes

170 **Dispatch from the End of a Three-Mile Dirt Road:** Recovering "Church"

CHAPTER 6 ~ Inside the Emergent Church   175

175 It's a Great Day at Jacob's Well!

180 Wikichurch

192 Tightly Knit: Journey

201 Binitarians

203 The People's Liturgy: Church of the Apostles

209 Time to Rethink Seminary

210 MyChurch: A Paean to Solomon's Porch

EPILOGUE: Feral Christians   219

APPENDICES   221

222 Appendix A: "Emergent Village Values and Practices"

227 Appendix B: "A Response to Our Critics"

233 Appendix C: "Disastrous Statements"

NOTES   237

ACKNOWLEDGMENTS   253

THE AUTHOR   255

INDEX   257

"A Living Way: Emergent Visions" Series Foreword

For a decade now, a group of friends has been gathering under the banner "Emergent Village: a growing, generative friendship of missional Christian leaders." The friends within Emergent Village share life in profound ways, care for one another, and laugh a lot as they together forge a way to follow God in the way of Jesus Christ for the twenty-first century. Out of this cauldron of friendship and disillusion with religion-as-usual have come some ideas and some practices that have influenced the church in North America and around the world. New ways of being Christian, of being spiritual, of following God have bubbled up in this group.

"A Living Way: Emergent Visions" is a partnership between Emergent Village and Jossey-Bass/Wiley to capture some of what God is doing in the world and to provide encouragement for God-seekers to cooperate with what God is in that kingdom work. These books are meant to start conversations and provoke imaginations, to encourage action and inflame passion. They are meant to help us all lean into God's future.

We welcome the conversation that we hope these books will call forth. And we look forward to meeting you down the road so that we can have this conversation together.

FOR SARAH AND DOUG JONES

WHO ALWAYS TOLD ME THAT I COULD DO ANYTHING

PREFACE

As I was working on this book, I was also on the road, speaking about this content to a variety of groups. In May 2007, I visited these five events in a whirlwind of travel:

- A Reformed Church in America seminary, where I spoke to youth pastors about ministry amidst postmodernity

- A Pentecostal church in Massachusetts, where I participated in a conference titled "God for People Who Hate Church" and shared the stage with witches and druids as they reflected on how they've been treated by Christians

- The National Cathedral in Washington, D.C., where I spoke about the challenge that emergent Christianity poses to the Episcopal Church at a conference called "Church in the Twenty-First Century"

- Yale University Divinity School, where I spoke about the interplay of faith and politics and the upcoming presidential election

- National Presbyterian Church, back in Washington, D.C., where I addressed the nature of orthodoxy at a conference of Christian visual artists

Two themes, I think, are noteworthy about my presence at these events. The first is their diversity. I don't know of another item on the menu of American Christianity that is currently being tasted by such a wide array of Christians. Within a week, I'd gone from sitting with Pentecostals who interpret one another's dreams and break out in "Holy Spirit laughter" to addressing collared Episcopal priests in the second-largest cathedral on the continent. That's theological whiplash.

Across the spectrum, people are interested in the emergence of a new church and a new way of practicing Christianity. This "new" way, to be sure, is rooted in the old, which is part of the reason that so many are intrigued by it. Many in church leadership today—not to mention everyday believers—feel that the church made a wrong turn somewhere in the twentieth century. At the dawn of a new century, the emergents are one of the few groups offering a way out of this mess, and lots of people are listening.

The second theme of these five visits is that my message of emergence has not been universally acclaimed. At each stop, both personal interaction and the now powerful blogosphere indicate that significant discomfort results from my visit. To one, I'm playing fast and loose with sacred doctrine, and to another, I'm cursing the very institutions that pay their salaries. At the last event, I was mocked outright by my copresenter.

But following each visit, e-mails and blogs and Facebook tell another tale as well. People write to say, "Thanks for giving a voice to a new generation of Christians; thanks for standing up to the powers that be." These commenters don't necessarily buy everything I'm selling, but they do appreciate the conversation, the evolution of what it means to be a follower of Christ in the twenty-first century.

My hope is that this book is yet another voice in the ongoing conversation that is Christianity, always emerging.

Tony Jones
Edina, Minnesota
Feast of Saint Francis of Assisi
October 4, 2007

INTRODUCTION: WHAT IS "EMERGENT"?

On June 21, 2001, a group of pastor-theologians convened a conference call. We were homeless. Brian McLaren and Doug Pagitt, Tim Keel from Kansas City, Chris Seay from Houston, Tim Conder from Chapel Hill, and Brad Cecil from Dallas had all been pushed out of the nest of our hosting organization a year earlier, and we were looking for some identity, some banner under which we could rally. We needed a name. In previous iterations, we had been called the "Young Leaders Network," the "Theological Working Group," and the "Terranova Project." Under that last rubric, we (and several others, including Sally Morgenthaler, Alan Roxburgh, Danielle Shroyer, Rudy Carrasco, Todd Hunter, and Jason Mitchell) had met less than a year earlier at my family's cabin in the north woods of Minnesota and had spent a couple of days thinking and arguing and dreaming about the future of Christianity.

We'd already been tagged with phrases "emerging church" and "emerging leaders" in years past, and those phrases came up again on this conference call. In the midst of the conversation, we settled on a variant of that word: we'd call ourselves "emergent."

E·mer·gent

—*adj*. 1. coming into view or notice; issuing; 2. emerging; rising from a surrounding surface or liquid; 3. coming into existence, esp. with political independence; 4. arising casually or unexpectedly; 5. calling for immediate action; urgent; 6. *Evolution:* displaying emergence—*n*.7. *Ecology:* an aquatic plant having its stem, leaves, etc., extending above the surface of the water. (*Source:* Adapted from *The Random House Dictionary of the English Language.*)

A couple of months later, that name made perfect sense when someone approached us at a conference and said, "You know, when a forester enters a forest to determine that forest's health, she does not look at the vitality of the tops of the old-growth trees. Instead, she gets on her hands and knees and examines what's growing, what's emerging on the forest floor. That's how she can gauge the well-being of the forest."

Later we reflected on this, and it made perfect sense: when it comes to the ecology of the American church, a lot of organizations exist to measure the health of the old-growth institutions, pruning their branches, fertilizing their roots. But there's a lot happening and emerging down below on the forest floor. The new communities of faith, the innovative forms of monasticism, the adventurous theology—that's the emergent church. The soil of that growth is deep and complex, a mélange that includes the advent of "new media" (blogs, e-mail, social networking sites, podcasts, Webcams, instant messaging, and so on), disaffection with politics as usual, the postmodern turn in philosophy, and cracks in the foundations of mainline and evangelical Christianity. Emergents—and I consider myself one—think that this movement is but one manifestation of the coming dramatic shift in what it means to be Christian.

There's a lot at stake. The ecclesial elites on both the left and the right of modern Christianity have spent the past century endowing denominations; founding colleges, universities, and seminaries; launching publishing houses and magazines; building enormous churches; and getting face time on CNN and Fox News. In general, they look skeptically at the young, emergent usurpers. Some of them have even endeavored to spray herbicide on the emergent growth.

But they haven't succeeded. Emergent Christianity has taken root, and it's growing like a weed—a lot of different weeds, actually. Young evangelicals are forsaking their suburban birthright and moving into America's toughest cities to found "new monastic communities." Young theologians are rejecting the siren song of academic tenure for the pioneering life on the emergent frontier. And young pastors are snubbing the safety net of denominations for the adventure of church planting among the relational networks of the emergent church. The conversation among people who think of themselves as emergent is robust, and it's taking place in books and blogs and conferences and spontaneous "meet-ups." As we'll explore throughout this book, the emergents are in some ways pioneers and in some ways expatriates. They do come from somewhere—most often a conventional Christian upbringing—but they are forsaking their homelands and choosing life on the frontier. They tend to be young, urban, and educated, but as emergent sensibilities spread around the world, those characteristics are becoming more tenuous as descriptors.

Like the electronica music of the 1980s and 1990s, the emergent church is a mash-up of old and new, of theory and practice, of men and women, and of mainline, evangelical, and, increasingly, Roman Catholic Christians. What started among leaders (a.k.a. clergy) is now spreading into the humus of everyday Christians (a.k.a. laypeople).

In some ways, there's nothing new here. Since the Gospel writers penned their witness to the faith, theologians have argued about how we talk about God, who Jesus is, and how humans relate to God. And since the earliest Christians transformed their Roman peristyle homes into *domus ecclesiae*, followers of Jesus have found new and innovative ways to orient their lives, collectively and individually. But too often in our history, the innovative theoreticians have sat safely ensconced in their tenured chairs, rarely deigning to speak with the lowly churchfolk. Meanwhile, innovative church leaders think the theologian and the biblical scholar have lost all touch with reality and instead busy themselves with the latest technical innovations in "how to do church." If the emergent church has anything rare, or even unique, it's this nexus of theory and praxis, of innovative theology and innovative practice. These twin impulses of rethinking theology and rethinking church are driving the nascent growth of emergent Christianity.

And love it or hate it, it can't be ignored.

Some Working Definitions of Terms Used in This Book

emergent Christianity

The new forms of Christian faith arising from the old; the Christianity believed and practiced by the emergents.

the emergent church

The specifically new forms of church life rising from the modern, American church of the twentieth century.

the emergents

The adherents of emergent Christianity.

Emergent

Specifically referring to the relational network which formed first in 1997; also known as Emergent Village.

Postmodernism . . . is not relativism or skepticism, as its uncomprehending critics almost daily charge, but minutely close attention to detail, a sense for the complexity and multiplicity of things, for close readings, for detailed histories, for sensitivity to differences. The postmodernists think the devil is in the details, but they also have reason to hope that none of this will antagonize God.

—JOHN D. CAPUTO

Either Christianity itself is flawed, failing, [or] untrue, or our modern, Western, commercialized, industrial-strength version of it is in need of a fresh look, a serious revision.

—BRIAN D. MCLAREN

I do believe; help me overcome my unbelief!

—ANONYMOUS MAN
(SPEAKING TO JESUS)

THE NEW
CHRISTIANS

CHAPTER 1

LEAVING THE OLD COUNTRY

WHEN SHE SAT DOWN NEXT TO ME IN FIRST CLASS ON THE flight to New York, I knew that she was the kind of person who regularly traveled there, up front. I was bumped up from coach by the airline, but I suspected that she paid for her seat. To be honest, I was intimidated by this woman, who was probably around my age. She wore torn jeans—the kind that are *really* expensive and come pretorn—complemented by a shabby chic wool sweater. And she was pregnant.

I never spoke to her, just observed. As we were taking off, she was editing a very hip-looking graphic novel with the blue pencil of a savvy New York editor. I, meanwhile, was attempting to hide the fact that I was reading a Bible—how uncouth! And once we reached cruising altitude, she pulled a sleek MacBook Pro out of her bag. I hesitatingly opened my Dell dinosaur and began typing up a Bible study.

I was outmatched. A very vanilla suburbanite Christian pastor from Minnesota next to the hippest of New York editors. "I write books," I wanted to say. But I dared not, for a New York editor is like a unicorn—if

1

you talk to her, she'll disappear. Or she'll stab you in the heart with her horn.

But then, about halfway through the flight, she closed her Mac and tilted her seat back. What happened next has stuck with me ever since. She took a rosary out of her pocket, draped the prayer beads over her pregnant belly, and spent the next hour surreptitiously praying with her eyes closed.

Neurons in my brain began to misfire. "Does . . . not . . . compute": a New York editor of graphic novels praying the most traditional of Roman Catholic rituals. I thought she was an enlightened, liberal member of the "East Coast elite." But instead she was praying to the Blessed Virgin. I would have been less surprised had she tried to blow up her shoe.

Is there something in the air? Is there a spiritual itch that people are trying to scratch but it's just in the middle of their back in that place that they can't quite reach?

It seems incontrovertibly so.

We are not becoming less religious, as some people argue. We are becoming *differently* religious. And the shift is significant. Some call it a tectonic shift, others seismic or tsunamic. Whatever your geological metaphor, the changes are shaking the earth beneath our feet.

lAs the second half of the twentieth century began, most sociologists, social theorists, and social philosophers were proclaiming that the death of religion was nigh. They were bards of an impending secularism that was lapping onto the shores of all Western countries. We are losing our religion, they calmly—and often approvingly—lectured from behind their podia. We're leaving the myths of this god and that god behind and establishing a new spirituality that is unhinged from the oppressive regimes of conventional religion. New Ageism is a nod in this direction: as we mature intellectually and scientifically, we'll realize that traditional religions are holding us back. We'll achieve our liberation by relying less on the strictures of religions and moving into the promising horizon of "spirituality."

This was, of course, a natural consequence of God's death, first declared by Friedrich Nietzsche in 1882 and touted again by *Time* magazine in 1966.

Nietzsche himself wasn't out to kill God per se, nor was he saying that no one believed in God anymore. He was announcing that that the modern mind could no longer tolerate an authoritarian figure who towers over the cosmos with a lightning bolt in his hand, ready to strike down evildoers. That deity, he said, had been murdered. With the death of that version of God, the Christian morals that upheld all of Western society had been undermined. We were, Nietzsche feared, on a fast track to nihilistic hell. So he went on a search for some sort of universal moral foundation that was not dependent on an unacceptable and medieval notion of God.

That same sensibility was seen by many observers as a move toward a universal (and secular) spirituality: we would realize how much we had in common; we would become more enlightened; we would teach the world to sing in perfect harmony.

But a funny thing happened on the way to the twenty-first century: we became more religious, not less. Fundamentalisms now thrive in all major religions, churches and religious schools keep popping up, and religious books outsell all other categories. Nowadays you can't find a self-respecting social theorist proclaiming secularism. Instead, they're studying religion and getting face time on CNN explaining to often oblivious journalists how religious Americans really are. Back in the pulpits, ironically, pastors continue to bewail that we're living through the decline and fall of the Judeo-Christian American empire, that secularism is a fast-moving glacier, razing the mountains of faith that have been a part of America since its birth.

But the data just don't back up this interpretation. Just ten percent of Americans are not affiliated with a church or synagogue, and another five percent hold a faith other than Judaism or Christianity. That leaves *eighty-five percent* of Americans who can write down the name and address of the congregation with which they are affiliated.[1] Yes, that bears repeating: eighty-five percent. There are about 255 million church-affiliated Americans.

What *can* be questioned is the level of commitment that Americans have to their churches. They may know the address, but do they know the doctrinal statement? Or the denominational affiliation? Do they care? The answer to the last question is most decidedly no. American Christians care less and less about the denominational divides that are so important to their seminary-trained pastors.

"CHURCH IS DEAD"

In the twenty-first century, it's not God who's dead. It's the church. Or at least conventional forms of church. *Dead?* you say. *Isn't that overstating the case a bit?* Indeed, churches still abound. So do pay phones. You can still find pay phones around, in airports and train stations and shopping malls—there are plenty of working pay phones. But look around your local airport and you'll likely see the sad remnants where pay phones used to hang—the strange row of rectangles on the wall and the empty slot where a phone book used to sit.

There are under a million pay phones in the United States today. In 1997, there were over two million.[2]

Of course, the death of the pay phone doesn't mean that we don't make phone calls anymore. In fact, we make far more calls than ever before, but we make them differently. Now we make phone calls from home or on the mobile device clasped to our belt or through our computers. Phone calls aren't obsolete, but the pay phone is—or at least it's quickly becoming so.

Modern

As an adjective, *modern* can mean current or up-to-date. (For example, a highway rest area with "modern facilities" has indoor plumbing.) In our discussions, however, *modern* refers to an era in Western society following the Enlightenment and the Industrial Revolution and reflective of the values of those social upheavals.

Similarly, the modern church is changing and evolving and emerging. To extend the analogy a bit, no one is saying that the pay phone was a bad idea. Most people would agree that it was a good idea at the time—it was an excellent way to communicate. But communication was the goal, and pay phones were merely a means to an end.

The modern church—at least as it is characterized by imposing physical buildings, professional clergy, denominational bureaucracies, residential seminary training, and other trappings—was an endeavor by faithful men and women in their time and place, attempting to live into the biblical gospel. But the church was never the end, only the means. The desire of the emergents is to live Christianly, to build something wonderful for the future on the legacy of the past.

SIGNS OF DEATH–AND LIFE

As a police chaplain, I've witnessed a few deaths, and the death rattle is a sound that sticks with you forever. In the throes of death, a person often loses the ability to swallow, and fluids accumulate in the throat. In the moments before expiration, the breath barely rattles past these secretions. It is an ominous sound.

We may now be hearing the American church's death rattle (at least the death of church-as-we-know-it). Exhibit A: the fabric of the traditional denominations is tearing. The Episcopal Church in the United States of America appointed a gay bishop, and now African bishops walk out of the room and won't take communion with the presiding bishop of the U.S. church. The Anglican Communion, a worldwide collection of denominations who gather under the rubric of the Church of England, claim that it's the rites of the church and their shared history that hold them together—and that's worked for four hundred years. But those commonalities probably cannot withstand the current pressure of liberalism versus conservatism. Ironically, conservative Episcopal churches in the States are placing themselves under the authority of like-minded bishops in Africa rather than recognizing that the real problem is an outmoded denominational structure and outdated categories of left and right.

That's happening in the "high church" world of Anglicanism. Meanwhile, for over a decade now, conservative forces have been attempting to purge the "low church" Southern Baptist Convention (SBC) of all liberal and moderate influences. Exhibit B: recently, the rapid growth of Pentecostalism in the global South has inevitably encroached on Southern Baptist missionaries stationed around the world, including the biblical "gift of tongues," which some interpret as a private prayer language between the believer and God. The SBC response to this incursion has been to purge its denomination of these influences, so the Southern Baptists are attempting to cast out all missionaries who speak in tongues. Concurrently, they've retrenched in their stance against the use of alcohol. As a result of these and other initiatives, moderate and liberal

Baptists have been sent packing, and they've gone on to set up their own new denominations or join other ones. That won't solve the problem, though, because it's not necessarily the theology but denominationalism itself that's the issue.

The irony of the struggles in the SBC is that the conservative shift is being spearheaded by leaders like Al Mohler, the president of Southern Baptist Theological Seminary. He's also a radio host, frequent guest on CNN's *Anderson Cooper 360*, and all-around Baptist celebrity. But the Baptist revolution in church life started with the Pilgrims and others in Jolly Old England in the seventeenth century who expressly rejected the hierarchical structure of the Anglican Church. But at least genealogically, what is Al Mohler other than a de facto bishop of Southern Baptists?

So we've got Baptists who aren't supposed to have bishops with Bishop Al Mohler and Bishop Paige Patterson excommunicating liberals and moderates, and we've got real-life Anglican bishops who won't break bread with one another. Do we need more evidence that the church in America is in trouble? How about when, in 2007, Focus on the Family's James Dobson called for the resignation of Richard Cizik, the vice president for governmental affairs of the National Association of Evangelicals (NAE)? Then it turned out that Dobson and his cronies aren't even members of the NAE! Or on the left, the silly television ads from the liberal United Church of Christ, virtually begging people to come to their dying denominational churches by caricaturing evangelicals as having bouncers and ejection seats in their churches.

I could go on.

This might be an overly bleak picture of church life in America. Maybe the church you go to is fine, and maybe you're relatively happy with your church, even if there's a little uneasiness that things are not quite right. That's what the surveys say. But if the evangelical pollster George Barna is correct, upwards of twenty million "born again" Americans have left conventional churches for home groups and house churches—or no church at all.[3] And that's the real story here, that a generation of Christians—many of them under forty—are forsaking the conventional forms of church and gathering in new forms.

Some 225 million Americans voluntarily claim Christianity as their religion, and ninety percent of them can tell you what church they belong to. But out on the fringes, on the frontier of American Christianity, is another ten percent who are leaving their parents' churches, vowing never to return. It's not the faith they're forsaking but the particularly polarized form of church life—the attitudes, forms, and institutions—they've been offered at the beginning of the twenty-first century.

This phenomenon is not simply a fad (although there are faddish elements) or youthful hubris (though there's some of that, too) but rather a harbinger of the future of church life in America. A new church is emerging from the compost of Christendom. Many in conventional Christianity, both on the left and the right, are concerned about the emergent church; others find it a hopeful trend. In any case, it is significant.

But what led to the emergent church movement? Disaffection with the theologies, attitudes, and institutions of American church life surely played a part, particularly with the poles of left and right that have become so prominent in the last quarter-century. Often segregated into the "mainline left" and the "evangelical right," they've both got irresolvable problems, from an emergent perspective.

> **A new church is emerging from the compost of Christendom.**

THE PROBLEM ON THE LEFT

Potential mainline preachers have to pick a flavor of Christianity early on in their careers—Presbyterian, Methodist, Catholic, Quaker, Baptist—the list could go on and on. Like ice cream, these are the main flavors, but there are also all kinds of exotic variations—Baptist Chip, Baptist Swirl, Low-Fat Baptist Lite, and Double Baptist Chunk.[4] The pastor then becomes a one-flavor guy. He goes to *that* seminary, learns *that* theology, buys into *that* pension plan, and goes to *that* annual trade show. This is not to disparage the erstwhile pastors—they really have no choice; they don't get to pick a new flavor on a whim. That's how the system of getting to be a pastor is set up; those are the rules by which the players are bound to play.

Mainline Protestantism

The older, established Protestant denominations, including Episcopalian, United Methodist, United Church of Christ, and Presbyterian. Also known as "name-brand Christianity." Mainliners tend to lean to the left, both theologically and politically.

But as young pastors are learning every nuance of their flavor of the faith, nearly everyone else in America is becoming less interested in a steady diet of one flavor. Americans are moving to Church of the Van-Choc-Straw (a.k.a. Neapolitan). American Christians care little about the denomination label on the sign in the parking lot or the church's stand on predestination. I found this out a few years ago as a young pastor myself. I stood before a "new members" class at Colonial Church, an old-line denominational church, and asked how many of the seventy-two persons there wanted to join Colonial because it's a Congregational church. Just two hands went up. The other seventy said they were drawn to Colonial by the choir, the preaching, the children's ministry, or by a friend. The proud Congregational heritage of Colonial Church—represented by a glass-encased chunk of the *Mayflower* in the entryway—meant nothing to them.

Dispatch 1: Emergents find little importance in the discrete differences between the various flavors of Christianity. Instead, they practice a generous orthodoxy that appreciates the contributions of all Christian movements.

It's similar to the way that being a European has changed. Before 1995, a French citizen had to stop at every border in Europe, show her passport, and get it stamped; the borders between countries were definite, and they were guarded by soldiers with guns. She also had to visit a bank and change her francs into lire or pounds or kroner. But with the formation of the European Union, every European in the twenty-seven EU countries now gets an EU passport, and the borders are unguarded—Europeans now travel freely between EU countries, and most use the same currency.

Similarly, Americans pass from church to church with little regard for denominational heritage—their passports say "Christian," not "Lutheran" or

"Nazarene" or "Episcopal." Some in the American clergy have gotten hip to this new reality, but far more are beholden to denominational structures for their self-identity (and their retirement funds).

What's interesting is that when asked, most mainline clergy express great chagrin at this situation. They agree that denominations are an outmoded form of organized Christianity, but they can't seem to find a way out.

Although denominations existed in nineteenth-century America, the first three-quarters of the twentieth century can really be seen as the Golden Age of Mainline Protestantism. In fact, the flagship magazine of mainline Christians, founded in 1900, is titled *The Christian Century*.

The postindustrial era was one of big organizations: universities, corporations, and nation-states were all growing in size and adding layers of administrative bureaucracy to cope with the other big organizations in the world. Christian leaders at the beginning of the twentieth century wanted to play in this arena too, so they followed suit and founded denominational headquarters in New York and Chicago; they added layers of bureaucracy (called "judicatories") and middle managers (often called "bishops" or "district superintendents"); and they started their own publishing houses, colleges, and seminaries.

The well-meaning members of denominations built these institutions to advance the gospel in a world of large, monolithic organizations. But we've now come to realize three problems: first, the gospel isn't monolithic; second, it's inevitably destabilizing of institutions; and third, for all their benefits (like organizing society and preserving communal wisdom), bureaucracies also do two other things well: grow more bureaucratic tentacles and attract bureaucrats.[5] So a crust of bureaucracy grew over the gospel impulses of the denominational founders, thickening over a century to the point that according to conservatives, the gospel has been suffocated right out of the mainline denominations.

Lillian Daniel is a pastor in the United Church of Christ, a notoriously left-leaning denomination founded in 1957. She's also active in the labor movement and an outspoken proponent of progressive causes—a passionate person. Reflecting on the biannual General Synod national meeting, she moaned, "We used to be a group of revolutionaries. Now we're a group of *resolutionaries*." Operating by the distinctly nonbiblical Robert's Rules of Order, she said, the convention has devolved into a gathering of persons who read resolutions that are then voted on and promptly ignored or forgotten. The resolutions range from those for gay marriage to those against gay marriage, from a call to study the imprisonment of native Hawaiians to "saving Social Security from privatization." The resolutions pile up; then they're read, seconded, discussed, voted on, and filed.

Lillian thought she was joining a movement, but she was joining a bureaucracy. And that bureaucracy tends to quash the passion of the many Christ-centered and enthusiastic persons therein.

A CASE STUDY: GO WHERE I SEND THEE

A seminary professor told this story with tears in her eyes. She had an outstanding student, a young man who'd hung around seminary for an extra year so that he could earn an extra master's in youth ministry on top of his master of divinity degree. Throughout his childhood, adolescence, college, and seminary years, he'd been a loyal Methodist, following in the path of his father, a United Methodist pastor. And during seminary, while going through the labyrinthine process of United Methodist ordination, he also fell in love with the idea of being a college campus chaplain. He just sensed that was the right spot for him—in his language, he felt "called." So he applied at a couple of colleges and was selected as a finalist at one of them. But at 10:00 P.M., the night before his final interview at the college, he received a call from his bishop. She told him (on his answering machine) of his first church assignment, a small Methodist church in rural upstate New York. He'd be a solo pastor. Upon hearing the message, the young man swallowed hard and called her back. "Could I have a week to get back to you?" he asked, "because I'm in the running for a college chaplaincy."

"No," the bishop replied. "You need to tell me in the morning. And let me just inform you, if you reject this placement, the next one I give you will be even worse."

The next morning, through tears, the young ordinand accepted the placement of his bishop and withdrew from the college chaplaincy position.

Although the bishop's actions seem indefensible, her power play was merely an attempt to stanch the bleeding. *We can't lose another young pastor*, she must have thought. *I've got too many pulpits to fill to let this guy go to a college*. She might have even considered that he would have a significant pastoral impact on a college campus, but she had little choice. While United Methodist Church vacancy rates hover around ten percent, the vacancies in churches with fewer than one hundred members—the majority of UMC churches—is far higher.[6] It's been well documented that young seminary graduates rarely want to serve in small, rural congregations. Couple that with the fact that only five percent of UMC clergy are in their twenties,[7] and you can see why the well-meaning bishop didn't want to lose her young charge to the allure of college chaplaincy.

She needed him in the system, like the Matrix needs human batteries. If she let him get away, he might never plug back into the United Methodist Church, and that's not just one less pastor in an already overstretched system; that's one less payer into the pension fund, one less recruiter of future pastors, one less name in the annual yearbook.

In other words, her tactics are understandable in a system that needs more young pastors if it is to survive. But how many potential pastors will continue to play by these rules?

THE PROBLEM ON THE RIGHT

While the mainline Protestants know that they are hemorrhaging members and money at alarming rates, the grass seems greener on the evangelical side of the fence. Fourth-ring suburbs of major metropolitan cities sport glossy new megachurches, their lots full of minivans on Sunday mornings and Wednesday nights. This is a bloc of the folks who elected George W. Bush, and since then, there's been no dearth of journalistic interest in American evangelicals.

Evangelical Protestantism

The loosely aligned "born again" Christians who hold a view of the Bible that tends toward literal interpretation, emphasize personal conversion to Christ, and generally lean to the right, both politically and theologically.

But if the problem with liberal Christianity is more dire and more obvious, the evangelical movement has its own problems. A century and a half ago, the United States was coming out of the Civil War, and the country was rent in two. Conservative churches in the South were reeling because they had supported the sinful and corrupt practice of slavery.[8] The liberal churches in the North, by contrast, were enjoying success in the wake of military and moral victory. At the same time, a new kind of biblical scholarship was in its ascendancy in Europe: German professors were using critical literary and historical methods to investigate the veracity of the biblical texts, culminating with Albert Schweitzer's *Quest for the Historical Jesus* in 1906. Schweitzer concluded, famously, that Jesus of Nazareth wasn't God after all but instead a wild-eyed apocalyptic rabbi who threw himself on the wheel of history only to be crushed by it.[9]

The majority of leaders in the American church embraced these academic trends. These were the mainliners, and they were in the majority. The only other choice in American Christianity was fundamentalism, and this was the backwoods, snake-handling, poison-drinking, Bible-thumping version of fundamentalism.[10]

Fundamentalism

A particularly rigid adherence to what is considered foundational to a religion. In American Christianity, fundamentalism began in the early twentieth century as a reaction to modernism and codified the "Five Fundamentals" of Christian belief: the inerrancy of the Bible, the virgin birth of Jesus, physical resurrection at the end of time, individual atonement of the believer by Jesus' death, and the Second Coming of Jesus in the future.

A group of men started meeting in the 1940s, tired of this liberal-fundamentalist polarization. They wanted to remain faithful to a more conservative interpretation of the Bible but not retreat from society into the woods—they were looking for a "third way" to be Christian in America. They claimed the title "evangelical," which had in fact been around for at least a century already. These men, including Carl Henry, Charles Fuller, Harold Ockenga, and Billy Graham, committed themselves to rescuing the Bible from the fundamentalists and liberals alike, and they did so by forming a network of like-minded organizations. They didn't have a headquarters or a central committee, but they spun a web of connection that now spreads across the United States in the form of Christian youth camps, college ministries, radio stations, publishing houses, magazines, and colleges. Over half a century, these evangelicals—focusing on conservative biblical interpretation, evangelism, and cultural suasion—increased their influence to the point of electing presidents and appointing Supreme Court justices. Though there are evangelical denominations, their histories are relatively short, and their identities are not nearly as reified as those of their mainline peers.

But it may be that evangelicals gained cultural prominence at the cost of real spiritual, societal, or intellectual transformation. And when measured by the present moral fiber of the United States, the evangelical revolution is a qualified failure—America, it seems, is no more "Christian" in its ethos than it ever was; some people argue that we're less Christ-like than we've ever been. Indeed, one can make the argument that evangelicals have been duped, selling their votes for a mess of pottage. For example, having played an important role in the Republican revolution and the eventual capture of all three branches of government, evangelicals have come to realize that Republican politicos have no serious intention of overturning *Roe* v. *Wade*—in fact, in the six years that Republicans had the White House and both houses of Congress (and, arguably, the Supreme Court), they passed virtually no significant antiabortion legislation,[11] even though many of them had been elected on just that promise. Add to that the relentless assault on Christian values in the form of video games, Coors Light ads, and gun violence, and you simply don't have a "Christian nation."

The evidence is in: millions of individuals "inviting Jesus Christ into their hearts as their personal Lord and Savior" at megachurches and Billy Graham crusades has done little to stem the moral dissolution of America. And ironically, it's the very individualism engendered by evangelicalism that has resulted in this predicament. The primary emphasis of evangelicalism is the conversion of the individual, but that emphasis has also handicapped evangelicals in their attempts to tackle systemic issues like racism and poverty and thus has left them open to manipulation by political forces.

A CASE STUDY: DON'T ASK US ABOUT THE CHICKENS

Known for chicken, Tyson Foods acquired Iowa Beef and Pork Company in 2001, making it the largest producer of meat in the world. Actually, the preferred corporate-speak for meat when you're at the Tyson headquarters in Little Rock, Arkansas, is "protein solutions." They refer to themselves as a producer of "affordable protein solutions."

I visited Tyson Foods in 2006 with a group from Yale University Divinity School's Center for Faith and Culture as part of an initiative called Faith as a Way of Life. Our trip to Tyson was meant to provoke our thinking about faith and business.

We began the day at a "kill plant." That's the industry name for a factory where animals are slaughtered and prepared; they're turned into things like chicken nuggets elsewhere. The plant we visited produces Cornish game hens, which I was surprised to discover are not a particular type of bird but are simply twenty-eight-day-old chickens. In other words, they're young, small birds. Outside of the plant, half a dozen trucks full of live, twenty-eight-day-old chickens are in the driveway. One at a time, they back into a loading dock and dump their squawking load into a trough. Six men, immigrants from the Marshall Islands (a U.S. territory in the Pacific), stand in the "dark room"—lit only by black lights, in order to keep the chickens calm—and hang the chickens upside down in stirrups. The men are amazingly agile, picking up a live animal and hanging it in one fluid movement. One hundred and thirty-five birds per minute leave the dark room, and that same number per minute wend their way on a conveyer system to the kill room. The head of each chicken is dragged through an electrified pool of water, stunning it briefly. That way, the animal is basically unconscious as its throat is slit a split second later by a whirring razor blade.

I really can't describe what it's like to watch 135 birds slaughtered in a minute or, even more overwhelming, to know that there are another 135 coming the next minute and the next minute, hour after hour, twenty-four hours a day, six days a week. Compound this by two dozen, which is how many kill plants Tyson operates. It's a staggering number of chickens that are killed for our consumption each day. Millions.

(Let me be clear: I'm no vegan. I eat protein solutions almost every day. I even hunt for protein solutions in fields and over ponds.[12] So I have no ideological objection to the raising and slaughter of chickens. Still, it was an overwhelming experience to witness the inner workings of a kill plant.)

Because I have no ideological ax to grind, I thought I'd ask a question to each of the groups we met with about the chickens. Scripture is clear: in Genesis 1:24–31, human beings are given the task of caretakers of the earth and the animals and plants that inhabit it. Christians (as well as Jews and Muslims, and indeed all spiritual people) are pretty well agreed on this idea. No one really debates whether we're supposed to care for God's creation. It's a given. So with this supposed theological consensus in mind, I figured I'd ask, "What about the chickens?"

Before lunch, we gathered in a little, wood-paneled board room at the front of the kill plant. A few workers, on their break, were ushered into the room. They stood against the wall while we Yalies sat around the table. It was a bit awkward. Here we were, the epitome of the "East Coast elite," questioning workers who make about $7.00 an hour slaughtering and prepping chickens. But these line workers immediately put us at ease—they were friendly and gracious. One woman had worked in the plant for thirty-five years; another was a Marshallese immigrant who'd been there for just four months. They talked about how much they appreciated the Tyson Corporation, the health care plan, and the plant's manager. The thirty-five-year veteran told of her daughter's bout with cancer and how the entire plant rallied around her and raised money to support her. They spoke openly about their faith and about the little Baptist and Pentecostal churches that they attend—some of them go to church three times per week. When I asked about the chickens, they answered candidly about the stewardship of the animals. I thought to myself, *A generation or two ago, these people would have been farmers and would have been slaughtering chickens by hand in their barns. All that's really changed for them is the technology and efficiency by which the chickens are dispatched.*

At four in the afternoon, we sat down with John Tyson at the company's headquarters. Tyson's grandfather founded the company, and his father turned it into a massive, multinational corporation. John is a prodigal son. A child of privilege, he became a drug-addled young man with no interest in his dad's company. But after a divorce and chemical dependency treatment, he became a follower of Jesus. Tyson is no towering figure; he stands about five foot nine. He's balding, a bit portly, and dresses in jeans, a golf shirt, and a worn Tyson Foods windbreaker. One could characterize him as a quiet, humble evangelical Christian. He wears his previous failures on his sleeve, and employees and friends speak of him as a truly good person.

And he makes about $5 million per year (plus stock options).

Tyson spoke openly about his life; his children, whom he's raising as a single parent; and the doubts he still has about whether his acquisition of Iowa Beef and Pork was a good idea. Then I asked, "What about the chickens?"

I elaborated: "I'm not asking you to feel guilty about slaughtering chickens; I think you're providing meat to millions of people every day, and I appreciate what your company is doing. But you're also a Christian, one whose job it is to act as a steward of God's creation. You have literally millions and millions of animals under your care. Do you ever *think* about them?"

He paused for a moment before answering. "Yes," he said, "I do." He paused again, and then continued, "As you might guess, I am hated by some people. I get lots of angry e-mail from PETA [People for the Ethical Treatment of Animals] activists, for example. But we've worked hard to develop the most humane ways to kill chickens. We've had significant studies done on what is the least painful and most hygienic way to slaughter chickens, and we invented the electrified pool of water because that's the best way to kill the chickens humanely. Yes, I think about the chickens, and I take my responsibility to them very seriously."

But in the middle of the day, we had gotten quite a different response. After lunch, we met with a couple of different groups of middle managers at Tyson. All men, they were dressed in khaki pants and golf shirts emblazoned with the Tyson logo. These men occupy the vast American strata between $7.00-an-hour kill plant line workers and $5 million-a-year John Tyson. They live in four-bedroom homes in suburban subdivisions, coach soccer, and belong to country clubs. And they all go to church—in fact, many of them told us they attend First Baptist Church of Springdale, pastored by the Southern Baptist celebrity Ronnie Floyd. They have four-year college degrees and maybe an M.B.A. They mow their lawns on Saturday and cheer for the Razorbacks. They're white, educated, and relatively wealthy. To be honest, they're my people. If I worked at Tyson, I'd be a middle manager. I say that because if my forthcoming judgment of them seems unduly harsh, I am also implicating myself.

We had a nice, civil chat, although they were significantly more standoffish toward us due to our Yale connections than were our interlocutors earlier in the day. We were the people that Pastor Ronnie had warned them about. They talked about their churches, their faith, and Pastor Ronnie. But when I asked, "What about the chickens?" the looks on their faces responded loud and clear: *Don't ask us about the chickens.* One man even said as much, implying that I was a leftist tree-hugger with an anticorporate agenda.

That night, as our group debriefed the day, a heated and not very civil conversation broke out. The group—made up of an artist, a novelist, a teacher, a business consultant, a businesswoman, a couple of theologians, and a few pastors—could not agree on the sincerity of the middle managers. Some of us were disturbed at their responses, while others argued that this is the very Sunday-Monday divide that afflicts many American Christians.

For my part, I was disheartened at their answers. But as opposed to laying the blame at their feet, I lay it at their churches'. The church that doesn't challenge its members to face the core ethical issues that confront them every day at work is the church that has abdicated its responsibility. Many churches, particularly evangelical ones, make this mistake, and here's why: too many evangelical churches have emphasized the vertical, just-me-and-Jesus relationship to the exclusion of the horizontal relationships with other human beings and with all of creation. In fact, a major study in the 1990s showed that the individualism inherent in American evangelicalism is directly responsible for evangelicals' inability to diagnose and solve systemic social issues like racism and abortion.[13] In other words, the formula for evangelical growth—namely, individual conversion—also precludes many evangelical churches from affecting the very changes that rally its members. So when I asked about the chickens, it was a theological non sequitur to the middle managers; as long as their relationship with Jesus was all right, everything else would take care of itself. Questions about animal rights or national health care or the minimum wage or immigration rights aren't theological questions. Instead, they're flagged as the "liberal agenda."

As is well known, the permissible range of issues that can be on the theological or ethical agenda at some conservative evangelical churches has been narrowed to two: abortion and gay marriage. In their salvos against other issues—such as global warming—evangelical leaders like James Dobson and the late Jerry Falwell have said as much. A specific example of this kind of thinking comes from Ronnie Floyd himself. In the days following the April 2007 Virginia Tech shooting massacre, Floyd posted extensively about the tragedy on his blog, "Between Sundays." He warned the American church to *"get serious"* and to "WAKE UP!!!" Thirty-three persons had died, he wrote, and they each went to heaven or hell. He then urged his readers to get busy with evangelism because "death is real," and the job of Christians is to "bring others to Christ" so that they won't go to hell when they die.

In Floyd's blog posts about the Virginia Tech shootings, there was nary a word about Seung-Hui Cho's ready access to guns and ammunition. No comment about the epidemic of clinical depression in our country. Not a mention of the prevalence of hurting people in our culture, often adolescents who are shrouded in anonymity, lost on college campuses with tens of thousands of other students. In other words, Floyd said nothing about the systemic issues that become acute to many of us during times of tragedy. Floyd's question is not how this young man's mind became so twisted in his own mental illness, how he fell through the cracks of our societal net, or how he was able to purchase two handguns and hundreds of bullets with no more than a driver's license. The question was about whether he and his victims had invited Jesus into their hearts before they died.

A stereotypical evangelical response to tragedy? Indeed, but not uncommon either. Jerry Falwell and Pat Robertson are rightly lampooned, even by their evangelical peers, for announcing that natural disasters are God's retribution on homosexuals, but their pronouncements are just one step beyond the theology harbored by some evangelicals: there's little we can do about the worsening situation in the world, so let's save as many souls as we can before it all goes up in flames.

But here's the good news: evangelical churches around the country are countering this trend and rejecting the narrow political agenda pushed by their leaders. I recently attended a conservative Baptist church that devoted an entire weekend to mobilizing their people to stop the genocide in Darfur. They brought in a survivor of the genocide in Rwanda, Celestin Musekura, to speak, and they screened the powerful and graphic documentary, *The Devil Came on Horseback*.[14] There was nary a word about saving souls or activist judges on the Supreme Court. In fact, there was a healthy dose of skepticism about why the Bush administration has dragged its feet on getting involved in Darfur. Some evangelical churches, it seems, can't be stereotyped, and they won't be pushed around by conservative radio hosts.

THE *REAL* PROBLEM: LEFT VERSUS RIGHT

Ironically, the "liberal" Christians in America and the "conservatives" suffer from the same illness. Both are beholden to a scheme that philosophers call "foundationalism," and that leads to their intractable fighting.[15] Since their foundations are different (though related), they are cursed to shout past one another forever, for they are each caught in a philosophical hell called *infinite regression*.

Foundationalism

The theory that at the bottom of all human knowledge is a set of self-inferential or internally justified beliefs; in other words, the foundation is indubitable and requires no external justification.

For the conservative, the sacred text of Christianity is indubitable, established by an internal and circular reasoning: "The Bible claims to be God's truth, so therefore it's true." Many evangelicals have a more sophisticated view of scripture than this, but they're still destined to a life of establishing the veracity of the Bible in the face of contravening evidence and opinion:

"I believe X, Y, and Z because it says so in the Bible."

"Well, how do you know the Bible is true and accurate?"

"I believe the Bible because the apostles died for its truth, and people don't die for a lie."

"What about the 9/11 terrorists?"

"They were deceived. They didn't know they were dying for a lie. The apostles had seen Jesus and lived with him, so they knew he wasn't a lie."

"What about the followers of Jim Jones and David Koresh?"

"Well, the Bible is *really* true because of the reliability of the original manuscripts."

"Do we have the original manuscripts?"

"No, but we have some pretty old ones that are close to the originals."

"How do we know they weren't changed in the early years?"

"Because we have faith in the historical process by which the early manuscripts were copied and distributed."

"So your faith is in history?!? *Does that mean you believe that history is indubitable?"*

"Not all history. Just our history."

"Based on what? Why is biblical history certain and sure?"

"Because it accords with reality."

"What reality? Whose reality?"

And so on, ad infinitum.

This is *infinite regression*, and it's inherent to foundationalist systems. Once presented, an "indubitable" foundation needs to be justified by a whole lot of other beliefs, and they, in turn, need to be justified. An eternal digging ensues, a search for that rock-bottom foundation that is perfectly self-evident. (Spoiler alert: no such foundation exists!)

For the liberal Christians among us, the foundation is what the theologian Friedrich Schleiermacher (1768–1834) called the "feeling of utter dependence." He posited that every human being has a sense that there's something Out There, bigger and better than oneself; religious systems are simply fallible human constructs that attempt to articulate things about and worship that Being Out There. Religion, he lectured, is essentially a feeling or an intuition, and dogmas are attempts to pin down that feeling.

Following Schleiermacher, some liberal Christians claim that Christianity is the best way we know of to make sense of the Being, while others say that Christianity is merely one of many ways. The infinite regression for liberals begins when confronting the work of the Big Three of the modern era, each of whom likened the "feeling of utter dependence" to the morning after a bad burrito. Karl Marx (1818–1883) said it's the opiate of the people. Sigmund Freud (1856–1939) claimed it's a fantastic illusion used as a psychological abjuration of every boy's sexual love for his mother. And Friedrich Nietzsche (1844–1900) said that God was merely the way that human beings reassign the misery they feel at living, and he called the coroner. Liberals, with an admirably high view of the intellects of these three, have had a hard time getting out from under their shadows.

So these two boxers, "Liberal" and "Conservative," tired, bedraggled, and lacking enough power to land any more punches, come back to the center of the ring for the next round of their eternal match, and they can do little more than grasp at each other, wrap each other up. There's a lot of clutching and grabbing, and an occasional shouting match on *Larry King Live* or *Hardball with Chris Matthews*. The referee can't separate them, and neither of them has the strength to land the winning blow. But they keep fighting.

Dispatch 2: Emergents reject the politics and theologies of left versus right. Seeing both sides as a remnant of modernity, they look forward to a more complex reality.

Meanwhile, a generation of Christians aren't even boxing anymore. They're flying kites. They've entered an entirely different conception of what game we're really playing. They've opted out of the boxing match between liberal and conservative. They're finding a third way between the bipolar strife that has racked our churches and our society.

CAUGHT IN THE *CROSSFIRE*

Tragically, the polemically charged culture of American politics has seeped into the American church. In an effort to get people's attention, maybe even to get on a TV or radio program, Christian leaders resort to unnuanced attacks on one another. Spokesmen (yes, they're usually men) from the right and the left are continuing the infighting that has so damaged the church in the past and even ratcheted it up a notch. To quote just a few of the more recent, and more inflammatory comments:

> From the left: "The Religious Right doesn't care about the poor."
>
> From the right: "Emergent is limp-wristed, faggoty, homo-evangelical theology."
>
> From the left: "Emergents are nothing more than angry evangelicals."
>
> From the right: "The emergent church is al-Qaeda's ally."

In an era of sound bites and polemics, Christians have too often followed suit. As with the building of denominational bureaucracies in the first half of the twentieth century and the spinning of a web of evangelical parachurch groups in the second half, Christians at the beginning of the twenty-first century are once again allowing the culture at large to dictate public Christian behavior. Christians have once again taken the role of reactionaries.

While emergent Christians are sometimes baited to enter these debates in the blogosphere, most have little interest in the bipolarities of a bygone era, and the constant posturing of the left and the right often seems more successful at raising money than it does at actually solving problems. With reactionaries on one side and resolutionaries on the other, emergents are attempting to reclaim Jesus' role in society: revolutionary.

A couple of years ago, *The Daily Show*'s Jon Stewart went on to CNN's vitriolic *Crossfire* program, looked hosts Tucker Carlson and Paul Begala in the eye, and said, "You're hurting America.... Stop, stop, stop, stop hurting America." Stewart was tired of the sophomoric shouting matches that epitomized "debate" on *Crossfire*, and his plea became an overnight sensation. CNN canceled *Crossfire* just a couple of months later, the president of the network explaining, "I agree wholeheartedly with Jon Stewart's overall premise."[16]

Stewart's appearance on *Crossfire* was a sensation on YouTube, as was Stephen Colbert's bitingly sarcastic routine at the White House Correspondents' Dinner in 2006. Both of these Gen X heroes walked into the palace and said, "The emperor has no clothes," and a generation of young, thoughtful, disillusioned, cynical Americans cheered. Much of "left versus right" confrontation is a farce to prop up television ratings, keep radio talk show hosts employed, and fill the treasuries of the two political parties. And the church has not been immune to this financially lucrative fear-mongering.

But more and more people are checking out, becoming savvy to the moral bankruptcy on both sides of the "debate." They're looking for a new, third way, both in the church and in society at large.

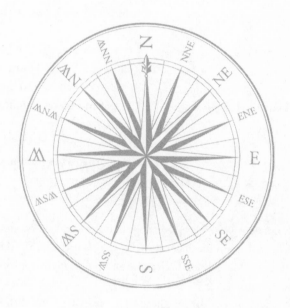

DISPATCH FROM THE BLOGOSPHERE:
MUSINGS OF A
POSTMODERN NEGRO

When I first ran across the blog "Musings of a Postmodern Negro," it caught my eye. And it made me a bit uncomfortable. *Negro* was a word I'd been taught to avoid back in middle school. Culturally and politically inappropriate, I was told. Archaic. Offensive.

Yet there it was, across the masthead of a particularly insightful blog. And stranger still, it was paired with *postmodern*. An unlikely couple, to be sure.

The blog was sharp and articulate. Long posts referred to the black liberation theology of James Cone and the radical pedagogy of bell hooks, the hip-hop lyrics of Mary J. Blige, the sermons of Martin Luther King Jr., and the philosophy of Jacques Derrida. Here's a taste of one such post, a reflection on Martin Luther King Day:

The Dream, as I have come to understand it, is an eschatological hope but [also] a liturgical practice whereby the people of God [are] on a journey to do a particular kind of work. That work being a Spirit-intoxicated performance of the gospel and giving a signification/foretaste to the kingdom of God...or as King called it the Beloved Community.[17]

The author also wrote openly about the inherent racism in American evangelicalism, yet he did so without anger. Passion, yes, but not anger. And sometimes he wrote with weariness,

As one who has been engaging a mostly white evangelical community for a couple of years now (three to be precise) I am getting tired. I find myself psychologically and spiritually drained. I find myself battling unconscious racial habits, aesthetics, and narratives all the time. This stuff wears you down. I am almost at a point where I feel the desire to retreat back into a non-white Christian world. Some days I feel burnt-out with the effort. Pray for a brutha![18]

And intriguingly, he wrote about his great interest in the emergent church movement. Emergent churches are overwhelmingly white, at least thus far in the still-young movement. So white, in fact, that the satirical religious newspaper *The Holy Observer* once ran a story, "Frightened Black Family Flees Emergent Church."[19]

I received an e-mail from the "Postmodern Negro," in the summer of 2005. Already an avid reader of his blog, I was thrilled to hear from him. He wrote to express interest in the emergent church movement and in Emergent Village specifically and to get information on emergent churches in his city, Charlotte, North Carolina. That e-mail led to a few phone conversations, a couple face-to-face meetings, and a lasting friendship.

Of all that I've learned about the "postmodern Negro," the most astounding discovery for me was that Anthony is not a professor, a philosopher, a theologian, or a pastor. He works for the Social Security Administration.

Anthony Smith grew up in Birmingham, Alabama. "Growing up in the eighties," he told me, "I saw everything: the crack epidemic, the beginning of the AIDS epidemic, the rise of gangs." In his own working-class home, he saw domestic violence and a parent using crack. "Most of my friends from growing up are either dead from gang violence or the drug trade, or they're in the penitentiary. My closest friend growing up, he's in jail for life for murdering someone.

"That's the bad stuff," Anthony continued. "But the good stuff is that I grew up in a black community that still had a sense of self, a sense of community. All in all, I had what black scholars call a 'thick black cultural experience.'" His grandmother brought him to a black Baptist church every Sunday through middle school, even though his own home was decidedly nonreligious; she was also the first African American woman to be a principal in the school district, and Anthony's grandfather was the first African American elected to the school board. But his father was on the streets, Anthony says, "an old-school brutha."

His mother, on the other hand, read a lot, and she was skeptical of religion. She marched with Martin Luther King in Birmingham in 1963 and stood up to the police water cannons. When Anthony was ten, she gave him a copy of Karl Marx's *Communist Manifesto*. A few years after that, she divorced Anthony's father, and they moved, he says, "to the white side of the mountain." There, in an upper-middle-class neighborhood, Anthony actually felt he had more in common with the working-class white kids than the bourgeois black kids.

Meanwhile, his interest in religion waned after his grandmother's death. First, he had philosophical problems with the idea of an all-loving God since he'd seen so many friends gunned down. And second, his image of a black preacher was a man with alcohol on his breath and a gold tooth—"He looked like a pimp," Anthony chuckled.

After high school, Anthony joined the Navy and served on a nuclear submarine. It was there that he became a devout Christian, making a profession of faith on January 2, 1994, in a storefront Pentecostal church. "I remember having a very profound religious experiece," he told me, "a profound awe." His pastor, James Lewis Giles, "was a serious autodidact, an organic intellectual.

Up until I met him, I thought Christianity was basically European, racist, white supremicist religion. But here was an African American pastor who blew that out of the water. He taught me that Christianity is two thousand years old, and I realized for the first time that Jesus was not British!"

Anthony, an autodidact himself, was drawn to Giles and his aberrant—at least in the black storefront Pentecostal world—interest in theology and history. Anthony's journey in Christian intellectualism began when Giles handed him a copy of C. S. Lewis's *Mere Christianity*. From there, Anthony began reading voraciously.

And he still reads voraciously. On his lunch break at work, he reads philosophy texts. The floor of his car is littered with books on spirituality, theology, and culture. He's been known to read while driving. He's even infamous among his friends for bringing a book to the movie theater and reading right through the previews by the light of his cell phone.

When I asked him why he reads so much, Anthony said, "I guess I just need to understand the world I live in. I mean, I had this profound religious experience in the Pentecostal church, but I needed to understand it. And I needed to understand Western civilization and the whole intellectual tradition behind Christianity."

Anthony's journey into the emergent movement began when he moved out of Pentecostalism, and he felt like a man without a home. An Internet search for the theologian Stanley Hauerwas led him to the Web site of Emergent Village, which led him to read a couple of books by Brian McLaren, which led him to the Emergent Village cohort—a monthly meeting—in Charlotte. Anthony now leads that group together with Steve Knight, and he contributed an essay, "Practicing Pentecost: Discovering the Kingdom of God amid Racial Fragmentation," to *An Emergent Manifesto of Hope*.[20]

When asked what it was about emergent Christianity that would attract such an unlikely proponent, Anthony mentioned two characteristics. "First," he said, "there is an epistemological humility with this particular movement. Christianity, especially American Christianity, for so long, because of its context, was wedded to imperialism, racism, and sexism. What I see in the emergent church are the conceptual tools and practices that can break out of that imperialistic past.

"What I saw in emergent is that we are wanting to see the **shalom** of God breaking out into the world in God's people."

I thought, 'This is what we need: we need white Christians who can shut up and listen to other folks.'

"And second," he continued, "is the notion of friendship, which I see in continuity with Dr. King and the civil rights movement. King didn't just march with black folk; he marched with Jews, with whites, with liberals. He marched with all kinds of different folks. So in this practice of friendship I saw some very real potential for a shared journey toward shared goals.

"What I saw in emergent," he concluded, "is that we are wanting to see the *shalom* of God breaking out into the world in God's people."

CHAPTER 2

DISPATCHES FROM THE FRONTIER OF THE AMERICAN CHURCH

AN ALLEGORY

Many years ago, a young woman, Abigail Church, well bred in a large East Coast city, fell in love and married. Both she and her husband were filled with wanderlust—they desired the adventure afforded by the American frontier. Upper-class society life was stultifying their spirits and their young marriage. So over the objections of her parents, the young couple packed up all their belongings and moved west.

Abigail's parents heard nothing from their daughter for many, many months. But they did read reports of the American West in their daily newspaper. Those stories were filled with disease, blizzard, hunger, battles with natives, and often, ignominious death. Gun battles blazed in those faraway towns, and scofflaws, cowboys, and renegade sheriffs were common characters.

Abigail's parents, George and Henrietta Church, worried incessantly, wondering if their daughter was even still alive. As they worried, they were able to keep up appearances: they still wore nice clothes, went to the opera weekly, and kept their Philadelphia mansion looking fine. But they failed to notice that their own lives were falling apart around them. Mr. Church's railroad business verged on bankruptcy, most of their household servants had quit, and their mansion was dilapidating from the inside out.

They kept up the extravagant landscaping but failed to notice that weeds had invaded their plant beds. They had the mansion painted but ignored the fact that termites infested the foundation.

Then, one day, they received a letter from their daughter. It had been written months earlier, coming to them by a combination of Pony Express, stagecoach, and rail. Mrs. Church, home alone in the afternoon, delicately opened the envelope, trembling with anticipation, and began reading:

Dearest Mother and Father,

My deepest apologies at not writing sooner, but circumstances have conspired against my timely correspondence. The two years since I left you have been filled with sorrow, trepidation, and hardship.

Samuel and I traveled by rail and stage to Saint Joseph in the state of Missouri. There we sold most of our earthly belongings for two horses and a parcel of land in the Nebraska Territory. We arrived at our quarter section of farmland in October, only to find our land in the possession of another family. A brawl ensued, and my dear Samuel was mortally wounded. I attended to him for a month before he finally expired on 17 November.

Winter on the Plains is severe, and I discovered that I was with child. With no husband and little money, I was taken in by Indians, and they nursed me through the birth of my child, which took place too soon in a tepee on the coldest night of February. I deeply regret that your first grandchild, Samuel Eli, died that very same night.

At that point, Henrietta Church, upon reading of her daughter's travails, fainted. The letter fluttered from her hands into the nearby fireplace, where it was consumed by flames.

Hours later, her husband found her, still unconscious, on the floor. George Church carried his beloved if beleaguered bride, Henrietta, up to their bed, where she died later that night of a broken heart. Consumed by grief, the once proud railroad baron took his own life with a pistol, dying alongside his wife.

Upon discovering their bodies and the state of their affairs, the authorities sold their possessions to remunerate their debts and buried them in a paupers' grave. Their mansion, its integrity irredeemably compromised, was razed.

AN ALTERNATIVE ENDING

At that point, Henrietta Church, upon reading of her daughter's travails, fainted. The letter fluttered from her hand to the threshold of the nearby fireplace, where it lay precariously near the glowing embers.

Her husband found her later that afternoon, still unconscious on the floor. Reviving her, he helped her to a chair and retrieved the letter from the brink of flames. Perching his reading glasses on his nose, he read the balance of the epistle aloud:

However, dear Mother and Father, all of this heartache has been mitigated by the great joy of my present situation. Contrary to opinion in the East, the Indians are not lawless savages but a people filled with grace and love and a beautiful rhythm of life uniquely suited to the rugged Plains. They took me in as one of their own, and I learned their ways, skills invaluable for life on the frontier.

After the snowmelt, my Indian friends escorted me back to Saint Joseph. They sold many of their furs (buffalo mostly) and paid for my three months' lodging at the Patee Hotel, the finest in the West.

Whilst at the Patee, I was courted by a fine young man of good stock named Jonathan Hawthorne. Jonathan and I were wed June last in Saint Joseph's Church of the Incarnation. It was a beautiful ceremony—O Mother, how I wish you could have seen it!

Having worked with the railroad for several years, Jonathan was named a supervisor for Union Pacific—surely you have heard of this most incredible innovation, the transcontinental railroad! He is supervising the laying of tracks through the South Pass, which will link the East and the West through the Rocky Mountains. Dear Father, I do so hope that you will make the journey westward and witness the next generation of your industry! You and Jonathan would surely become fast friends!

We have moved farther west, as Jonathan's work has taken us to Cheyenne, in the Wyoming Territory. We own a beautiful clapboard house in town, with plenty of room for you to stay, should you pay us a visit. And I do believe you should, since just this month I have given birth to twins! Please do come and visit little George and Henrietta Hawthorne.

I do miss you so! My heart longs to see you again.

The West is beautiful: the air is clear, the mountains majestic, the people proud and adventurous—won't you please come to Cheyenne?

Your always loving daughter,

Abi

George and Henrietta Church did indeed travel west to visit their daughter, her husband, and the twins. In fact, they stayed the rest of their lives, living well into their nineties. They lived out their days among their children and grandchildren, blessing them with wisdom and gifts.

Even today, you can visit their graves in Cheyenne.

And if you look closely, you can see George and Jonathan in the famous picture taken May 10, 1869, when the golden spike completed the transcontinental railroad at Promontory Summit, Utah Territory: father and son-in-law, side by side, looking into the future.

GEOLOGICAL MUSINGS

What's happening on the adventurous frontier of the American church seems like very good news to those on the frontier. But the residents of the old, established mansion-churches don't always know quite what to do with the rumors they're hearing about the emergent pioneers. Some disparage the emergent church as the new liberalism, while others decry it as little more than hip, faddish evangelism for the cynical set. Some say it's anti-intellectual because emergents are forsaking traditional academia for the more populist route of church work, while others vilify the emergents for overquoting postmodern philosophers and literary critics like Jacques Derrida and Stanley Fish. They're nothing but overeducated elite white males, they say.

Postmodern

That which comes after, and in reaction to, the modern. Although the definition of the term varies widely from discipline to discipline, it often entails a revival of older styles and methods, an abandonment of sharp differences between fields of knowledge, and a flattening of former hierarchies.

Each of these criticisms has merit, but the emergents are a tough group to pin down. The gospel is a destabilizing force, emergents respond, an inexorable movement of God, and this makes for unusual bedfellows. The gospel of God's uncompromising love for human beings and all of creation, incarnated most perfectly in the person of Jesus of Nazareth, is just as unpredictable as the wild-eyed Messiah himself was. Jesus refused to be domesticated by the cultural, political, and theological forces of his day. For instance, scholars have tried to prove that Jesus was in fact an Essene or maybe a Zealot—each a political faction of his era—but all attempts at getting Jesus to register with a political party fail. He shattered the demarcations that we use to give ourselves some sense of identity. And the gospel, which he breathed into fullness, calls Christians to affiliate first and foremost—if not exclusively—with him.

But it's been two millennia since Jesus invoked this radical claim. Like the scorching-hot lava that bubbles in the mantle of the earth, the gospel is scalding-hot and dangerous—and also strangely compelling. And although it has been crusted over for eons, it will inevitably find a time and a fissure, an opportunity to blast through that crust and explode, volcano-like, into the atmosphere. It would be no stretch to argue that God's radical love has burst through the crust of human institutions at regular intervals for the past six thousand years. Roman Catholics will claim Augustine, Francis of Assisi, and Aquinas as surfers on the lava. The Orthodox will point to Athanasius, Basil the Great, Gregory Nazianzus, and John Chrysostom.

And Protestants will claim this is exactly the kind of volcanic activity that happened in the sixteenth century, when reformers like Martin Luther, John Calvin, Ulrich Zwingli, and Menno Simons were used by God to break through the crust of institutional Roman Catholicism. These men, and their immediate successors, railed against the institutional excesses of Rome, against the power of the bishops, the "infallibility" of the pope, and the selling of indulgences to spend fewer years in the fabled purgatory.

Dispatch 3: The gospel is like lava: no matter how much crust has formed over it, it will always find a weak point and burst through.

But today the beautiful, scary, messy lava-gospel has again been crusted over by layers of bureaucracy, institutionalism, and dogma. As we've already seen, the battle of left versus right, telegenic though it may be, is one major symptom that the politics-transcending gospel has been crusted over. It's also been crusted over by the individualism inherent to our democratic system of government. The Lockean and Jeffersonian concept of individual rights stands at odds with the gospel's call to communal, shared, selfless living. And the rampant consumerism of postmodern America is another crust, exemplified by the abundance of "Jesus junk" in the marketplace. Christianity is big business. A friend of mine met the managing editor of a major newsweekly, and he was told that the magazine's editors have a calculus for determining how many times per year they can get Jesus, Mary, or angels on the cover, for when they do, they sell nearly twice as many issues as during a normal week. Trillions of dollars are tied up in massive church buildings and property, in the output of Christian publishing houses, and in the production of worship music.

It's not that Rick Warren has any malice in his heart as his book, *The Purpose-Driven Life*, tops thirty million in sales. It's just that the gospel cannot possibly be commodified into "Forty Days of Purpose" (as Warren himself has admitted). People may want their gospel in forty days, but the gospel can't be packaged, and its calling on a human life cannot possibly be completed (or even figured out) in six weeks.

Jesus can't be domesticated. Every time someone tries to house-train him, he breaks off the leash and starts causing trouble.

So regardless of the crusts of isms that form—individualism, consumerism, institutionalism; Presbyterianism, Methodism, Catholicism—the gospel will eventually once again volcanically explode, producing a river of fascinating, if dangerous, lava.

For there is no such thing as Gospelism.

WHAT EXACTLY IS EMERGING?

When responded to by human beings, the gospel causes people to do strange and beautiful things. They leave their mothers and brothers behind and leave the dead to bury their own dead, and they go off to fight AIDS in Africa. They quit their jobs and go to seminary. They confess their sins and promise Jesus that they will go and sin no more.

At its essence, emergent Christianity is an effort by a particular people in a particular time and place to respond to the gospel as it (once again) breaks through the age-old crusts. And it's the shifting tectonics of postmodernism that have caused the initial fissure.

The emergent church cannot be separated from the postmodern situation in which it was born. Like the emergents, postmodernism is notoriously slippery and difficult to define. François Lyotard famously described the postmodern condition as an "incredulity toward metanarratives"[1]—that is, a suspicion of "grand stories" that claim supremacy. More recently, it's been described by Cornel West as the "decentering of Europe."[2] Still others, like the philosopher Emmanuel Levinas and the theologian Jürgen Moltmann refer to it as the reality of the world "after Auschwitz," their point being that the Enlightenment promises of human progress, rationality, and peace died in the gas chambers of the Holocaust.[3]

The Enlightenment

An eighteenth-century movement in western Europe and America that vaunted reason as the primary, if not sole, basis for authority. Both the French and American revolutionaries were heavily influenced by Enlightenment philosophy.

Those of us born in the aftermath of the bloodiest century in human history are acutely aware that while the Enlightenment rationality brought some real good (for example, the Bill of Rights, advances in science and medicine, the civil rights movement), it also brought some incredible evil (the atomic bomb, Agent Orange, Nazism). As a species, we became more knowledgeable about our DNA and more efficient at killing one another. Many of us feel one thing about the legacy of the modern movement of enlightenment, rationality, industrialization, and science: ambivalent.

As a result, we're unsure about a lot of things and cynical about others. But it does seem clear that we need to start paying close attention to details and to start listening intently to one another's stories (hence my selection of the epigraph from Jack Caputo at the front of this book).

The Other

Postmodern shorthand for anyone differing in any way from "us," born of the reality that in an era of radical pluralism and globalization, we are constantly confronted with people who are indeed different from us.

Into this mix, what many have called a cultural watershed—the transition from the modern to the postmodern—came a group of younger Christians who had been reared in the modern church (albeit before the left-right battle lines were so definitively drawn) and educated in the postmodern world. Confronted with the radical pluralism—the globalization—of postmodernity, human beings seem to have three choices.[4] The first is *secularization*, characterized by the desire to downplay all differences of belief. For decades, social theorists were convinced that in the face of "otherness," human beings would become less and less religious. That religion would be seen for what it really is: a myth, based in ancient and medieval superstition, that serves only to divide what should be united.

But of course, it was clear by the waning days of the twentieth century that human beings weren't losing religion; they were getting *more* religious.[5] This leads to the second response to pluralism, *fundamentalism* (and its secular cousin, *ethnocentrism*). Here is the opposite posture, turning inward and circling the wagons with like-minded people. Consequently, the focus narrows to two questions: what makes us distinct, and how can we keep ourselves pure?

The emergent Christians are attempting another tack, one that steers between the Scylla of secularism and the Charybdis of fundamentalism. It's what might be called the *postmodern* posture: an attempt to both maintain one's distinctive identity while also being truly open to the identity of the other. Unfortunately for those who like models and paradigms, "twenty-one irrefutable laws," and "seven steps," the emergent response to pluralism is always ad hoc, always contextual, always situational. It does not lend itself to tidy books or simple blog posts. It means that emergent churches—including those profiled herein—look quite different from one another. They share little in the way of leadership structures or church architecture or forms of worship. What they share is an ethos, a vibe, a sensibility. And that's squishy.

This causes no end of frustration to those who criticize the emergent movement and would like to stomp it into oblivion. Each book against emergent Christians seems to miss the mark. One antagonistic blogger has said that criticizing the emergent church is like "nailing Jell-O to the wall." When someone writes that emergents don't believe in truth, they respond, "Yes, we believe in truth; we just think of it differently than you do." When another charges that emergents disregard history, they say, "We just interact with history in new ways." When yet another argues that emergents don't claim a particular theological tradition, they reply, "We find truth and beauty in many traditions."

Although these answers can be written off as postmoderns being intentionally slippery, something larger is at play. Emergents are unwilling to blindly accept the underlying assumptions of the stories they've been given. A few years ago at an emergent conference on theology, the Old Testament scholar Walter Bruegemann told the crowd that all of us live according to cognitive frameworks, which he called "scripts." American Christians, he charged, too often live by a "technological-therapeutic-militarist-consumerism" script, and he warned the emergents to live, instead, by the biblical script.

In an effort to follow the alternative biblical script, emergents often press hard at questioning the underlying assumptions in any previously articulated framework. For instance, they ask, "How is Reformed theology beholden to sixteenth-century assumptions?" And "How did early twentieth century socioeconomic structures affect the birth of Pentecostalism?" This constant questioning, often reserved for the academy, can seem obsessive at times, but emergents really are trying to understand how the gospel is understood and lived in various contexts.

The new context, the locus of emergent Christianity's birth, is the globalized, postmodern twenty-first century. Of course, just as many assumptions lie here as anywhere, so one must tread carefully, even suspiciously. But both observers and participants in the emergent phenomenon must also take care not to import their own preconceived notions onto the new Christianity.

The way to attend to the new, emergent Christians is to listen carefully to their stories, to visit their churches, to read their books (and to read between the lines of their books).

Deconstruction

A mode of literary analysis in which the unspoken assumptions underlying a text are revealed and even disassembled. Coined in the 1960s by postmodern guru Jacques Derrida, it has become important in other fields, including theology.

The emergent church defies simple explanation and categorization. It is pluriform and multivocal. It is, as I have written elsewhere, like a conductorless choir singing medieval polyphonic chants. The parts are in harmony and disharmony, and sometimes folks sing off-key, but taken as a whole, it's a thing of beauty.[6]

THE BEGINNINGS

In the mid-1990s, Jack Caputo hosted a conference at Villanova University on postmodern philosophy featuring the inimitable Jacques Derrida, as well as others. Caputo heard that an evangelical pastor from Texas was in the crowd, along with some of his young charges. "If Brad Cecil is here, I'd like to meet him. Please come and see me," Caputo said from the stage. Brad, a volunteer pastor of young adults at the conservative megachurch Pantego Bible, had been reading Derrida and Richard Rorty and other postmodern philosophers for a couple years, and hearing of the conference, he knew he couldn't miss it. Caputo, for his part, couldn't understand what a Texas evangelical was doing at an academic conference featuring Derrida, who could, in Derrida's own words, "rightly pass for an atheist."

Dispatch 4: The emergent phenomenon began in the late 1990s when a group of Christian leaders began a conversation about how postmodernism was affecting the faith.

Meanwhile, Tim Conder, a youth pastor at Chapel Hill Bible Church in North Carolina, was invited to a meeting with the top American evangelists to determine how they could reach out to the nascent "postmodern generation." Doug Pagitt was another youth pastor at another megachurch, growing increasingly disheartened with the stultifying theology therein. Karen Ward was struggling as a bureaucrat at the Evangelical Lutheran Church in America's national headquarters in Chicago. Tim Keel was finishing up at Denver Seminary and interning at Ron Johnson's Pathways Church in Denver, fighting to maintain the intuitions he'd gained as an artist in college. Andrew Jones was starting a church for Goth kids in Portland, Oregon, and Mark Driscoll was up the road working with skaters and punks in Seattle. Chris Seay, who was planting a church for Baylor University students in Waco, Texas, hired a young guitar player named Dave Crowder. Danielle Shroyer, a student at Baylor, was Chris's intern. Mark Scandrette had moved his family to San Francisco, to see what God had in store. Dan Kimball was watching his youth ministry at Santa Cruz Bible Church take on a life of its own at the "Graceland" Sunday evening service. Theologians Stan Grenz and John Franke were writing a book called *Beyond Foundationalism*, an evangelical justification for new forms of theology.[7] And other theologians and pastors, too, were starting a significant interaction with the most cutting-edge postmodern theory of the day.

I was just out of seminary, where I had first heard the word *postmodern* on the lips of Professors Nancey Murphy, Jim McClendon, and Miroslav Volf. And what I experienced was like new life.

Others could be named, too, and more names surface every year, names of people who were on the same journey in the mid-1990s, people who realized that *something* was wrong with the way Christianity was being practiced and the way that churches were being led. But the ability to articulate that had not yet come.

In 1997, Doug Pagitt left Wooddale Church in Minnesota to run a new initiative of the Dallas-based Leadership Network. Doug was charged with gathering the next generation of evangelical leaders; his quest: to find the next Bill Hybels, the next Rick Warren. One of the first gatherings he hosted took place at the Glen Eyrie Mansion outside of Colorado Springs. He had tapped a dozen young leaders to come to this meeting to discuss ministry to Gen Xers—"GenX 1.0" was the name of the gathering. Midway into the two days of meetings, Doug turned to Brad Cecil and asked, "Brad, what do you think?" By this point, Brad was on the floor in the corner of the room, literally balled up in the fetal position.

"I don't belong here," Brad responded. But after being pressed a little more, Brad finally said, "OK, I think you all have it all wrong."

While all of the previous talk had been about attracting Gen Xers back to church, the same way that Hybels and Warren had gotten the boomers to reengage, Brad said that now something totally different was going on. He went to the white board in the room and began to draw diagrams, explaining that the shifts under way were much more profound than simple generational differences.

"The Middle Ages," he said, "were characterized by *mysticism*. God was the author of all. But in the modern period, starting in the seventeenth century, man was seen as the author, and we entered an age of *empiricism*. Now," he continued, "we're experiencing the *postmodern turn*, toward an age of *enlightened mysticism*."

By the time Brad was done, the board was covered with a timeline stretching from Jesus to the present, littered with names like Foucault and Descartes and Rorty and Kant. (Brad later turned that talk into a PowerPoint presentation that has attained legendary status among emergents.) Most of the young evangelicals in the room had never heard these names before, or if they had, they had been warned against them. Here was Brad Cecil, once considered a protégé of Jerry Falwell, deferentially referring to secular philosophers!

After Brad's outburst, Doug, Chris Seay, and Mark Driscoll—the triumvirate of the "Young Leaders Network"—put their heads together. They decided that Brad was on to something, that he "got it"—whatever "it" was. They called Brad over to a corner of the room during the next coffee break and began pointing at others in the room. "Does he 'get it'?" they asked him. They were splitting up the room between those who understood Brad's presentation and those who didn't. And for their part, Doug, Chris, and Mark were interested in spending time with those who "got it."

"Get what?" Brad answered.

"You know. *It*. The stuff you're talking about."

The four of them couldn't yet articulate *it*, but they could feel it. It felt like the beginning of something new and the overthrow of something old. It felt to them like the burgeoning of a whole new way of understanding who they were as Christians. And they knew that they needed to do something about *it*. They began traveling the country, looking for others who *got it*.

My entrée into the group came a year later.

"THE BIBLE IS PROPAGANDA"

One very hot night in August 1998, I found myself sitting in a restaurant in Arlington, Texas, called Papacito's Cantina. I had been flown down to DFW by Doug to participate in a meeting about which I knew almost nothing.

Doug and I had met months before in Minneapolis. He and I were youth pastors just down the road from one another—he at an evangelical church, I at a mainline. We'd met for lunch at his request in the fall of 1997. We ate and talked about youth ministry, our churches, and ideas for how we might work together in the future. A few months later, I received a letter from the his church's senior pastor, Leith Anderson, stating that Doug had left for a new job, and the congregation was looking for someone to take his place. I figured that was the last time I'd hear of Doug. But a few months later, he called me from Texas and asked if I could fly down for a two-day meeting. I agreed.

I arrived in Texas somewhat disoriented and suffering from a nasty head cold. Knowing no one—even Doug and I had only met that one time—I mainly sat and listened. I don't recall everyone who was there, but I remember that we were in an entirely forgettable Embassy Suites hotel meeting room, not far from the airport. Chris Seay was there, and Mark Driscoll, Brad Cecil, Andrew Jones, and a couple of others.

The meeting was called to plan an event, a conference of sorts, to be held that fall at Glorieta Conference Center in Santa Fe, New Mexico. Following up on the smaller meeting in Colorado, they wanted this Glorieta event to be a sort of "national anticonference" that would be more of a free-for-all than your average pastors' meeting. Participants would be placed in cohorts, and they'd travel through the conference together, meeting to debrief one another on their experiences.

Doug had invited me to lead the youth pastors' cohort along with a couple of other guys. It seemed like a reasonable request, so I accepted.

When I got into that meeting room at the Embassy Suites, I was pretty sure that something interesting was going on in this group. These guys had a confidence that belied their age—most of them were under thirty—and the women in the room had a similar bravado. The event, to be called the National Reevaluation Forum, was already pretty well planned. I was coming in a little late to the game, but I didn't mind.

When we took a break for dinner, I followed the group across the parking lot and into Papacito's. I ended up sitting across from Brad Cecil, and the two of us got to talking. I can't remember the exact trajectory of the conversation, but I do remember saying at a somewhat inopportune time, and in far too loud a voice, "The Bible is propaganda!" It came out even though I don't believe I had ever thought it before. To be honest, I was a bit amazed that I had even said it. Everyone else at the table looked at me, their faces betraying the thought "Who's the new guy?"

As one does in these situations, I began to fervently defend my position, even in the face of Brad's stupefaction and his cries of "You've got to be kidding me! That's crazy!"

"Propaganda has a point and a purpose," I retorted. "It doesn't claim to be objective. It's trying to convince someone of something. It's trying to get people to join a cause, to join a movement. Isn't that exactly what the Bible is?"

Particularly torqued at my insouciance was Mark Driscoll, the fireplug sitting to Brad's left. The guy has an uncommonly sharp mind—and a tongue to match. (The story of his conversion, the rapid growth in membership at his church, and his subsequent disavowal of all things emergent is well documented in his own books.) Mark definitely did not appreciate my take on the sacred text of Christianity, and he let that be known. But in time, the conversation shifted to other ideas and arguments, and we finished our dinners.

The next morning, however, Brad approached me again. He said that he'd been consumed with this idea that the Bible is propaganda, and I had to once again hide the fact that I had never thought or said such a thing before—the phrase just popped into my head and tumbled out of my mouth. But it did indeed articulate something that had been bubbling in my spirit for a couple years, and it resonated with Brad's own theological intuition. I was trying to make the case that the Bible is not an object, to be read and studied dispassionately. In my experience, evangelicals read the Bible like a science book, looking for clues that would establish its truth, in order to prove that the events recorded in the Bible actually took place and to justify what they say it says about women's roles in the church and the abomination of homosexuality. I knew mainliners, on the other hand, who read the Bible with a healthy dose of skepticism, almost visibly uncomfortable with the extraordinary claims of miracles and items of faith like the resurrection. But I had started to think that either of these approaches is a misappropriation of the Bible. It is a living, breathing document that makes a claim on its readers' lives. It's like the pamphlets surreptitiously printed by Paul Revere and his compatriots in 1776—propaganda in that sense. It's God's manifesto, Jesus' *Little Red Book*.

These kinds of thoughts about the Bible had been burgeoning in me for years, but I didn't have people to talk to about them. And that was true for the others at the Dallas meeting as well. Brad was not quoting Jacques Derrida at the weekly staff meeting of Pantego Bible Church. New Zealander Andrew Jones, though financially supported by the Texas Baptist Convention, was doing off-the-map ministry with street kids and organizing 2:00 A.M rave parties in warehouses during which people danced their way through the biblical narrative. Chris Seay, an assumed future star in Texas evangelicalism—destined for one of the "big steeple" churches—had forsaken that promise to start small churches in inner cities. And Doug had left Wooddale Church when it became clear that his theological adventures into things like "open theism" meant that he'd never be allowed to plant one of Wooddale's daughter churches.[8]

We were, in some sense, a group of church misfits and castoffs. Surely, this was a group of competent people, convinced of their strong opinions, but many of them felt they were working without a net. They'd opted out of the systems that had nurtured them, and the relationships that would become "emergent" were the beginnings of a new way of being Christian and a new way of leading churches.

An unmistakable strain of the DNA of the early emergents is that we were all reared during the golden era of American youth ministry. Pioneered by organizations like Youth for Christ and Young Life and individuals like Mike Yaconelli and Wayne Rice, Protestant youth ministry in the 1970s and 1980s crackled with innovation. "Relational ministry" it was often called, wherein relationships between adult leaders and teenagers had primacy. The old catechetical routines and confirmation programs of earlier periods seemed stuffy and dull compared to the wild games and overnight camping trips of our youth. In 1965, it was unheard of for a church to have a paid youth worker; by 1985, it was virtually unthinkable not to have one. And the stereotype of the Young Life leader—a twenty-three-year-old, hot-enough-to-be-a-model guy driving a Jeep with a golden retriever in the back and a surfboard on the top—wasn't too far off the mark. But for all the magnetism of this model of ministry to teenagers, it was a mistaken syllogism: *if* kids love leader, *and* leader talks about Jesus, *then* kids love Jesus. The advent of relational youth ministry was also at the cost of justice ministries and the very catechesis that teaches young Christians that they're not the first generation to follow Jesus. Happily, justice ministry and catechesis are currently experiencing a renaissance in youth ministry.[9]

In a related way, most of the guys in Papacito's that night had cut their teeth in megachurch evangelicalism. Unlike my own mainline, Lake Wobegon adolescence, which taught me to be hardworking but demure, evangelicalism vaunts entrepreneurs and big personalities. From Billy Graham to Bill Hybels, having a big voice on a big stage is a sign of God's blessing on one's ministry. Notoriously, evangelical leaders spend as much time reading books on leadership by Harvard Business School professors as they do theology books by Dallas Seminary professors. So these young emergents had been tapped in their early twenties—some of them in their late teens—to be the next generation of megachurch pastors. They had great charisma and the right genitalia, and they were the kings-in-waiting. But then, in their mid- to late twenties, they opted out of that system due to problems with both evangelical theology and evangelical methods of church. But they were still leaders with charisma, charm, and several "dynamic communicators' workshops" under their belts. Looking back, it should come as no surprise that someone who commanded a youth ministry of two or three hundred teenagers at the age of twenty-three would have planted a church of that size by the age of thirty-three.

But trouble was already brewing by 2000. Following Brad Cecil's seminal outburst in 1997, "It's about theology!" became the mantra of the first emergents.

Theology

Reasoned discourse about God, religion, and spirituality. Literally, "words about God," from the Greek *logos* (word) and *theos* (God).

While the church life that we knew—both evangelical and mainline—was preoccupied with filling large churches and honing the methods thereof, early emergents were interested primarily in the theologies that undergirded the various practices of American Christianity. It seemed that the methodologies of the churches from which they had become disenfranchised were built on a whole host of assumptions, and these underlying assumptions had gone unchallenged for at least a generation. We figured that the way to unmask these assumptions was via theological questioning. We looked at the architecture of church buildings, at the structure of the leadership, at the form of the liturgy, at the denominational and seminary structures, and we asked, What does this say about what we believe about God? In some ways, it seems, we were following the lead of Derrida and other postmodern deconstructers in questioning the very premises of the Christianity that we had inherited.

Honestly, at the time the group harbored no ill will (though there was a bit of arrogance). We simply wanted to know *why* the churches we were serving did what they did. Why the quest for growth? Why the patriarchy? Why the robes and organ? And it seemed the only way to get answers to those questions was to investigate the foundations on which they were based. This led some to study foundationalism itself and ultimately to reject that system of knowledge.

This was unwelcome news to the funders at Leadership Network; the clear message from them was "We convene pastors to talk about best practices. Theology just causes people to argue. We don't do theology." The funding for the Young Leaders Network's good times was about to come to an end.

In 1999, Doug left the employ of Leadership Network and moved back to Minnesota to plant a church called Solomon's Porch with his wife, Shelley, and a few friends. Jason Mitchell, a church planter from the West Coast, was hired and put in the untenable position of both keeping the first generation of emergent leaders in-house and discovering the next wave of church pioneers. He lasted less than two years. Today, one can find nary a word on the Leadership Network Web site about the emergent church, and Leadership Network founder Bob Buford is vocal about his distaste for the movement.

Meanwhile, things with Mark Driscoll had become uncomfortable. Sitting on a panel at a Seattle event in 1999, he vehemently stated that women should not be pastors. Everyone else in the room was dumbfounded, since he was breaking an assumed consensus in the group. He was also becoming known as the "foul-mouthed preacher."[10] When Brad Cecil invited Mark to guest preach at Axxess Church in Arlington, he explained to Mark that unlike Seattle, swearing from the pulpit in Texas just wouldn't fly, and he asked Mark to please keep his language clean. Mark used the F-word in the first sentence.

The young emergents were gaining a reputation as arrogant, foul-mouthed, and angry young preachers, very much as a result of Driscoll's outbursts. This resulted in a couple of meetings and conference calls, an attempt to quell his vituperations. But nothing worked. Driscoll's increasingly conservative theology and his unrepentant attitude led to an eventual distancing from the rest of the group. By 2003, he was publicly denouncing his former fellows.

THE *NEW KIND OF CHRISTIAN* EFFECT

In 2000, the wheels were coming off the relationship between Emergent and Leadership Network. A meeting, led by Leadership Network's Brad Smith, was convened in San Antonio, Texas, one of several over a two-year period in an attempt to salvage the relationship. For a while, the group that would come to be known as Emergent had been known internally as the Group of Twenty. No one quite knew who was in the Twenty, although there was a gravitational center to the group. Those on the margins were invited to a meeting or two, after which it was determined whether or not they *got it*. Brian McLaren had been to a couple of meetings, but he hadn't quite been included in the Group of Twenty until San Antonio. A decade older than most of the early emergents, a baby boomer, and a suburbanite, McLaren was a bit of a misfit. But Doug had read the manuscript of his next book and was convinced that Brian *got it*. That book, released the next year, was *A New Kind of Christian*.[11]

Part parable, part Socratic dialogue, *A New Kind of Christian* follows the conversion of "Pastor Dan Poole," a burned-out, middle-aged evangelical pastor who is approaching a crisis of faith and leadership. Pastor Dan meets Neo, a former Presbyterian pastor cum Episcopal layman (and the high school science teacher of Dan's daughter). Early in the book, Dan agonizingly admits, "I feel like a fundamentalist who's losing his grip—whose fundamentals are cracking and fraying and falling apart and slipping through my fingers. . . . I feel that I'm losing the whole framework for my faith."

Neo tells him, "You have a modern faith, a faith that you developed in your homeland of modernity. But you're immigrating into a new land, a postmodern world."[12]

Thereafter, the two converse about most, if not all, of the issues that evangelicals consider essential. At every point, Neo tries to push Dan beyond the confines of conventional evangelicalism, into the new territory of postmodern Christianity.

- Neo on the Bible: "What if the real issue is not the authority of the text . . . but rather the authority of God? What if the issue isn't a book that we can interpret with amazing creativity but rather the will of God, the intent of God, the desire of God, the wisdom of God—maybe we could say the kingdom of God?"[13]

- On Christianity as the exclusive truth: "Look, my understanding of the gospel tells me that religion is always a mixed bag, whether it's Judaism, Christianity, Islam, or Buddhism. Some of it reflects people's sincere attempts to find truth, and some of it represents people's attempts to evade the truth through hypocrisy.... Look, Dan, I believe Jesus is the Savior, not Christianity. Is that so bad?"[14]

- On salvation: "I don't think it's our business to prognosticate the eternal destinies of anyone else."[15]

- On evangelism: "Stop counting conversions, because our whole approach to conversion is so, I don't know, mechanistic and consumeristic and individualistic and controlling. Instead, I'd encourage us to count conversations, because conversation implies a real relationship, and if we make our goal to establish relationships and engage conversations, I know that conversions will happen. But if we keep trying to convert people, we'll simply drive them away. They're sick of our sales pitches and our formulas."[16]

That summer, in 2001, Brian attended the Christian Booksellers Association, where he was a little-known author promoting a little-known book (and with a secular publishing house!). But Phyllis Tickle, the associate editor for religion at *Publisher's Weekly* and oracle of all things religious, was holding a press conference with a group of reporters. One asked her, "Other than Rick Warren's *Purpose-Driven Church*, what is one book here that you think will be around for a long time? A book we haven't heard of?"

Tickle replied without hesitation, "*A New Kind of Christian* by Brian McLaren."

Legend has it that the reporters and publishers left the press conference and walked en masse to the Jossey-Bass booth, where Brian was besieged with book-signing requests. He went on to write two sequels tracing the friendship of Pastor Dan and Neo,[17] and *A New Kind of Christian* has gone on to sell well over one hundred thousand copies. Brian has vaulted into the leadership of American Christianity—much to the chagrin of many evangelicals—culminating with *Time* magazine's recognition of him as one of "America's 25 Most Influential Evangelicals" in 2005.

Looking back, it's clear that *A New Kind of Christian* touched a nerve. Brian's e-mail inbox has been besieged with correspondence for the past half-decade, many of which begin "I feel like Pastor Dan!" In his books, he has articulated that "*it* factor" that was nascent but unnamed in a growing number of American Christians. An expanding cohort of evangelical leaders, many of them in their twenties and thirties, had grown disillusioned with what the evangelical establishment offered them and felt alone in their inner turmoil. Another common theme in Brian's inbox is, "I thought I was the only one thinking these things." Brian's writings have become a rallying cry, a public recognition of a broad but largely silent dystopia.

But they've also garnered vitriolic criticism. Book-length critiques have been published,[18] and entire Web sites are devoted to listing his heresies. Recently, Brian has been disinvited from several conferences at which he was scheduled to speak, usually after nasty letter-writing and blogging campaigns by his critics. And his follow-up book, *A Generous Orthodoxy*[19] (also a best-seller), caused a rift within the editorial staff at the evangelical publishing giant Zondervan; in a storm of leaked e-mails and surreptitious phone calls, a few key editors wanted to deep-six it, while others fought to keep it alive.

The intense passions ignited by McLaren's writing and speaking indicate yet again that the American church is in a liminal space, a time between times. To some, he is the sage of a new, generous Christianity. To others, he blurs the very sharp lines that have been drawn over the past half-century. And Brian's more recent turn to political and governmental concerns have only increased the attacks. In 2005, he was arrested for protesting federal budget cuts to welfare, and in 2006, he took the board chairmanship of Jim Wallis's left-leaning Sojourners/Call to Renewal organization. This has provoked longtime friend and former coauthor Len Sweet to charge, "I think that any intrusion of Christianity into politics—whether Left or Right—is ugly."[20]

Undaunted by charges of heresy, bad epistemology, and anti-Christism, McLaren soldiers on. In 2006, he retired as pastor of Cedar Ridge Community Church, and his speaking tour that year brought him to over two dozen countries around the globe. And he still gets letters and e-mails from readers, though now they're as likely to say, "Brian, I just got fired from my church for promoting your ideas in staff meetings."

One person has joked, "Evangelical pastors have to read *A New Kind of Christian* wrapped in a *Playboy* cover."

MEANWHILE, ACROSS THE POND

The emergents in the United States were also aware that a parallel movement was afoot in the United Kingdom. In fact, the English pioneers of a new iteration of Christianity had been at it there for over a decade, albeit along a slightly different tack. My first exposure to the British scene was via Jonny Baker, a staff member at Youth for Christ-London who, along with some of his mates, had invented an interactive labyrinth that was touring churches in the British Isles. Unlike a conventional labyrinth, this one consists of pilgrims wearing headphones and lighting candles by touching LCD screens.[21]

Jonny brought the labyrinth to the States at some youth conferences. He also happened to be one of the early bloggers, so his influence was immediately felt across the emergent church movement.

But in the UK, the movement was not called "emergent," nor was it primarily theological. The common rubric for Jonny and his mates in Britain is "alt.worship," which in itself suggests that their entry point into emergence was through forms of worship. In the mid-1990s, the alt.worship crowd in the UK was pioneering some very edgy ideas, like rave worship.

Dispatch 5: The emergent movement is not exclusively North American; it is growing around the globe.

The economy of churches in the UK is decidedly different than in the United States, which contributed to the different angles on the emergent phenomenon. The Anglican Church, being the state church, is deeply ensconced in the culture of Britain. And the Anglican communion is not a particularly theological collection of people; the Anglican connection is liturgical, leaving a wide latitude for theological expression. There are Anglicans of all stripes—conservative, liberal, charismatic, and so on—and they're all held together by a thin layer of glue called *The Book of Common Prayer* and occasional meetings of the thirty-eight geographical primates. But for all the problems this latitude has caused the Episcopal Church (that's the American brand of Anglicanism), in the UK it allowed the alt.worship people a wide berth. In addition to labyrinths and raves, they took over musty (and relatively empty) Anglican churches on Sunday nights, filled them with beanbag chairs and trance music, and hosted experiential worship services. In their book *Alternative Worship,* Jonny and his coauthor, Doug Gay, point to liberation theology as another influence in their progression.[22] Rowan Williams, the archbishop of Canterbury and thereby the most authoritative voice in the Anglican Church, even lent his imprimatur to the movement by writing the foreword to *Mission Shaped Church,* a report to the Church of England on these new forms. Williams wrote, "If 'church' is what happens when people encounter the Risen Jesus and commit themselves to sustaining and deepening that encounter in their encounter with each other, there is plenty of theological room for diversity of rhythm and style, so long as we have ways of identifying the same living Christ at the heart of every expression of Christian life in common."[23]

This acceptance by the church hierarchy didn't come easily, however. One of the first large, contemporary worship gatherings in London was the infamous "Nine o'Clock Service." Known as NOS, it began as an alt.worship youth ministry of Saint Thomas Anglican Church in Sheffield in 1986. NOS grew—attracting as many as six hundred each week to its "rave-in-the-nave worship"—and moved out of Saint Thomas in the mid-1990s. But it all came crashing down amidst a scandal including sexual and cultic accusations in August 1995. "This was a textbook cult," wrote the *Guardian,* and the *Daily Express* called NOS a "Rave for Jesus Cult." Jonny told me that he and other avant-garde young Anglicans had to go underground for several years because the scandal caused the Anglican leadership to suspect anything postmodern of being cultish.

Whereas NOS was, in Jonny's words, "loud music and lasers," the alt.worship movement was resurrected in the late 1990s with more reflective, ambient, contemplative services. Grace, the alt.worship led by Jonny; his wife, Jenny; Steve Collins; Mark Waddington; and their friends, meets at Saint Mary's Anglican Church in Ealing on Saturday evening, once a month, and it has a mellow vibe.[24] The evening consists of trance music, some readings, time for quiet contemplation, a short testimony, and occasionally communion.

It's a highly creative evening that the conveners readily admit they do for themselves—that is, Grace is not an "outreach" of Saint Mary's but a worship gathering by and for some "post-Anglicans" in London. "We wanted a service that was a genuine place for us to worship," Mark told me, "with the music we were into at that time. And it's evolved as time's gone by, as any service should."

I asked if that means a hyperconsumeristic approach: a new church for every little subgroup, as opposed to joining the grand tradition of the Anglican liturgy.

"We're working on a value of 'minimal exclusion.'"

"Every group, to be a 'group,' necessarily excludes some, even if that's by someone's self-exclusion" Jonny responded. "But at Grace we're working on a value of 'minimal exclusion.' We want to minimize exclusion as much as possible."

Other folks in the UK are emerging as well. Jason Clark, a Vineyard pastor in London, began inviting Brian McLaren to speak at conferences in London in 2001.[25] He became the point person for "Emergent-UK" in 2003 and has often consulted with emergent leaders in the United States. Other charismatic youth churches, such as Soul Survivor, were emerging in the UK, as well as the "24-7" prayer movement, a round-the-clock prayer revival that has spread around the globe. Each of these versions of UK emergence has influenced the development of emergent Christianity in the States.

And across the globe, Christians have been emerging at a rapid rate. In 2006, Brian McLaren met with emergents (and conservative evangelical protesters) in France, a theological consortium in Latin America called Red Del Camino,[26] and other groups throughout Europe, Asia, Africa, Australia, and New Zealand. In May 2007, a historic meeting called Amahoro Africa was held in Uganda. Leaders from North America, Europe, and Asia gathered to listen to young Christian pastors and theologians in Africa discuss the biggest challenges to their own emergence.[27] And new emergent networks are bubbling up each year.

What's most noteworthy about these various networks is how they've plugged into the emergent phenomenon. Through advances only possible in the last few years, including electronic means of communication and relatively hassle-free worldwide travel, emergents from around the world have found one another online and then developed those relationships into true friendships. Someone reads a blog or listens to a podcast, then sends an e-mail, and six months later is sleeping on a couch in that person's living room. In fact, the Web site for emergent Christians in Denmark boasts a page called "The Emergent Couch," on which emergents can register their sofa in expectation that others would come, visit, and sleep over.[28] This kind of denominationless connection among Christian leaders simply would not have been possible prior to the advent of the Internet. As it is, the global connections between emergents are bound only to increase.

THEN TILL NOW

But the Internet has meant more than connections among emergents. It's also meant that emergent Christians have been subjected to a constant onslaught of virtual criticism for the past several years. A Google search is likely to turn up these recent headlines:

> "The Emergent Church Is a Duplicitous Daughter of Apostate Rome"
>
> "The Emergent Church: 'Christian' Gay Is A-OK"
>
> "Gobbldygook Orthodoxy"
>
> "Brian McLaren: Even Satan Disguises Himself as an Angel of Light"
>
> "Tony Jones Is Not a Christian"

Of course, truth and accuracy matter little in some corners of the blogosphere, but the power of these anti-emergent Web sites cannot be denied. In an era when many people gather their information online, the fact that these sites turn up high on search engine lists has played a part in the evolution of emergent Christianity, occasionally putting emergents on the defensive. (See Appendix B for one such *apologia* for the emergent church.)

But these Web sites point to another change in the emergent phenomenon: in the past five years, the emergents have been deemed a threat in some parts of the American church. The visibility of emergent Christianity has surely risen. The media—both secular and Christian—have taken notice; books are selling;

Web sites are expanding; and churches around the country have used emergent language in their marketing materials.

One harbinger of the pervasiveness of all things emergent in the church is the number of seminaries and divinity schools that now offer courses on the emergent phenomenon. Pro, con, or neutral, emergent texts have taken up residence on syllabi across the theological spectrum. And emergent leaders are regularly invited to speak and lecture at seminaries.

Few scholars have yet attempted to sum up the emergent phenomenon in print. The one exception is the book *Emerging Churches* by Eddie Gibbs and Ryan Bolger. Gibbs and Bolger categorize their interviews with scores of leaders in emergent churches into nine categories, which they consider the core characteristics of the emergent movement: identifying with Jesus, transforming secular space, living as community, welcoming the stranger, serving with generosity, participating as producers, creating as created beings, leading as a body, and merging ancient and contemporary spiritualities. Based on their interviews, they conclude, "Emerging Churches are communities that practice the way of Jesus within postmodern cultures."[29]

The possible critique of that definition is that it is so broad that it could be applied to any church. Homing in a bit more is über-blogger and North Park University professor Scot McKnight, who defines the movement thusly: "Emerging churches are missional communities emerging in postmodern culture and consisting of followers of Jesus seeking to be faithful to the orthodox Christian faith in their place and time."[30]

In the end, what makes the emergents difficult to define is the relational nature of the movement. Whereas traditional groupings of Christians are either bounded sets (for example, Roman Catholicism or Presbyterianism—you know whether you're in or out based on membership) or centered sets (for example, evangelicalism, which centers on certain core beliefs), emergent Christians do not have membership or doctrine to hold them together. The glue is relationship. That makes it difficult to put one's finger on just what emergent is; to the question "What do you all hold in common?" the answer is most likely "We're friends."

And the friendship has grown significantly in just a decade. One observer of the movement put it to me this way: "It's like the emergents grew tired of the ocean liner that we call the traditional church," he said, "and one day a small band of them decided to get in a life raft, lower it into the ocean, and sail off in their own direction. What they didn't expect was that scores of others would see that, jump overboard, and try to climb in the raft with them." In other words, the challenge for the emergents has been the sustainability of the relational life raft.

The relational quality of the emergent phenomenon has caused anxiety among theological critics and frustration among journalists, but to a generation of Christians weaned on social networks, it makes perfect sense. In the end, the new definition of "Christian" may not be what particular doctrines one believes or which flavor of church to which one belongs but whether (and how thoroughly) one is woven into the fabric of global Christianity.

THE CHURCH'S CHOICE

Like George and Henrietta Church in the (not-so-subtle) allegory that leads this chapter, the American church has a choice to make about emergent Christianity. Or to be less abstract, Christians—both leaders and run-of-the-mill believers—need to decide what to do with the dispatches they're receiving from the emergent frontier. To be sure, one response is outright hostility and fear. For some, the frontier faith of the emergents is an out-and-out assault on all that is good and pure and holy in the church. To some, emergents pose a threat to orthodox doctrine. To others, they threaten to abolish time-tested forms of worship and structure. For either of these, the hope is that emergent Christianity is a fad that will soon disappear. But those critics should be chastened by the prediction of one of their own number. The evangelical intellectual Os Guinness went on the record at the beginning of the emergent movement and said, "I don't think postmodernism will be around in ten years' time." He said that in 1997.[31]

A more common way to read the dispatches from the emergent frontier is with caution, to stay put in the drawing room of the Old World manse and read about the adventures on the frontier. "Interesting," such a reader says, taking another sip of tea and stroking his Vandyke, "I really should try to implement some of those interesting innovations they're using on the frontier."

"Indeed," his wife says, dispassionately. "But let's not rush into anything."

"Indeed," he intones flatly, flipping the page to the business reports.

Many in the church have tried to catch just a little of the emergent virus—just enough to make them "relevant," but not enough to make them sick. At a typical pastor's conference, one of the five keynote speakers represents emergent Christianity, and the attendees stroke their chins thoughtfully and earnestly take notes. Then the next speaker talks about the latest in evangelism techniques—"Try these new evangelistic urinal screens! Get them embossed with your church's Web site, and drop them in the toilet at the local sports arena!"[32]—and the pastors earnestly scribble more notes. But many emergents will tell you that you can't be "a little emergent" any more than you can be "kind of pregnant." It's an all-or-nothing state, and a half-hearted embrace of these dispatches from the frontier will inevitably lead to frustration.[33]

The third response—the one chosen by most of the characters in this book—is to move to the frontier, where the action is. The most apt analogy for many emergent Christians comes from the 1999 movie *The Matrix*. Thomas Anderson, a.k.a. Neo (it's more than a coincidence that this character shares the name of McLaren's protagonist), is given a choice by his mentor and guide, Morpheus. At their first meeting, Morpheus challenges Neo, saying, "Let me tell you why you're here. You're here because you know something. What you know you can't explain, but you feel it. You've felt it your entire life. There's something wrong with the world. You don't know what it is, but it's there, like a splinter in your mind, driving you mad. It is this feeling that has brought you to me. Do you know what I'm talking about?"

Neo does. Kind of. But as Morpheus guessed, he can't quite explain it. He can feel it, but he can't put it into words. It's the Matrix, and Morpheus is offering Neo the chance to unplug from the massive system in which human beings are no more than batteries. After a little more explanation, Morpheus holds out a red pill and a blue pill and says, alluding to *Alice in Wonderland*, "This is your last chance. After this, there is no turning back. If you take the blue pill, you wake up in your bed and believe whatever you want. You take the red pill, you stay in Wonderland, and I show you how deep the rabbit hole goes."

Neo begins to reach for the red pill. "Remember," Morpheus says, "all I'm offering is the truth, nothing more."

It may be the coincidence that the release of *The Matrix* coincided with the birth of Emergent, but it's a frequent reference point in conversations: "When did you take the red pill?" The answer to that question is often when someone read a book or attended a conference or visited an emergent church. Some convert to an emergent way of faith, while others profess, "When I read my first emergent book, I realized that I've always been emergent." Back to the first analogy: some have to pull up stakes and move to the frontier; others are born there.

There's a lot at stake. It's not easy to leave the security and comfort of a mansion for the rugged life of the frontier. Honestly, most people do it because they see no other choice: it's leave or die (spiritually speaking).

Much more could be written about the first decade of the emergent phenomenon, more than a chapter can hold. I've only lightly touched on some names who deserve more prominence: Don Kimball, author of *The Emerging Church* and pastor at Vintage Faith Church; Scot McKnight, author of *The Jesus God* and the eponymous blog; and Andrew Jones, the "Tall Skinny Kiwi" blogger. More should be said about the theology of John Franke and Stan Grenz and LeRon Shults, more about the advent of the "missional church movement" and about the "new monastic" communities that have begun in many urban areas, and about the "emerging women" who blog and hold conferences, and about the influence of Youth Specialties in the early days. Suffice it to say that each of these occupies an important place in the story, and each deserves to have their story told, too. My telling of the story, of course, comes from my vantage point.

Regardless of the particularities, each of their stories would tell the same tale: something significant is taking place. At a recent theological conference, I ran into a pastor of a large Bible church in Texas. He was on a road trip, stopping first at Wheaton College for the annual theology conference and then driving to Philadelphia for the Emergent Village Theological Conversation. These were two intense and high-level dialogues about theology and philosophy, and I asked him what motivated him to take a two-week road trip and listen to theologians wax on about God. "Without Emergent, I wouldn't be a pastor anymore," he told me. Then, after a pause, he continued, "In fact, I'm pretty sure I wouldn't be going to church at all."

Somehow, the emergent way of faith had given him enough hope to carry on in ministry and even in the faith. His story is not uncommon, as you will see.

DISPATCH FROM THE ROCKY MOUNTAINS: KATIE AND KRISTEN

Sitting at a coffee shop recently, I was approached by a couple of women in their early sixties. They'd overheard me talking about the emergent church with a Web guy I'd met there.[34] They begged my pardon for eavesdropping on our conversation and then asked, "How is the emergent church different from normal Christian believers?" Frankly, I was stunned that these two had even heard of the emergent church movement, so I responded with a question: "What do you mean, 'normal Christian believers'? Which flavor of Christianity are you talking about?"

"Just normal," said one. "I'm a born-again Christian. How is an emergent Christian any different from that?"

As I did my best to answer, they kept peppering me with questions:

"How do you know you're saved?"

"How does someone get to heaven?"

"Do you think we are the 'New Israel'?"

"What is the foundation of your belief?"

"Do you believe in the Holy Spirit?"

"Do you believe in prayer?"

"Do you think the Bible is inspired?"

I'm not so naive to think that there weren't "right" and "wrong" answers to these questions, but I didn't know where these women were coming from. If they were conservative evangelicals, one set of answers would be correct, and if they were liberal mainliners, another would. I wasn't trying to be deceptive, but I didn't want to step on a grenade either. So I tried to ferret out their own church affiliation to discover the agenda behind their questions, and they ultimately told me that they attend Grace Church, a large and very conservative megachurch in Eden Prairie, Minnesota. I knew enough about Grace to know that these women would be highly skeptical of emergent Christians. In fact, I knew that their pastor, Daniel Henderson, had preached a sermon warning his flock about the dangers of the emergent church movement not long before.[35]

Although one of the women had to leave, the other, Katie, and I kept talking for over an hour. I found it fascinating that the more we spoke, the more she agreed with all of the emergent critiques of conventional Christianity and the church. "The church has lost its relevance," she declared.

When we got onto the topic of the Holy Spirit, I proffered that emergents tend to have a stronger belief in the third person of the Trinity than many evangelicals. "Emergents trust in the Holy Spirit," I said, "more than they trust in the methods of doing church."

"I totally agree!" she almost shouted. "I really think that prayer is the answer and that the Holy Spirit moves in ways totally unknown to us! So," she continued, "why would I want to come to an emergent church?"

"Well, I don't imagine you would want to," I said, "but I can tell you why others do. Let me read to you an e-mail I received just today."

Does God work & act in Absolutes?

Tony,

I am a part-time youth leader/Starbucks barista/inner-city after-school program worker in Colorado and was recently in Austin at the Youth Specialties Conference. I sat in on your talk on the emerging church, and I left very hopeful and surprised by my rare sense of feeling understood and in harmony with someone else. Your example of finally meeting someone who loves the same film or book, that no one else has appreciated, described how I felt after your talk—and how I often feel when I meet others who are looking for the layers and shades and colors of God.

I appreciated the lack of arrogance in which you spoke of this movement. You did not speak of it as a solution or the right way or even an alternative but rather as something ancient and new and hopeful. I see followers of Jesus everywhere looking for deeper truth underneath what has been claimed as "absolute truth," wondering whether God really works in absolutes. I see people looking at the Bible, in its abstract and poetic language, as a start of interaction with God and humanity, rather than a way to keep God inside a book and a source of answers to throw at people in a debate. I see people asking what it looks like to love without an agenda, to care and live among the poor and forgotten. I am hopeful because I see it happening everywhere—making me actually believe what I always tell my youth kids—that there is no absence of God anywhere.

I have conversations every week with coworker friends at Starbucks who are completely respectful of Jesus and who live far more compassionate and selfless lives than a lot of Christians but who want nothing to do with Christianity. They speak with me honestly because there is respect and laughter and a genuine sense that we are learning together and from each other. I am so grateful for these friend-ships and ongoing conversations—people of various traditions and experiences and religions and sexual orientations coming together and rethinking the distortions of Americanized Christianity that have become accepted as the Way. The sense I always get from these friends is a tiredness toward a commodity-driven culture and a deep skepticism of a commodity-driven church that sometimes resembles very little if anything having to do with Jesus.

I have grown up in the church and have worked within it long enough to know that I love it as much as I am hard on it. It has been just as hard on me—I have actually been accused of having a too hope-ful and loving perception of God, which I find ridiculous and funny. I have also been accused of being too tolerant and accepting—that non-Christians like me too much and that Jesus says we should be persecuted. Somehow I do not think that is what Jesus meant when he said those words[36]—that we would be persecuted for being intol-erant and presumptuous, uncreative and uninspired. I think maybe he meant that we would be persecuted for our love, for our pas-sionate commitment to bringing out awareness of social injustice, for trying to level the unequal distribution of wealth as a result of greed and power that results in poverty and oppression and vio-lence.

At the same time, this is the community that has shaped me and caused me to think and become and question myself. It is also a community that has loved and supported me and given me the humbling and beautifully messy context of working with teenagers who are looking to me for some sort of understanding of God.

All of this said, I suppose I just wanted to thank you, and possibly give you a sense of feeling understood. Peace to you.

—Kristen

"I see people asking what it looks like to love without an agenda, to care and live among the poor and forgotten. I am hopeful because I see it happening everywhere."

"I don't know why *you'd* want to get involved in the emergent church," I told Katie, "but that's why Kristen does. And if I may be so bold, she speaks for thousands of younger Christians."

Katie nodded and smiled. I gave her my card, and we went our separate ways. But I do wonder if Katie might have a daughter a lot like Kristen. Or a granddaughter. Or indeed, if Katie herself might have found Kristen's e-mail a compelling apologetic for the emergent church.

CHAPTER 3

WHO ARE THE EMERGENT CHRISTIANS?

THE VERY FIRST PREEMERGENT GATHERING IN COLORADO—
the one with Brad Cecil's catatonia-cum-whiteboard presentation—was not
about postmodernism at all. Not, at least, until Brad turned the conversation that
way. Instead, that meeting was called to discuss how evangelical megachurches
might reach out to eighteen- to thirty-five-year-olds. The baby boomers had
come back to church in droves (albeit not always to their parents' churches).
They'd dropped out of church in the 1960s and 1970s, while they were in
college, but they flooded back into the megachurches in the 1980s, often after
the birth of their children. But by the mid-1990s, it was clear that the Gen
Xers were not trending the same way. The first Xers were having children, but
they weren't enrolling them in Sunday school. Under the aegis of Leadership
Network, a bunch of evangelical youth pastors, college pastors, and church
planters met to solve the problem. Church needed to be gussied up to attract
the Xers. "Let's make it more *relevant*," they said. "Let's use grunge music and
wrought-iron candleholders."

And that's about when Brad went catatonic.

Brad's spontaneous presentation on the history of Western philosophy took the conversation—which has now gone on for a decade—in a completely different direction. This is not about generational ministry, he was saying. This is about a complete shift in worldview, about the first major philosophical watershed in four or five centuries.

Thus the emergent conversation has never been about age, but the emergents do tend to skew younger than the average American churchgoer. I surveyed eight emergent congregations in May 2006, and the average age was 32.5,[1] whereas the average age of an American in church on any given Sunday is 50.[2] Emergents also tend to be whiter and more educated than the average American churchgoer.[3] These numbers reflect that emergents are generally of the coveted Generations X and Y, but numbers don't tell the whole story. Peppered throughout each congregation that I visited were older folks and nonwhite folks and others who insisted that emergent Christianity does not fit in the usual categories. These comments are reminiscent of the postmodern skepticism toward metanarratives. Instead, our concern should be with the details, the micronarratives, the actual stories of actual people.

HUNCHES AND INTUITIONS

Like Kristen at the Colorado Starbucks, another barista at another Starbucks— this one in Grand Rapids, Michigan—led to another e-mail I received recently:

Tony,

I just heard the BEST emergent put down! The manager of Starbucks in our town is apparently a fairly conservative Christian guy. Well, one of the girls in my church works for him. He assumed that since she's gay, she doesn't go to church. She informed him that we have a new kind of community that most evangelicals would consider "emerging." He told her, "You know what I hate about those emergent people? They love everyone."

Isn't that great?

–Chad

Chad's e-mail wouldn't seem so shocking had it come from a New England Episcopalian or a Chicago Congregationalist, from someone whose church has "Open and Affirming" on its marquee. But Chad's no mainliner. He's an evangelical in a capital of evangelicalism: settled by Dutch Reformed immigrants, Grand Rapids is home to multiple evangelical publishing houses, colleges, seminaries, megachurches, and ministry headquarters. Among the evangelical intelligentsia, it's often listed alongside Colorado Springs, Colorado, and Wheaton, Illinois, as an evangelical ghetto.

Chad grew up the son of a Presbyterian pastor. In high school, his family switched to the Reformed Church in America, a smaller and more evangelical denomination. After college, Chad spent ten years as a youth pastor in Reformed and Evangelical churches, growing more dissatisfied each year with not only the systems of the churches but also the way in which the faith was being disseminated—he

> "You know what I hate about those emergent people? They love everyone."

was particularly disenchanted with the political assumptions at play within evangelicalism. Through his contact with Emergent, Chad began to sense a need to create a new kind of church, more representative of his understanding of Christianity. After leaving his evangelical church in 2003, he began to meet with a group of people in local coffeehouses in Lansing, Michigan. In these gatherings, Chad saw the potential of a more free-form and life-giving expression of the faith, a vision that included small, simple churches that met in homes and focused on shared life and teaching. Though Chad and his friend, Eric, had thought to focus their new ministry in the Lansing area, word of their "simple church" vision leaked out, and they began attracting interest from all over Michigan.

Meanwhile, Chad and his family have some deep relationships with some people in Grand Rapids who follow Jesus and are also a part of the gay, lesbian, bisexual, and transgender (GLBT) community. These friends had been active in a large and famous church nearby, but after they came out, they were told that they could not rise into the ranks of leadership in that church. Soon after that painful episode, Chad and Eric decided to create a church around these new friends rather than see them be further alienated by Christianity. Notably, this has not entailed a big ideological or political adjustment for Chad, at least not yet. By developing their idea of "simple church," Chad and Eric have avoided many of the political land mines that threaten more traditional and more institutional churches.

Across the emergent church landscape, characters like Chad defy easy classification. Is he an evangelical? He's unhinged from any denominational structure, and he obviously feels the freedom to start up a church wherever and whenever and with whomever he wants. These are evangelical characteristics. Or is he a mainliner? His openly gay barista friend feels welcome at his church, and her boss would surely like to expel emergent churches from the evangelical fold. This kind of inclusive spirit is characteristically mainline.

As a result of these category-defying characteristics, many emergents feel homeless in the modern American Christian church. In 2006, I visited eight emergent congregations across the country. At each, I performed one-on-one interviews and facilitated focus groups, listening for articulations of just what emergent Christianity offered these people.

First, these are largely people who feel great *disappointment with modern American Christianity*. The bipolarities of left versus right were often noted. And although the majority are evangelical expatriates, quite a few are former mainliners and Roman Catholics. Some of their self-identity comes from who they *were* and what they came from. So it's not uncommon to ask an emergent Christian about something and have the response begin "Well, I know we're *not* like..." This has provoked a fair amount of criticism, especially of the early emergents. Some have charged that emergents are a little too much like adolescents in rebellion from the parents who gave them life. "We rebelled, too," say former Jesus Movement members, "but then we settled down and joined the establishment. You can only fight the system for so long." Of course, nothing raises the hackles of emergents more than patronizing comments like that.

But if emergents are overly sensitive to this charge, it's because there's just enough truth in it to sting. Most emergents are children of the twentieth-century church. Like most Americans, they grew up going to Sunday school and church camp. Some went on to evangelical colleges. But somewhere along the way, they lost faith in the church, if not faith in God. That is, while many of their peers disengaged from faith altogether, the emergents found the problem to be the way the gospel had been presented to them, the way it had been lived out, and the way that churches had been structured to promulgate that message. They report that the churches of their youth are too big, are too focused on capturing a greater "market share," and preach their message with too much certainty. More than one emergent reported sentiments similar to one young man who said, "This emergent church is my last attempt at church. If this doesn't work, I'm out. I don't think I'll ever give up on God, but I'm on the verge of giving up on the notion that human beings can form organizations that faithfully represent God in the world."

The second characteristic of emergents is a high—if tortured—*desire for inclusion*. In interviews, similar comments were repeated in all eight churches: "openness," "nonjudgmental," "wherever you are on the journey," "inclusive." But they were quick to point out that this doesn't necessarily mean liberal or relativistic. One emergent stated, "Just because our church is open to various viewpoints doesn't mean that anything goes. We really

> "This emergent church is my last attempt at church. If this doesn't work, I'm out."

believe things. We just also really believe that we might be wrong." This is a tricky middle path between the certainties of evangelicalism and the openness of liberalism, and the jury is out as to whether this middle ground is really a tenable place to stand.

The struggle to maintain a distinctive identity while valuing inclusion was articulated by Danielle Shroyer, pastor of Journey in Dallas, in 2006. The annual Emergent Village Theological Conversation that year was with Miroslav Volf, a Christian theologian at Yale. Best known for his book *Exclusion and Embrace*, Volf makes a compelling case that at the very heart of the Christian life must be the ability to embrace the Other, to forgive one's enemy (his own youth as a Christian in communist Yugoslavia has been the impetus for his work in this area).[4] Sitting on a stool across from Volf, Danielle told of her church's struggle with the issue of homosexuality. Despite the lack of consensus in the church, the congregation and leaders were working together to determine what posture they would take on this contentious issue. "What worries me," she confessed to Volf, "is that either way we go, we'll be excluding someone. If we go one way, we'll exclude homosexuals, and if we go the other way, we'll exclude fundamentalists." The tone of Danielle's voice betrayed the honesty of her plea: she was not looking for a new way to be liberal and inviting to all. She was looking for a way to navigate the rocky shoals on either side of this issue, each of which holds the wreckage of many a church. She was trying to find a third way, an alternative answer. Emergents, as a whole, are navigating these same turbulent waters.

#3   The third defining characteristic among emergents is a *hope-filled orientation*. Emergents generally view the future with optimism, in stark contrast to the large number of American Christians who decry the present state of affairs, confident that Jesus' imminent return hinges on disasters, wars, and evil.[5]

The hope of emergents is not an Enlightenment-influenced hope in human progress but what theologians call "eschatological hope." That is, they interpret the Bible in such a way that Jesus brought good news (a.k.a. gospel), and there's more good news to come, even on Judgment Day. In an emergent church, you're likely to hear a phrase like "Our calling as a church is to partner with God in the work that God is already doing in the world—to cooperate in the building of God's Kingdom." Many theological assumptions lie behind this statement, not least of which is a robust faith in God's presence and ongoing activity in the world. Further, the idea that human beings can "cooperate" with God is particularly galling to conservative Calvinists, who generally deny the human ability to participate with God's work. This posture, however, is too passive for most emergents, who see the Bible as a call for us to contribute to God's purposes.

(A caveat: lists are dangerous, and emergents are rightly suspicious of them. These three characteristics of emergent Christians are not conclusive, nor are they necessarily provable—or disprovable. They are simply my intuitions based on scores of conversations with emergents, and I expect—and hope—that they will provoke much debate.)

INFLUENCING CULTURE OR INFLUENCED BY CULTURE?

American Christians have struggled with just how to appropriate resources, especially those from outside of the faith, in considering their religion and their amusements. In 2007, the flagship magazine of evangelicalism, *Christianity Today*, allowed itself to be wrapped in a false cover, an advertisement for the movie *Evan Almighty*. Inside, editor David Neff described the false cover as a "bold symbol of the new cooperative spirit" between evangelicals and Hollywood. "Yet," he cautioned, "the relationship is still cautious and tentative."[6] In the next issue, he was excoriated in several letters for this marketing partnership.

Aside from the journalistic question of whether *Christianity Today* writers can be relied on by evangelicals to write honest reviews of movies that they've promoted and prescreened, this turn of events is noteworthy in evangelical-land. Not long ago, evangelicals were intent on setting up an alternative to most spheres of culture. Christian radio stations and television stations appeared not long after the advent of those media. For years, the Billy Graham Evangelistic Association underwrote Worldwide Pictures, Inc., a company that produced feature-length evangelistic movies and then screened them in rented movie theaters. And when a recording artist from the "Christian" subgenre had a "crossover hit" (think Amy Grant and Michael W. Smith in the 1980s), it was big news.

Now evangelicals truck heavily in everyday culture. The massive sales of *Your Best Life Now* by Joel Osteen and *The Purpose-Driven Life* by Rick Warren were fueled, in part, by bulk purchases from Sam's Club and Costco. *American Idol* Carrie Underwood sings openly, "Jesus, Take the Wheel." And Hollywood unashamedly woos evangelicals, often by courting evangelical leaders. The consequences of this newfound admiration, however, comes at a cost. Dozens of evangelical leaders attended prescreenings of the 2004 film *The Passion of the Christ*, personally hosted by its megastar director, Mel Gibson. They then went on, predictably, to promote Gibson's film as "the single greatest evangelistic tool in the history of mankind." It was only later that the *New York Times* uncovered that Gibson is part of a breakaway sect of Catholicism called Traditionalist Roman Catholics. These old-order Catholics are extremely conservative, rejecting the innovations of the Second Vatican Council (1962–1965) and narrow in their understanding of salvation. Gibson holds to the doctrine of *extra ecclesiam nulla salus* ("outside of the church, there is no salvation")—and by "the church," he mean *his* church, the "true" Catholic church. In other words, Gibson likely thinks that the evangelical leaders who were touting his movie are all bound for hell.[7] And that's not to mention Gibson's anti-Semitic rant in 2006 or his ambivalence about the reality of the Holocaust (Gibson's father, also a Traditionalist Catholic, is a vociferous Holocaust denier).

Navigating culture as a Christian is notoriously tricky, as evangelicals have discovered. This discovery might prompt them to be a little less critical of liberals, whom they've often taken to task for selling out to culture. The story of the twentieth-century mainline church was a story of co-option, according to evangelicals. The line between church and culture was erased, and in biblical terms, mainline Christians lost their ability to be the "salt seasoning" in the world.[8]

How ironic that the tables have turned. Today, evangelicals are reveling in their newfound influence in Hollywood and on Capitol Hill, and major mainline voices are promoting a retraditioning of the church, a return to church as a distinctive community, set apart from culture.

The problem with these postures toward culture is that they don't really understand what culture is. "Culture" is not some monolithic entity out there that Christians can either resist or acquiesce to. Etymologically, *culture* comes from the Latin word *culturus*, from which we also get *cultivate*. Technically speaking, culture is the vast array of symbols (language, clothing, icons, ideas, hairstyles, stemware, obscene hand gestures, and pretty much everything else) by which human beings cultivate our experiences of life. If life is a messy field full of dirt and weeds and rocks and plants, culture is the chisel plough pulled behind the tractor that fashions the mess into an assemblage of rows so that we can make some sense of it.

Or in the words of the Christian essayist Frederica Mathewes-Green, "A culture is just a fleeting human creation, a spontaneous uncontrolled collaboration, and we shouldn't expect it ever to be perfect or even to be very good."[9]

It's with this understanding of culture in mind that emergents can respond to the charge that they are "too cultural," a criticism that has been leveled often in recent years. Usually, the subsequent explanation is that emergent Christianity is simply the cool, faddish new way to be Christian—that it's a Christianity engendered by blogs and cell phones and hip clothing and postmodern philosophers. Emergents, it is claimed, have allowed culture, as opposed to the Bible, to dictate their ministry.

But when seen as the means by which we cultivate our experiences of life, culture is everywhere and everything. Every pastor who stands in a pulpit to proclaim the Sunday morning message is beholden to culture: he's using language and a microphone, she's got some scribbled notes and glasses perched on her nose, she's got her hair combed a certain way, and he's wearing his favorite tie. Likewise, every parishioner in every pew is completely enveloped in "culture." There's no escaping it.

Nor is there any such thing as a "sacred-secular divide." Regardless of the City of God versus City of Man of Augustine (354–430) or the "two kingdoms" of Luther (1483–1546) or the myriad other articulations of a Platonic divide between the things of God and the things of world, emergents see the whole of culture and creation as one big mess in which God is moving. There's the beautiful and godly—the birth of a child—and the horrific and satanic—the killing of a child—inelegantly intermixed. And between those two poles lies a vast array of objects and events and people and ideas that reflect some of God, some of us, and even a bit of evil.

Dispatch 6: Emergents see God's activity in all aspects of culture and reject the sacred-secular divide.

The emergent way of interacting with the multifarious resources of "culture" is not monolithic either. There's no one-size-fits-all method for parsing out the good from the bad. Instead, it's an art of looking for the intersections between theology and other disciplines, looking for truth wherever one can find it.[10] In other words, Christian theology does not have the sole claim to truth; what Christian theology can do is find truth elsewhere and then translate that truth into the idioms given to us by the biblical narrative. Truth is wherever God deigns to expose it; it is most perfectly and poignantly instantiated in the person of Jesus, and from him it flows out into all creation.

So, for instance, one might wonder about the inordinate success of the show *American Idol*, in which amateur singers place themselves at the mercy of three judges and a judging nation for the minuscule chance of becoming a superstar. We hear the incomprehensible platitudes of judge Randy Jackson, the passive-aggressive deferrals of Paula Abdul, and the vitriolic assaults of Simon Cowell and wonder, Are we just a nation of sadists? Then we see the true brilliance of the show, the one who (literally) picks up contestants when they've fallen down in joy or in sorrow, who often stands in the singers' stead and takes Simon's barbs, who gives the hug and smile when a contestant gets voted off the show: it's Ryan Seacrest. I daresay, without the redemptive presence of Seacrest, *American Idol* would not have taken off like it has. His ability to humanize the contestants, even as the judges attempt to dehumanize them, is, in microcosm, a testament to the desire that we all have for redemption. It's been said that every good story is a version of the biblical story, and *American Idol* is no exception.

Now, is this simply an exercise in self-delusion, an attempt to justify our co-option by the market forces of American pop culture? No. It is, instead, an attempt to bring theological reasoning to bear on a major cultural phenomenon, an attempt to understand *American Idol* Christianly. It's an attempt to find truth even in the banality of *American Idol*. Or postmodern philosophy. Or evolutionary psychology. Or you name it. Emergents look for the intersections and connections between the overarching biblical narrative—the story that orients our lives—and the many ways that human beings cultivate their experiences. Assuming that God is at work in the world, emergents also assume that they will find traces of God in the many articulations of scientists and artists and philosophers and politicians. Really, the ways that God, in Christ, can be revealed to us are limitless. So to catalogue the many influences on emergents—both "theological" and "nontheological"—would be impossible. Suffice it to say, if God is in it, then emergent Christians will find God there.

AN "ENVELOPE OF FRIENDSHIP"

When the pastor accepted my invitation to lunch, I was happy, if a bit anxious. This man is the pastor of a large Baptist Church, the president of a ministry, and the author of several best-selling books. He sits atop a pyramid of conservative Reformed Christians that has been particularly critical of emergents.[11] I sent him an e-mail after seeing the promotional material for his pastors' conference, the language of which made it clear that the emergent church movement was one of his targets for criticism. My e-mail was an olive branch: an invitation to lunch and an assurance that we both share a commitment to proclaiming Christ.

The pastor is a gentle-looking man, but his theology is anything but gentle. He believes that God's anger burns with holy fire against human sin. Words like *wrath*, *hate*, and *blood* peppered his sentences as we dined at the Olive Garden (his choice). Slight of stature, he has a piercing gaze. He brought three of his compatriots, and I brought Doug Pagitt, the pastor of Solomon's Porch and my best friend. He carried a Bible and a notebook; Doug and I each brought books that we'd written to give as gifts.

The pastor began by admitting that he'd never heard of me before, and that he really didn't have anything against emergent Christians per se. His beef is with Brian McLaren and Steve Chalke, both emergent authors who have questioned the version of the doctrine of the atonement that he holds dear.[12] Early in the lunch, Doug said that he's long respected the ministry of the pastor's church and since we're in the same town, perhaps we could minister in partnership with one another. "Regardless of our theological differences," Doug said, "maybe we can find ways to work together." But as the lunch progressed, it became clear that the pastor felt that the beginning of any partnership was necessarily agreement on a particular doctrine, the atonement, a doctrine that he equates with an understanding of the gospel. To put it conversely, if you don't understand the atonement as he does, you do not understand the gospel. To put it even more bluntly, he said that if you reject his understanding of the gospel, you are rejecting the gospel *in toto*, and so, by logical extension, you are not a Christian. (To be fair, he didn't pass the same sentence on people who have never had the gospel explained to them in this way before, only on those who hear it and outright reject it.)

I mentioned the billions and billions of people who have lived and died as faithful, albeit not Reformed, Christ followers over the past two millennia, to no avail. Doug mentioned that there are lots of things that our two churches might work together on, like fighting sex trafficking, that have nothing to do with how one sees the atonement, but the pastor didn't budge. I mentioned that it might be arrogant and a bit deceptive to preach that one of them is the sole and exclusive means of understanding the single greatest event in the history of the cosmos: the crucifixion and resurrection of Jesus. "What do you tell your congregation about how Christians understood the atonement for the thousand years prior to Anselm?"[13]

The pastor paused, looked at me, and said, "You should never preach." He went on to state that in this confusing, relativized, and postmodern world, people need "fixed points of doctrine" around which they can orient their lives. In other words, a correct understanding of a particular doctrine is the beginning of all Christian ministry. If you don't have that, he was saying, you don't have anything.

Then I tried another tack in explaining emergent Christians. "For you," I said, "it's the fixed point of doctrine that is the litmus test of all ministry. But for us, it's the Apostle Paul's call to be ambassadors of reconciliation in the world.[14] Everything we do in the emergent church is surrounded by an envelope of friendship, friendship that is based on lives of reconciliation. And it's within that envelope that we have all sort of discussions and debates about the atonement and sex trafficking and baptism and AIDS in Africa.

"In fact," I continued, "I'm not sure it's even possible to be an orthodox Christian if you're not living a life of reconciliation."

Dispatch 7: Emergents believe that an envelope of friendship and reconciliation must surround all debates about doctrine and dogma.

The "envelope of friendship" is a powerful image, and it resonates with many younger Christians. A generation or two ago, defenses of Christianity that focused on human sinfulness were potent; a common metaphor showed God on one side of a diagram and a stick figure (you) on the other; the chasm between was labeled "Sin," and the only bridge across was in the shape of Jesus' cross. But emergents ask, "What kind of God can't reach across a chasm? Chasms can't stop God!" Indeed, many emergent Christians will concur that we live in a sinful world, a world of wars and famines and pogroms. But they will be inclined to attribute this sin not to the distance between human beings and God but to the broken relationships that clutter our lives and our world. Jesus' message and ministry are ultimately about reconciliation: bringing those on the margins back into the center of God's relationship with the world. And the crucifixion, when seen as an act of divine solidarity with the suffering and broken world, becomes *the* event of reconciliation. What happened, economically speaking—what was the cosmic transaction

on Good Friday—is a subject to be bandied about in theological circles until the end of time. But when seen as an event of beauty and
reconciliation, even in its tragedy, the crucifixion of Jesus Christ is the
impetus for healed and healing relationships in a world that desperately needs
them.

And the concentration on correct doctrine is also the reflection of an
earlier time. Beginning with the Enlightenment in the eighteenth century,
the modern era vaunted reason and the life of the mind above all other
aspects of human existence. As a result, we've seen the blossoming of science
and medicine, the advancement of technology, and great leaps forward in
almost every field of study. But as often happens, the pendulum swung too
far in one direction, and the human intellect was overvalued. Presently, we're
witnessing a culturewide renaissance in the life of the human spirit, a reembrace
of emotions, experience, relationships, creativity, nature, and the many other
aspects of being human.

In many ways, emergent Christianity is an expression of this worldwide
shift. The pastor's concentration on one aspect of Christianity—a doctrine that
is ultimately accepted or rejected by the human intellect—is an articulation
of modern Christianity, and it's one that is clearly helpful to a lot of people.
But many faithful followers of Christ are becoming more reticent to place so
much reliance on the human intellect. It's just failed us too many times. Each
of us can recount myriad times that we mistook something that we were quite
previously sure of.

And our collective human intellect has failed us, too, most poignantly in the
twentieth century. We look back now and wonder, How did we allow Hitler to
amass so much power in the 1930s? Why did we train and arm the Taliban in
the 1980s? How could we allow the Rwandan genocide to proceed unchecked
in the 1990s?

If we're wrong about stuff this big, surely we might be wrong about churchy
things like specific doctrines, just as our forebears have been. Martin Luther
was right about a lot of things back in the 1520s, and he rightly criticized the
Roman church. But he hated Jews. He was definitely wrong about the hating
Jews part, so isn't it reasonable to think that he might have been wrong about
some of the theological parts as well? When we look back on the successes
and foibles of the Christians who have gone before us, one thing is demanded:
humility. And the "envelope of friendship" is the mechanism in the emergent
church to ensure at least a modicum of humility.

AN EMERGENT VOTERS' GUIDE

I once asked a fellow Minnesotan why he voted for former professional wrestler, Jesse "The Body" Ventura, for governor in 1998. He said, "It was my way of giving the finger to the Democrats *and* the Republicans."

There's a growing sense among emergents that the polarization in American politics isn't real—it's a script written by the two political parties and the American media. They wrote this script, and they perpetuate it, because they have the most to gain from its perpetuation. The unnuanced maps showing states as "red" or "blue" disregards the fact that in a red state, as many as forty-nine percent of the voters are blue, and vice versa.

But even more important, it ignores what we all know to be true: each one of us is a complex mélange of viewpoints and opinions, and very few of us line up with every plank in a party's platform. Being that postmodern Christians are acutely aware of micronarratives and justifiably incredulous toward metanarratives, they are particularly suspicious of the spokespersons of left and right who often begin their pufferies with "Americans believe . . ." But having two sides makes for good television; having six nuanced positions does not.

From a theoretical point of view, both the good and the bad of our democracy in its present state seem to be driven by the concept of unalienable, individual human rights. Dubbed as believable as "witches and unicorns" by the philosopher Alasdair MacIntyre, the modern version of individual rights was invented by John Locke (1632–1704) and written into the Declaration of Independence and the U.S. Constitution by Thomas Jefferson and his posse.[15] Carried into the modern world by the French and American revolutions, individual rights became the foundation of liberal democracy, clearly the most robust and equitable of all systems of government yet conceived. And although it happened more slowly than many people would have liked, the concept of individual rights brought about great goods like ending government-backed slavery, women's suffrage, and the civil rights movement.

However, it is also responsible for some serious ills, including the rampant consumerism ("You *deserve* that new iPod!") that has led to the average American adult carrying a credit card balance of $8,000. And, it seems, the premise of individual rights means that some arguments just aren't winnable:

the rights of the mother versus the rights of the unborn child; *my* right to define "marriage" versus *your* right to define "marriage." For all its achievements, the shortcomings of social contract theory are now in view.

Dispatch 8: Emergents find the biblical call to community more compelling than the democratic call to individual rights. The challenge lies in being faithful to both ideals.

Emergents don't have a problem with Lockean individual rights per se; their problem is with the fact that unalienable, individual rights is not a biblical-theological virtue. The Bible's call is not to protect the self but to sacrifice the self. Jesus says clearly to his followers, "Drop everything and follow me.... Let the dead bury their own dead.... Sell everything you own, give the money to the poor, and follow me.... Take up your cross daily." An anecdote that corroborates this is supplied by the Roman Catholic spiritual leader Brennan Manning. Years ago, he asked his Jewish friend and poet Shel Silverstein what Jesus meant to him. Silverstein responded a few weeks later when he gave Manning *The Giving Tree*, now a perpetual best-seller in children's literature. In the simple story, a tree literally gives his life, piece by piece, to a boy as he becomes a man. It's beautiful and poignant, and it represents the self-sacrifice at the center of Jesus' life.

To that, the Apostle Paul adds a score of exhortations to self-control, forgiveness, and reconciliation. Supplement this with the fact that every word of the Hebrew and Christian scripture was written to human beings living in community (the nation of Israel in the former, the early church in the latter), and it becomes untenable for a Christian to base her life on the philosophy that "it's all about me and my rights."

Instead, emergents seek a theological rationale for their political engagement. The thing is, that rationale varies from issue to issue, which makes the emergents an infuriatingly moving target for those with more traditional political viewpoints. For instance, the Christian speaker Len Sweet, a longtime friend of Emergent, recently spoke out against the movement in *Relevant* magazine, saying:

> We got to this point in the '70s where you could not tell the difference between the Democratic Party platform and the Church's portrayal of the Kingdom of God. I think that any intrusion of Christianity into politics – whether right or left – is ugly. So I don't see Jesus as coming with a political agenda. Yes, there are radical social and economic consequences to His message, but to claim that Jesus' message was a political one [is incorrect]. It's Jim Wallis's evangelical updating of the Social Gospel movement, or liberalism's liberation theology of the '70s and '80s.[16]

In the article, Sweet charges that emergent Christians are nothing but the New Christian Left, based primarily, it seems, on Brian McLaren's increasingly political writings. But to those inside Emergent, the criticism missed the mark, as do the protestations of the lefties when emergents don't play by their rules either. For gathered around the Emergent table are Republicans and Democrats, pro-lifers and pro-choicers, laissez-faire free-market capitalists and communitarian socialists. There is no ideological requirement to join, just a shared commitment to robust, theological dialogue about issues that matter.

And surely, most emergents vehemently disagree with Sweet's claim that Jesus' message was apolitical. This school of thought—that Jesus was interested in the Kingdom of God, not in the machinations of human politics—is not shared by emergents. The emergents are activists—even political activists—just not in the conventional sense. If "politics" means the way that human beings collectively make things happen, then this supremely interested Jesus.

But where Sweet is right is to claim that Jesus was not co-opted by any of the political parties of his day. Emergents have grown up in the dire shadow of the Moral Majority and the Christian Coalition, who too closely allied with the Republicans in the 1980s and 1990s. From the emergent perspective, this partnership was a match made in hell, a marriage in which one partner (the Republican Party) will inevitably corrupt the other (the Christian Right). Thus in my travels, many emergents have expressed to me great hesitation about the building momentum of leftward or progressive groups (such as *Tikkun* magazine, Sojourners/Call to Renewal, and FaithfulDemocrats.org). Their fear is that these groups will make the same mistakes that their conservative brethren did thirty years ago: lose their independence by aligning with a political party. Politics is a dirty business, which is why political scientists refer to the compromises required as the "theory of dirty hands." In other words, for politics to work in a liberal democracy, elected officials cannot stand unbudgingly on principle. To get things done—like getting legislation passed—politicians have to compromise. That's just how it works.

But this very compromise has drawn the ire of Stanley Hauerwas, dubbed by *Time* magazine as America's most influential theologian[17] (and known by many as the theologian with the saltiest language). Looking back on the twentieth century, Hauerwas is supremely disheartened by the compromises of his coreligionists. The American mainline—Hauerwas is a Methodist—forsook many of their distinctives in order to have influence in society. Many flowery prayers have opened the session of the U.S. Senate as a result, but the radical and liberating gospel got lost. Hauerwas and his legion of acolytes respond by saying that Christians operate according to a rationality and language that is mutually exclusive from the compromises required in a democracy. Hauerwas himself has gone so far as to say that Christians should not run for political office.

While the Hauerwasian position appeals to many emergents, others find it an overreaction and agree with the Princeton University philosopher Jeffrey Stout, who charges Hauerwas with creating a "Christian enclave theory."[18] Emergents seem stuck in a no-man's-land: on the one hand, they're committed to a deep, political engagement in American society, but on the other hand, they vow not to be co-opted by a political party. This is driven both by the belief that the national parties are ultimately concerned with self-perpetuation (not a gospel value) and by the clear inference in the Gospels that Jesus remained independent from all of the political parties of the day: the Essenes, Sadducees, Pharisees, Zealots, and Herodians all appear on the biblical stage, yet Jesus identifies with none of them. The one thing predictable about Jesus' interactions with the powers that be: he was predictably unpredictable.

Consequently, emergents are looking for a couple of things. First, they're intent on finding and supporting politicians who will change the political landscape, those who will resist doing business as usual. This may not differ appreciably from many politically engaged Americans, but the emergents may be the generation of Christians to represent a critical mass, a tipping point to upset the political apple cart. Second, emergents will look at political engagement as an art rather than a science. Therefore, they will artfully look for points of intersection and moments of potential cooperation with politicians on both sides of the aisle. The junctures of the gospel and political engagement are myriad, and they will surely not line up exclusively with the ideology of one political party. But the independence of emergents does not preclude activism. In fact, it begets activism.

DISPATCH FROM I-35:
THE TERRIFIC TALE OF
TRUCKER FRANK

I can always tell when Frank Schutzwohl is at our church, Solomon's Porch, on a Sunday night. The big rig minus its trailer is a dead giveaway. Frank, the only trucker I know who attends our church, is there only every other week. He drives a route between Kansas City and Minneapolis. It's the sole route he drives, and he's driven it for the past ten years. In fact, he just passed the benchmark of a million miles without an accident. He leaves Kansas City in the morning with a load of industrial cleaning supplies and arrives in the Twin Cities in the late afternoon. He bums around for a while, and maybe takes a nap, before he has to open the trailer for the guys to unload at 10 P.M. Then he sleeps in his cab before making a pick up somewhere in the metro area—maybe paper waste or automotive chemicals—and heading back down to Kansas City. Since it's a two-day round-trip and there are seven days in a week, Frank's at church every other Sunday.

Frank wasn't always a trucker. He grew up in a German Catholic family in Salem, Oregon. His family immigrated from Germany when he was six. In his teens, he converted to Protestant Christianity through a friend who attended a conservative Baptist church. In Frank's words, it was a "Bible-thumping fundamentalist church, part of the Independent Fundamental Churches of America." After a year at Seattle Pacific University, Frank was prevailed upon by his pastor to transfer to the conservative Western Baptist Bible College (now Corban College) in Salem, from which he graduated.

Although he planned to attend seminary, Frank got work as a pastor immediately out of college, first at a small fundamentalist church and then at a larger Mennonite church in Salem. Both pastorates were short-lived. And although Frank's time there was brief, he was drawn to the Mennonite virtue of pacifism: "I didn't see the violent Jesus, the militaristic, nationalistic Jesus; I didn't see him in the Bible, and it's kind of like my eyes were opened." A stint as a carpenter followed, and then Frank and his wife moved to Missouri to be closer to her family. He was driving a school bus and teaching high school when yet another small Baptist church in the country asked him to serve as the part-time pastor, which he did for six years until his marriage broke up.

Because the dissolution of his marriage was due in part to the supervisor of the bus company, Frank turned to driving a truck, and he's been doing that ever since.

Frank and I met for a beer late one night while his truck was being unloaded. It was a slow night, and the bartender pulled up a stool and joined us, intrigued by our conversation. Frank's a big guy, probably six-foot-four, with a goatee and a shaved head, though he often wears a stocking cap pulled down low. Soft-spoken, he smiles easily, and he speaks with grace about his most difficult days.

"Trucking saved my life," Frank tells me (and the bartender). "I got through my divorce behind the wheel of a truck. There were times when I would literally beat my head against the steering wheel—good thing it was padded! There were other times that I would just scream. You turn the radio on, you hear a song that would remind you, and there you go, boom, right down into the pits again."

In the midst of the divorce, he swallowed a bottle of pills, but a friend got him to the hospital where they pumped his stomach in time to save his life. "I fully expected to wake up to the sounds of angel choirs," Frank told me, "so I was a bit shocked to instead see a nurse's face." Months later, arriving at a strange truck stop via a string of wrong turns, Frank told that story to a fellow trucker. "I've got a pistol under the seat of my cab," the trucker told him, "and

I was going to kill myself tonight because of my divorce. You just saved my life."

That convinced Frank that he was still around for a reason, and he recommitted himself to pursuing his Christian faith. After getting to Minneapolis in his truck, most nights he'd go to hang out at a local Christian bookstore. He became a regular there, sitting in the coffee shop, reading books, and listening to Christian music. As they became familiar with him, the employees would occasionally sit with him during their break time and talk about faith and theology. He'd also elaborate on his unconventional ideas for church, different ways that churches should be run, and the corruptions of the modern church. Even the manager, also named Frank, would join him in conversation.

Trucker Frank soon became the best customer at the store, according to Manager Frank. He'd buy six or ten copies of a book he liked and pass them out to people he met on the road. The employees, often college students, would ask his advice about books to recommend. They'd even point a Bible-shopping customer to Frank—"Go ask Frank which Bible to buy; he knows a lot about the different versions"—and they'd let him listen to all the new CDs that had come in that week.

Trucker Frank started playing practical jokes on his friends at the bookstore. He'd call the store from the road and ask for the Veggie Tales Nativity set, "You know, the one with Larry the Cucumber as Joseph. I saw it on the Internet." The best, according to Frank, was the time when he called up and asked in a German accent for the Shroud of Turin bedsheets. "When I go to bed at night, I literally want to be covered up with the image of Jesus on the shroud." As a young employee scoured the store for the fictional item, Manager Frank got on the line, laughing, "I'm gonna get you, Frank!"

In fact, Frank became so chummy with some of the employees of the Christian bookstore that they all went to the Renaissance Festival together; Frank and another guy dressed up as a monk and an archbishop, and the girls went as wenches. "We were friends," Frank told me. "We shared things."

About that time, a new manager was assigned to the store, and she posted the following memo in the employee break room:[19]

Trucker Frank

I know that some of you recently got together with trucker Frank outside of work. That was good to hear as you use time outside of work to enjoy your friendship with him.

One of the fun things about working here is the people we meet and work with. However, as a good steward of our working hours, extended conversations (like those that go on with Frank) are not at all appropriate, as you are getting paid to do a job. Neither is it appropriate for employees to spend work time with each other in that fashion. I know that a previous manager did not share this perspective about Frank, but I need to let you know how I view this situation.

Making times to meet outside of the work hours is the answer. Being attentive to other customers and the huge job before us here is the answer.

But what about Frank???? I have not talked with Frank, but if he thinks about it, I'm sure he would agree. Everyone here has just given him the OK to come in and chat anytime. Just tell him you now must arrange to meet with him when you are done with work.

Please talk to me about my perspective if you have any questions or comments you wish to share with me.

When one of the employees questioned the new manager about her perspective on Frank, she admitted that Frank's unconventional views on church and faith might be unsettling to some customers, and she'd just as soon if he didn't hang around anymore.

Frank has been fired as a pastor, he's been shunned by churches he used to attend, and he's even been told not to sit near the youth in worship because the kids were having too much fun in his presence. But he admitted that this was a first: he had never been excommunicated from a Christian bookstore.

But shortly before the posting of the memo, an employee told Frank about Solomon's Porch. "There's a church I think you'd like," she told him. "My roommate goes there. They sit on couches. It sounds like the kind of church you keep talking about."

Intrigued, Frank visited the Porch on a Sunday night. "As soon as I walked in, I looked around and I loved it immediately. It was just awesome," he says. "And then, when they allowed people to participate, I thought, this is great. They *actually want* people's input. And then when they said that the sermon that's done on Sunday night is put together on Tuesday by the group—that they come up with the sermon collectively—I thought, *this is perfect*."

> "When they said that the sermon that's done on Sunday night is put together on Tuesday by the group—that they come up with the sermon collectively—I thought, this is perfect."

So there was Frank, sunk low in an easy chair on a Sunday night recently. The discussion during the sermon turned to accountability in the church. This is a common sticking point for newcomers to emergent churches. Emergents seem so free-form, so loosey-goosey, so anything-goes. That leads some to believe that emergent churches are particularly susceptible to spiritual and theological abuses. In a somewhat aggressive tone, a visitor stood up and challenged us all to think about excommunication. "What would it take," he asked, "for someone to be excommunicated from this church?" Without waiting for an answer, he pressed his point: "Jesus is very clear in Matthew 18. If a brother sins against you, you confront him in private; if that doesn't cause repentance, bring two or three witnesses with you; and if that doesn't work, you bring the whole church. Finally, if the person still isn't repentant, you excommunicate him. It's right there in the Bible."

Indeed, I was familiar with this passage. So, it turns out, was Frank. From his chair, he raised his hand. "Do you know what it actually says should be the final step?" asked Frank.

The inquisitor was silent.

"It says we should treat that one like a tax collector or a pagan. And how did Jesus treat tax collectors and pagans?"

Another long pause.

"*He welcomed them!*" Frank nearly shouted. "He didn't excommunicate or ban them. He ate with them and forgave them! Jesus is saying that we should follow all the steps of reconciliation, and as the last step, we should treat them as though they never knew Jesus. And what do we do with people like that?"

Once again, silence.

"We invite them to church!" He said it like a punch line he'd been waiting his whole life to deliver.

I'll admit that I'd heard that passage dozens of times in my Christian life, often to condone the most un-Christ-like behavior, but I'd never seen it as Frank had just explicated it. The proverbial scales fell from my eyes. Of course, Frank was right! This saying of Jesus' doesn't call for excommunication at all but rather for opening the church doors wide, welcoming even those who've committed sins against people inside the church.

Later, at the bar, I asked Frank about this. He said that he'd been meditating on that passage just a few days before, engaging in an ancient Benedictine practice called *lectio divina*, or "holy reading." Considering how he'd been on the receiving end of a few excommunications himself, the passage had a special poignancy. As he prayed, he thought about the "publican and the heathen," harking back to the King James language of his youth. The final line of that passage in the King James reads, "If he neglect to hear the church, let him be unto thee as a heathen man and a publican."

The ban on publicans and heathens was meted out by the Pharisees, Frank thought, but Jesus did just the opposite: he opened the kingdom to those who were shunned. Jesus was turning the Pharisees' own practice of shunning publicans and heathens on its head!

Frank then went looking for versions of the Bible that corroborated his thoughts, and he immediately found it in Eugene Peterson's contemporary translation, *The Message:*

> If a fellow believer hurts you, go and tell him — work it out between the two of you. If he listens, you've made a friend. If he won't listen, take one or two others along so that the presence of witnesses will keep things honest, and try again. If he still won't listen, tell the church. If he won't listen to the church, *you'll have to start over from scratch, confront him with the need for repentance, and offer again God's forgiving love.*[20]

"I read that," Frank said, "and I thought, there it is! There's the key to that passage. I think Jesus calls us to *intensify* the love and compassion you have for that person who has sinned against you." But meanwhile, the latest Baptists who had shunned Frank were treating him in just the opposite way: they were acting as though he didn't exist, literally walking on the other side of the street when they saw him coming down the road in the little Kansas town where he lives.

Not every story in this book has a moral, but there is a moral to Frank's story. Here's a guy who has been through the wringer: divorced, suicidal, cheated on, and excommunicated. Try as he might, this pastor-trucker has struggled to find a place in the church. But out here, on the frontier of the American church, he's found a couch with his name on it.

And not only that. Most churches—I daresay, 99 percent of churches in America—don't allow just anyone to speak at any time, especially not members with checkered pasts. But because anyone, including Trucker Frank, can speak freely in this emergent church, my seminary-trained eyes were opened to find a truth in the Bible that had previously eluded me.

When we met at the bar that night, Trucker Frank said that when he retires from over-the-road trucking, he just might go back to school for a graduate degree, buy a pipe and a tweed coat, and become a seminary professor. I think that's a fine idea.

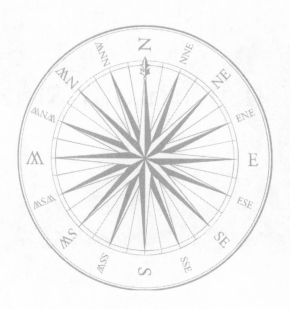

CHAPTER 4

THE THEOLOGY, STUPID

IF EVER THERE'S BEEN A POLITICAL STRATEGIST WHO BURNS away the dross of political verbiage and applies the "Keep It Simple, Stupid" principle, it's James Carville. Working for Bill Clinton's 1992 presidential campaign, Carville penned a haiku and pinned it to the wall in the campaign's Little Rock headquarters:

> Change vs. more of the same
> The economy, stupid
> Don't forget health care.

Since then, the middle line of Carville's poem has been often adapted and is culturally ubiquitous.

Carville was right, of course. Despite political bloviations about cultural and moral issues, most Americans vote according to what they think will benefit them most financially. The economy—both the national economy and the household economy—determines many elections, including Clinton's 1992 victory.

Similarly, despite all of the talk about worship styles in the emergent church—the return of ancient, Celtic prayers; the grungy music; the dialogical sermons—it's really the theology underneath the styles that is most important and provocative. Indeed, the emergent innovations in worship rarely raise an eyebrow among the critics. What's really intriguing about emergent Christianity? The theology.

For several years now, two camps have formed in the movement. Among some who are emerging, the methods of Christianity have become irrelevant, and they must change. But for this group, the message of the gospel is unchanging—it's been figured out, once and for all, never to be reconsidered.

But to another group, the methods *and* the message of Christianity are bound to be reconceived over time. Indeed, if one changes the methods, one will inevitably change the message.

Another way of saying this is that the Christian gospel is always enculturated, always articulated by a certain people in a certain time and place. To try to freeze one particular articulation of the gospel, to make it timeless and universally applicable, actually does an injustice to the gospel. This goes to the very heart of what emergent is and of how emergent Christians are attempting to chart a course for following Jesus in the postmodern, globalized, pluralized world of the twenty-first century.

So while the excurses into philosophy and theology that follow may seem far afield from what instigated the new, emergent Christianity, they actually drive to the very heart of the phenomenon. Now, please allow me to introduce this discussion by telling a bit of my own story.

DARTMOUTH DAYS

I don't know if they ever said it outright while I was in Campus Crusade for Christ in college, but the implication was there, and I didn't have to dig very deep to get at it: Jesus' Second Coming was predicated on *me*. Well, actually, on *us*. Our little band of fifty or so undergrads at Dartmouth College, along with our peers at campuses around the country, had a monumental task: to "tell the entire world about Jesus."

To that end, we knocked on the dorm doors after our regular "MnM" (Monday Night Meeting). We were expected to give money to the mission of Crusade and to spend our spring breaks doing evangelism in Panama City, Florida. We would play "slow-motion football" on the beach in order to attract a crowd; once the crowd had gathered, a player (at regular speed) would shout, "Thanks for watching our game! We want to tell you about someone!" Then the unsuspecting crowd would realize that about one out of every four crowd members was actually a plant, with an ample supply of tracts tucked into their appropriately conservative swimsuits. Some would flee, but others would stick around for the ten-minute presentation of the gospel. I don't know whether they stayed primarily due to social convention or out of true spiritual curiosity. It didn't matter.

We were also expected to seriously consider joining the Crusade staff upon graduation and go, as the Crusaders would have it, to the far corners of the earth and show the *JESUS* film on a bedsheet stretched between two trees to half-naked bushmen who had never seen a white man before. If it turned out that God hadn't called me to be a missionary in Burundi, I was expected to support heartily (meaning financially) those who were.

I was in college in the late 1980s, so the millennium was breathing down our necks. "One billion new Christians by 2000" was the oft-trumpeted refrain.[1] Of course, there are over two billion Christians in the world, but since half of those—Roman Catholics—weren't considered "saved" by Crusaders, and lots of others—the Orthodox and the mainline Protestants—were probably not really "believers,"[2] there were actually far fewer than one billion of "us" in the world. The rabidity with which the Crusaders pursued evangelism was not the result of a desire to expand the commercial Christian empire, as one might suspect. (Bill Bright, the founder of Crusade was, by all accounts, a financially modest individual.) It was, instead, the result of this theological axiom: When everyone on the planet has heard the salvation message, Jesus will return.

This belief comes primarily from a verse in the twenty-fourth chapter of Matthew's Gospel. There Jesus is recorded as giving a fairly horrifying account of the "end of the age": wars, famine, earthquakes, persecutions, false messiahs, and "love grown cold." Amid this chapter-long harangue, Jesus says, "And this gospel of the kingdom will be preached in the whole world as a testimony to all nations, and then the end will come."

Like many things in the Bible, it seems simple at first: an *if A, then B* proposition. *If* we preach the gospel to the whole world, *then* the end of the age will come. But a little reflection reveals more complexity. First of all, the exact nature of the "gospel of the kingdom" is a source of much debate among

Christians; while some relate it forensically to the atonement (which is hard to imagine, since Jesus says these things before he was executed), others consider it closer to Jesus' proclamation of the "year of the Lord's favor" in Luke 4, harking back to the Israelite custom of releasing all slaves and forgiving all debts every fifty years. Further, this passage is not a conditional in Greek. That is, in Greek, it is not constructed as an *if-then* statement. Instead, the verb *preach* is in the future passive tense (*will be preached* or *will have been preached*), and the verb *come* is in the future tense (*will come*). Although the original Greek lacks punctuation, we might punctuate it thusly: "And this gospel of the kingdom will be preached in the whole world as a testimony to all nations. And the end will come." In other words, these two things *will* happen, but the latter is not necessarily contingent on the former. And to add to the complexity, we don't know exactly how Jesus said it in his own language, Aramaic.

But most significantly, Jesus is talking about the immediate circumstances of the disciples, not about evangelism techniques two millennia hence. The entire passage is couched in the language of the here and now. Jesus is looking his closest followers in the eye and saying, "Many will come in my name—watch out that you not be deceived. . . . You will hear of wars and rumors of wars, but see to it that you are not alarmed. . . . You will be handed over to be persecuted and put to death, and you will be hated by all nations because of me. . . ." Most biblical scholars—evangelical, mainline, and Catholic—agree that these sayings of Jesus presage events that took place before or during A.D. 70, the year that the Roman emperor Titus sacked and destroyed Solomon's Temple in Jerusalem.[3] In other words, as Jesus concludes his predictions, these things would all happen within the disciples' lifetimes: "I tell you the truth, this generation will certainly not pass away until all these things have happened."

And finally, "the world" to which the gospel would be preached was not the planet Earth. The only "world" known to Jesus was the Roman Empire and its peripheral trading partners—large, to be sure, but not nearly the scope of our world today.[4]

But these grammatical and theological subtleties made little difference to the Crusaders. Nor did the verses just down the page in which Jesus makes it clear that no one, neither humans nor angels nor even the Son, can know the time of the end—only the Father knows.

But it didn't escape the notice of the Crusaders that Jesus doesn't say that all nations must *accept* the gospel of the kingdom, just that they must have it *preached* at them. What this bred was a new fashion of efficiency in the dissemination of the gospel—our ten-minute guerrilla evangelism dorm sessions and the *JESUS* film are good examples. The film's Web site (http://www.jesusfilm.org) boasts that it has been translated into over one thousand languages and shown to over five and a half billion persons. It has resulted in more than two hundred million "decisions to follow Christ" ("decisions recorded only at live screenings"), but of course, decisions aren't necessarily the point in the Crusader calculus. The point is to get it out and show it to every tribe and tongue so that Jesus will come back.

Here's the major theological flaw with this kind of thinking: it makes the assumption that the activity of God is contingent on the activity of humans, while the biblical narrative seems to indicate that God acts independently of us. God is not likely sitting on a lofty perch, looking down on the earth and saying, "Well, I'd like to come back, but I can't until the gospel is preached in all the world."

A similar defect afflicts the so-called dispensational view of the end-time made popular in the 1970s by Hal Lindsey in *The Late Great Planet Earth* and more recently by the jejune Left Behind novels. These propose the dubious theology that the world is going to get worse and worse and worse until it gets so bad that God *has* to intervene (but not before God whisks away all of the Christians and lets the rest of humankind rot in a satanic hell for seven years).

Again, the problem is that these theologies ultimately make God subservient to human beings—God is incapable of getting involved until we preach to all the nations, in the one case, or until the world is beyond redemption, in the other. Like the billboard I see every time I drive up to Brainerd, Minnesota, inscribed "Unless We Confess, God Cannot Bless," it requires the activity of the Creator to hinge on the activity of the creation, specifically on humans.

But God is a being whose activity is, by definition, not contingent. God can forgive whomever God wants to forgive, whether or not the forgiven person has adequately confessed his or her sins. And God can return whenever God pleases. In fact, classical theism posits that God is the one "necessary being" in the cosmos—all others (including humans) are "contingent beings."[5] That is, our existence is contingent on God's existence. That's why it's so farfetched to manufacture a God who's handcuffed until our human actions release him.

But what *can* be said for these theologies that dream up a contingent God is that they sure do motivate people to get things done. A lot of evangelism has been spurred on by the notion that we can tip that first domino that will eventually bring us to Judgment Day. And a lot of inactivity—on, say, environmental issues—has resulted from the dispensationalist view that the earth is bound to sink into a cesspool of sin, war, false teachers, and antichrists until Jesus' return.

Meanwhile back at college, I also visited the Congregational church on campus. Since I'd grown up as a Congregationalist, it seemed like a natural fit. The Church of Christ at Dartmouth College is a white clapboard building on the campus green, the quintessence of New England Puritan architecture. No one welcomed me, no one even smiled in my direction. I chalked this up as the aloofness that's part of the New England personality disorder, but it was a far cry from "Minnesota nice."

I recognized the opening prayer, the hymns, and the robes on the ministers (I grew up calling our clergypersons "ministers"—I didn't learn until my Campus Crusade experience at college that I was supposed to call them "pastors"). But as we got more deeply into the worship service, it seemed like I was in some kind of Bizarro Church. During the Lord's Prayer, the opening words were "Our Mother, who art in heaven." Other prayers were addressed to the "Great Spirit." Several of the hymns had the same tunes that I remembered but slightly different words—all reference to maleness and warfare had been purged. The sermon was hazily connected to the Bible but was really about politics. Jesus was rarely mentioned.

In short, it looked, smelled, and sounded like the church I knew back in Minnesota, but it was really quite different. I went back a couple of times, just to see if that first visit was a fluke. It wasn't.

What I'd experienced, for the first time, was liberal mainline Christianity.

Back on campus, I chafed under some of the policies of Campus Crusade. First, a glass ceiling inhibited women from ever achieving the coveted position of campus director. When I asked about this, I got fuzzy arguments from scripture—it turns out that Crusade doesn't necessarily bar women from top leadership positions, but the general discomfort with women's leadership is a part of a particular angle on biblical interpretation. This was lost on me at the time, since I'd grown up at a church with ordained women ministers.

;Second, we were being trained in so-called "cold-call evangelism." What that meant was, once per month, we left the MnM rally and spread across campus to evangelize the unbelievers. A partner and I (because Jesus sent out his followers two by two) went to the dorm we were assigned and began knocking on doors. When a door was answered, we'd ask, "Are you willing to take a short survey?" to which any undergrad who'd like to avoid homework answered, "Yes."

Once inside, the next question we were trained to ask was, "Are you interested in spiritual things?" Again, virtually any eighteen-year-old will answer this question in the affirmative (hell, if you can fog a mirror, you'll answer yes). From there we'd launch into Crusade's famous evangelistic tract, "The Four Spiritual Laws." There was no survey; we were not tabulating any results. It was a scam, a classic bait-and-switch. We used the premise of a survey to get inside the dorm room, steer the conversation, and get out in under ten minutes. We had to keep moving; we had a whole dorm to canvas.

This method of evangelism troubled me deeply. I found it horribly embarrassing to "share the gospel" with someone one night and then find myself sitting next to her in the cafeteria the next day. It was one thing to proselytize my anonymous seatmate on a plane ("God sat you next to that person for a purpose," the Crusade staffers told us)—I'd never see that person again. It was quite another to witness to my college classmates. I hated it, and I quickly refused to do it. Upon our release from MnM out into the front lines of evangelism, I'd quietly steal back to my dorm room, turn out the lights, and not answer the door.

The final nail in the coffin, it seems, came when I joined a fraternity during the fall of my sophomore year. Back home, I'd been schooled in what is alternatively called "lifestyle evangelism" or "friendship evangelism." The basic premise is that *how one lives* makes a more compelling case for Christian faith than *what one says*. Or as Saint Francis of Assisi purportedly said, "Preach the gospel always, and if necessary, use words." With this in mind, it seemed completely natural to join a fraternity—if any group of guys could use a Christian in their midst, it was the Dartmouth hockey players who made up the Heorot House.[6]

But when I pledged Heorot, that was the final straw for the Crusade folks. I guess it meant that I had slipped into the dark world of beer drinking and other nefarious behaviors. In January of my sophomore year, my "discipler" sat me down at a table in Collis Student Center at Dartmouth College and proceeded to tell me (I remember it verbatim), "The staff and student leaders of Dartmouth Crusade met over the break, and we've decided that you have an unteachable spirit.[7] There's no room for you in the leadership of Campus Crusade."

I sat there, stunned.

"You can still come to Bible study, though," he smiled.

Back in my dorm, I called Jeff Lindsay, my youth pastor back home, and asked him, "Can someone get kicked out of a Christian group?"

"I guess so," he said with sadness in his voice.

I was still angry when I arrived at seminary in the fall of 1993, and I attribute a lot of that anger to my excommunication from Campus Crusade. But I was not just angry; I was also wrong. I thought that the problem with Crusade at Dartmouth was with the *method*—that is, the way the Crusaders did Christian ministry. I thought the inherent misogyny was bad form; I thought the martial methods of evangelism were ill-conceived; I even thought the organization's name, reaching back to one of the low points in Christian history, was a poor choice. I had similar disappointments with the mainline Congregational church—I wondered why it seemed to jettison many of the distinctive aspects of Christianity, like the language, while maintaining the very things that I saw as outdated: robes and choirs and organs.

What I didn't see was that these methods of ministry were beholden to underlying theologies that are even more in need of overhaul than the methods themselves.

I had seen the lesions, which were the ways that these people went about living the Christian faith. But the cancer was the theology that they held. The Crusaders were good and noble people, but they saw other human beings as accomplishments, as possible conquests. I wondered what would cause someone to think that way.

The Congregationalists seemed to worry that talking a lot about Jesus so near an Ivy League campus would compromise their commitment to "diversity" (the official theme, ordained by the college administration, of my freshman class at Dartmouth).

The answer I found is that it's a flawed system of belief that begets such ruinous ways of being Christian (and human).

I began to understand this fact and, I think, began to forgive the fine people who were responsible for the hurt caused to me and others only when I fell into a new way of thinking while at Fuller Seminary. My professors there called it *postmodernism*. That was a word I'd never heard before, but it was like the chemotherapy that nuked what cancer cells I still had in me from college.

With the support of professors like Nancey Murphy, Jim McClendon, and Miroslav Volf, I began to investigate what a postmodern theology would look like. I found a way to be Christian and to think Christianly that was wholly unencumbered with the intellectual rigor mortis of the conventional systems part of Christianity. What I now know is the left and right camps of Christians were locked in an epic struggle for the heart of the faith, but they were both founded on the fallacious system, called *foundationalism*, that we discussed in Chapter One.

But isms aside, I experienced an existential freedom when I learned that there's a completely different way to conceive of being a follower of Christ. As a child, I had seen the black-and-white movies of 1950s polio patients, trapped in iron lungs—in fact, those iron lungs occasionally showed up in my childhood nightmares. If the conventional ways of understanding the Christian faith were like an iron lung, pressing down on my chest, this new, emerging way was a total release, freedom, liberation.

I could breathe again.

As I looked back on my experiences in college, both at the liberal Congregational church and in the conservative campus ministry, I came to terms with the fact that these weren't malicious people. Instead, the ways they lived out their faith were a natural response to the theologies they held. It was the theology that was broken. I'll put it this way: *theology begets a way of life*. The better the theology, the better the way of life. Therefore, I claim:

Good theology begets beautiful Christianity.

And so it follows that

Bad theology begets ugly Christianity.

That may sound supremely arrogant, but hear me out. A lot of us, emergents included, are disheartened by the complexion of Christianity in America. We're embarrassed by the Jesus junk we see in stores, by the preachers we see on TV, and by the ill-fated marriage of faith and politics. We're equally saddened by the $75 million evangelical megachurch campus in the suburbs and the shuttered mainline church in the city. While there is much that is good about being Christian in America

> A lot of us, emergents included, are disheartened by the complexion of Christianity in America.

today, very many of us think there needs to be a profound change in the way that Christianity is practiced and promulgated. All I'm saying is that the current practices that embarrass us are reflective of a deeply held theology. So, while we rethink how we live the faith, we must also reconsider what the faith *actually is*.

WHAT, EXACTLY, IS THEOLOGY?

Some readers might be tempted, at this point, to say, "All this talk of philosophy and theology is really a waste of time. Why bother with it? The only important thing is that we love Jesus. That's it."

Well, I submit that "only loving Jesus" *is* a theology. It's a paper-thin theology, a reductionistic theology. It's a theology that avoids many things; for instance, (1) two millennia of argumentation over the nature of God, (2) the great difficulties in reading the Bible, and (3) all of the grief in the world. The refrain "Can't we all just love Jesus?" uses that unseemly word *just* (a word that we Christians use altogether too often in prayer: "Father, we just ask that you would just be here with us tonight . . ."). *Just* is a term of minimization, of diminution, when used in this way. (Ironically, *just* can also be used to denote *justice*, which is at the very heart of the gospel.) But Jesus, the gospel, the Bible, theology, they're never "just" anything. They're always more, much more, than we might think. These items (Jesus, gospel, Bible) should *not* be qualified with the adverbs *just* or *only*. The gospel is always *more than* we imagine, the Bible always has something for us *greater than* we expect, and Jesus is always *beyond* what we can conceive.

So we must refigure our theology. Too much bad theology has engendered too many unhealthy churches and too many people who don't quite get the whole "following Christ" way of life. Too much thin theology is responsible for too many Christians who practice the faith in ways that are a mile wide and an inch deep. The hope of emergents, their ministry, their message is, more than anything, a call for a reinvigoration of Christian theology—not in the ivy towers, not even in pulpits and pews, but on the street.

As noted in Chapter Two, *theology* means "discourse about God." It's distinct, for instance, from what you find in most secular universities, which have departments of religion but long ago abandoned their study of theology. People who study religion today look at how human beings organize their experiences of God—the forms, structures, and practices. But such study is generally unencumbered by belief in the existence or nonexistence of God.

Dispatch 9: The emergent movement is robustly theological; the conviction is that theology and practice are inextricably related, and each invariably informs the other.

Theology, on the other hand, speaks directly of God. And anytime human beings talk of God, they're necessarily also going to talk about their own experience of God. So for our purposes, *theology is talk about the nexus of divine and human action*. In other words, it's how we talk about the points of intersection between God and us, the places where God's activity meets our activity.

But theology isn't just talk. When we paint scenes from the Bible or when we write songs about Jesus or when we compose poems about God or when we write novels about the human struggle with meaning, we are "doing theology." Augustine, the fourth-century theologian and bishop of Hippo (in northern Africa) wrote theology in his magisterial *City of God*. And Michelangelo sculpted theology in his *Pietà*. John Milton wrote theology in *Paradise Lost*. Peter Paul Rubens painted theology in *The Allegory of Peace and War*. Fyodor Dostoyevsky wrote theology in *The Brothers Karamazov*. And Bono sings theology in "Mysterious Ways."

Most human activity is inherently theological, in that it reflects what we believe to be the case about God—who God is, what God wants from us, how involved God is in the world, and so forth. The house I buy—where it is, how big it is, how much it costs—is a *theological* decision. It reflects what I believe about the following questions and more: Does God care where I live? Does God care how I spend my money? Does God favor the city or the suburbs? Does God care about energy use? Does God favor public transportation? Maybe I believe that God cares about none of these things, in which case my decision to purchase the biggest house I can afford in the nicest part of town reflects my *theological belief* that God is not concerned with such things. Similarly, decisions that are much more mundane also reflect our beliefs about who God is and how God interacts with us. Some people pray for a good parking spot when they're driving to the mall. Others ask, "If God is allowing genocide in Darfur, why would he intervene in the traffic patterns at my shopping mall?!?"

So theology isn't just talk, and it's not even just great works of art like *The Allegory of Peace and War*. Actors act theology and businesspeople work theology and stay-at-home moms change diapers and make lunch theologically.

So human life is theology. Virtually everything we do is inherently theological. Almost every choice we make reflects what we think about God. There's no escaping it.

THEOLOGY ON THE RISE

For many years, I've been at speaker at the National Youth Workers Convention, a trade show for thousands of youth pastors and church volunteers. Recently, I've been offering a late-night theological discussion—a kind of roundtable talk in which anyone can bring up anything, and the collected crowd will be invited to assault the idea theologically. It's a great time, and it's been growing in popularity; it's not uncommon to have a hundred youth pastors crowd into the room at 10 P.M. to discuss theology. I recently posted an entry on my blog about one of our sessions, and this telling comment came from an anonymous correspondent:

I was able to make the late-night theology discussion in Anaheim. Didn't have a headache when I got there, but did when I left.

I'm not seminary-trained. I have a journalism degree from a state university, and somehow I ended up in youth ministry. I feel inadequate a lot of the time and am intimidated by my senior pastor at times. So when we had our weekly staff meeting this past Tuesday, I shared about my experience going to the "late-night theology discussion." His response was "What did you guys decide?" I said, "Not much," meaning we didn't come up with a definitive answer for anything. He replied, "That's how it usually goes."

I felt about three inches tall because in my head, I heard him saying, "Those are useless because they have no grounding. We have our doctrine and theology that is the answer, and those crazy emergent, postmodern, heretic types don't ever come up with anything."

I know middle and high schoolers aren't usually great theological thinkers, but I've grown tired of regurgitating answers that some guy decided were fact 500 years ago. On one hand, I feel free to not be trapped in my denomination's doctrine (in my personal life), but I feel limited as to what I am able to pass on and reveal about my thinking.

I really appreciate other leaders more interested in pursuing youth and having them think rather than pray the prayer.[8] . . .

Do I want lots of youth finding out about God and living out their faith on a daily basis? Heck, yes! But how do I [tell my] my senior pastor [that I'm not interested in attracting big numbers of kids]? Maybe I just wrote my own answer.

Indeed, he did write his own answer. In my own experience with young people, they desperately desire *theological* answers to theological questions. In fact, the latest neurological research on adolescents shows unequivocally that teenagers' brains are actually wired to ask questions of transcendent meaning.[9] So it's no surprise that the teens in his church want to talk about God and about the "meaning of life." That's part and parcel of the adolescent journey toward self-identity. For the

> "I've grown tired of regurgitating answers that some guy decided were fact 500 years ago."

church to disregard this aspect of the adolescent condition by promoting a "we already know it all" security is not only disingenuous and untrue but also disastrous to the attempts to introduce young people to a life of faith. Like any of us, adolescents are theological beings, and they will develop in their theological savvy not because we offer them rote answers but because we allow them to explore the intricate depths of faith *and doubt*.

It's notable that many of the founders of emergent Christianity—myself included—spent time in the trenches of youth ministry. As a youth pastor, one is commonly afforded a great deal more latitude in the questions of faith than other Christian leaders—whatever it takes, you're often told, to keep the teenagers in church! But this openness to new answers, and even new questions, is infectious. So many emergents have become disheartened with a Christianity in which all the answers are already known, all the orthodoxies already reified. Instead—and emergents have been accused of being a bit puerile themselves in this regard—they're looking for a Christianity that's still exploratory, still adventurous.

Of course, it's not just teenagers and emergents who desire theological resources for their lives. It's a culturewide longing. By most accounts, traditional publishing has hit a rough patch, and it may never recover. With the advent of new media, Americans are reading fewer books and newspapers. Religion and spirituality books, however, buck the trend. They're the one sector of publishing that has consistently grown in the past several years, and, to the occasional dismay of the East and West Coast intelligentsia, books about religion often top the *New York Times* best-seller list. The popularity of religious books is a leading indicator of the theological and spiritual longing still prominent in our culture.

Sometimes, however, the books that achieve popularity lack a depth reflective of the Christian story. Rick Warren, who's sold many millions of his *Purpose-Driven Life*, recently told Charlie Rose that he spent twelve hours a day for seven months paring the book down to make it more reader-friendly: "I tried to make it very simple.... If I had a twenty-seven-word sentence, I'd try to make it down to nine," he said.[10] Warren's book, a forty-day experience of purposeful living, boasts about a thousand Bible verses, the vast majority of them coming with little explanation and no context.

Warren is humbled at the success of this book, and he's the first to admit that he's written nothing new. Further, Warren has nobly parlayed his enormous success into a fight against AIDS in Africa. But it should come as no surprise to us that his *Purpose-Driven Life* lacks the nuance and sophistication that many people in the emergent church desire. Just down the road from Warren's Saddleback Church in Southern California is the Crystal Cathedral, where Robert Schuller (borrowing a page from Norman Vincent Peale's playbook) transformed the gospel of Jesus Christ into the "power of positive thinking (with Jesus)." These populist versions of twentieth-century American Christianity wandered a bit from the Apostle Paul, who proclaimed that the cross on which Jesus hung was a "scandal."[11]

Both Schuller and Warren are progenitors of the "seeker-sensitive" church movement, which dominated American evangelicalism in the 1980s and 1990s. Massive church campuses in the suburbs were built to resemble shopping malls in an attempt to entice suburbanites. Traditional Christian symbols like crosses were removed lest newcomers be confused. And preaching about concepts like "sin" was avoided, opting instead for sermon series on "how to be a better Christian family." Many now see these as the sins of the seeker-sensitive churches, and even some of the founders of the movement have expressed regret.

This is an important backdrop for understanding emergents. Many of them were nurtured in these seeker-sensitive environments. Some even served on the staffs of these churches. But as the complexities of a globalized world have encroached on their psyches, the emergents have pursued a faith that spurns easy answers. If the seeker-sensitive church movement can be seen as a reaction to the failures of liberal theology or as a safe haven for people in a world awash with change, the emergent church movement is a counterreaction, a retrieval of the deep theological tradition of wrestling with the intellectual and spiritual difficulties inherent in the Christian faith.

Maybe you've seen this before: some well-meaning evangelist spray-paints "JESUS IS THE ANSWER" on the side of a railroad bridge. Then some smart aleck comes by later and adds "SO WHAT'S THE QUESTION?"

It seems to many emergents that the question is difficult, intricate: What is the meaning of life? Why is there evil in the world? How is God involved in our lives? Just what is the "Kingdom of God"? How can we be involved in God's work in the world? These are hard questions, and they demand nuanced, complex answers. So they fight back against a world that vaunts simple solutions to complex problems, and they do so, first, by encouraging the questions. As you've seen in some of the correspondence in this book, making room for the questions is one of the aspects of emergent Christianity that many seekers appreciate. As a result, emergent Christians often get labeled as "slippery." They're told they don't answer questions directly but answer instead with another (often deconstructive) question. As stated earlier, these are attempts to get to the assumptions underlying the initial question.

So questioning is not an act of defiance on the emergents' part. It is a trait of integrity.

The Gospel

The irreducible good news of God, ultimately delivered in the person of Jesus Christ. In other words, a reality that cannot be summed up in a call-out box.

When someone asks, "What is the Gospel, in a nutshell?" I often quote my friend, philosopher of religion Jack Caputo, who wrote of the philosophical impulses of "deconstruction": "Nutshells close and encapsulate, shelter and protect, reduce and simplify, while everything in deconstruction is turned toward opening, exposure, expansion, and complexification, toward releasing unheard of, undreamt of possibilities *to come*, toward cracking nutshells wherever they appear."[12]

This statement could just as easily be made about the gospel, the Kingdom of God, or Jesus himself.

Many Christians take great umbrage at the emergent assertion that the gospel is complex and irreducible. They argue that the gospel is simple and that emergents are making it too hard. They say the Bible has a "plain meaning," and that's the one meant by God. But emergents just don't see it. The more emergents read the Bible, the more complex it becomes. And in fact, that's a point in favor of the Christian Story, for that means it jibes with the complex realities of the globalized, pluralistic, often confusing world in which we live.

In other words, emergents are drawn to a gospel that meshes with our own experience of the world, a gospel that doesn't shy away from the tough questions. For, in the words of another emergent who is planting a church in a bar in Berlin, Germany, "to every answer there is a good question."

GOING DEEP

"Go deep!"

The same phrase used in youthful touch football games applies to the theological disposition of the emergent church. They want depth, regardless of the cost. If that means that they have to wade through philosophical texts with twenty-seven-word sentences, so be it. For if human beings want to be in touch with and in cooperation with the God of the universe, it's only realistic to acknowledge that it's not going to be simple. Far from it. It'll be difficult and complex and nuanced. There'll be no cutting corners, no easy answers, no magic bullets.

In that way, theology is not unlike many other human endeavors. Take physics, for example. I'm woefully ignorant of physics, though the principles of physics have everything to do with who I am and how I experience the world. When I hear physicists talk about physics, I know it takes an extraordinary amount of study and self-discipline to become conversant in their field. Yet I also believe that as the author of the physical properties of the cosmos, God is exponentially more complex and compelling than physics. So if physics is hard to grasp, why wouldn't God be hard to grasp?

Of course God is hard to grasp. One might even say that God is impossible to grasp (more on that in the next chapter). So what of this human endeavor of theology? Why attempt it? Is it pointless? Three traits, though not usually touted, actually make up the DNA of any theological reflection.

Dispatch 10: Emergents believe that theology is local, conversational, and temporary. To be faithful to the theological giants of the past, emergents endeavor to continue their theological dialogue.

First, theology is *local*. As a human being who attempts to communicate with other human beings, all of my communication originates within me. It's inescapable: what I say and how I say it, what I think and write, my facial expressions, and the clothes I wear are all iterations of me—of my mind and emotions and the rest of what it means to be "me." So in that sense, everything that emanates from me (like this book) is essentially local in that it proceeds from the *locus* of my person. Theology, since it is a human enterprise, is no different from any of my other activities. As *my* attempt to reflect on notions about God, theology is inherently local.[13]

To put it in the converse, theology is not universal, nor is it transcendent. The God about whom we theologize is transcendent, but our human musings about God are not. To think that our theology is not local and specific is a falsity that has been foisted on the church. Professional theologians, those men and women who sit on seminary faculties, are sometimes tempted to write and speak with the confidence that their theology is somehow clean or sterile or untainted—that they come to their task without any presuppositions, prejudices, or context. But of course, they're just as local as the rest of us. They live in a certain place, speak a certain language, talk with certain people, read a certain newspaper, and are held accountable for what they write and say by other theologians in their guild.

This localness of theology is a hallmark of emergent thinking and sensibility. As I hope you'll see in my profiles of some emergent churches in Chapter Six, these churches can also be considered *local theological communities*. Recently, I received an e-mail announcement that a local group of emergent Christian leaders was gathering in Pittsburgh. Their desire? To begin a conversation about "Pittsburghian theology." This is commonly acknowledged by many folks who understand that Dietrich Bonhoeffer's theology was shaped by Nazi Germany, that Augustine's was formed by his neo-Platonic environs in northern Africa and the Roman Empire, and that Martin Luther's was fashioned in a Roman Catholic monastery.

That brings us to the second trait of theological DNA: theology is *conversational*. René Descartes (1596–1650) reported that he heard God tell him in a dream that he would be the first philosopher to prove human existence, a quest that had eluded philosophers for two thousand years. He set about to solve this intellectual problem by retreating from others, often changing his address. And he frequently worked alone, sitting in a bread oven. There he sat, for years, and thought. And thought. And thought. Mainly, he doubted everything that had previously been thought by philosophers and theologians and mathematicians. Finally, he concluded that the one thing in the world that he couldn't *disprove* was that he was thinking. Eureka! he thought, I've proved my own existence: *I think; therefore, I am.* But the folly of his "solution" was at least twofold. First, he relied completely on his own brain, a fallible organ if ever there was one. And second, his intellectual journey was *solo*—or at least he thought it was.

In fact, Descartes wasn't really solo, since he was in conversation with all of the philosophers who had gone before him. He knew their work, and he took it into account as he developed his own scheme. Even though he claimed to write as though no one had ever written on these matters before, he was in relationship with his predecessors. Even in his opposition to their thoughts, he was bound in relationship to them.

The same goes for us when we muse about God. For emergents, there is no *ex novo* theology—there's only theology done in the aftermath of the multifarious theologies that have gone before. They are in conversation with two thousand years of Christian theology and four thousand years of Jewish theology before that. Some are in conversation with Islamic and Buddhist and Hindu and various other theologies (and a/theologies). And it's my sense, from reading lots of old theology, that this is exactly how most of the towering theologians from the past would like us to interact with their work. They weren't trying to close doors to future generations' conversation about God; they were seeking to solve the dilemmas of their own times and their own minds and spirits. They did the best with what they had, and they would expect us to do the same.

And the conversation isn't just between *me* and my theological forebears but also between me and those with whom I live. Descartes might not have made the philosophical errors he did had he put himself in a community with other people who could have challenged his assumptions (like his overconfidence in his own intellect). Emergent Christians hope to avoid the danger of solo theology by intentionally placing themselves in theological communities, and the more diverse the better. The biblical proverb that "iron sharpens iron"[14] explains exactly how theological ideas get honed in community. One of the ways emergents do this is to live by the motto "Anyone, anytime, anyplace"—that's a commitment to go anywhere (within reason) to converse with even their staunchest critics, to listen for the places they're wrong or misguided, and to respond to the charges against them. The posture during these conversations is meant to be open and earnest, not defensive.

Finally, theology is *temporary*. Since our conceptions of God are shaped locally and in conversation, we must hold them humbly. We must carry our theologies with an open hand, as it were. To assume that our convictions about God are somehow timeless is the deepest arrogance, and it establishes an imperialistic attitude that has a chilling effect on the honest conversation that's needed for theology to progress.

Greg Koukl, the president of Stand to Reason Ministries, is one of the most vocal critics of emergent Christianity. He and I have developed a friendship over the past couple years, in spite of our differences. Recently, when we were together, I asked him to name one big thing that he's changed his mind on in the last ten years, something he believes about God or the world or politics. After thinking for a moment, he said that, although he changed his mind on lots of things in his twenties, he was pretty much set in his beliefs by the age of thirty-five, and he's spent the last fifteen years publicly espousing those beliefs. As you might guess, Greg totally disagrees with my assertion that theology is temporary. In fact, he countercharges that emergents are mistaken to vaunt the temporality, fluidity, and plasticity of theology.

Contrary to Koukl's understanding of theology, emergents reject metaphors like "pin it down," "in a nutshell," "sum it up," and "boil it down" when speaking of God and God's Kingdom, for it simply can't be done. The Kingdom of God is expansive, explosive, and un-pin-downable (to coin a phrase). Consequently, our characterizations of God and God's Kingdom are necessarily fleeting.

Fleeting, but not unsubstantial. As Julie and I raise our children, new dilemmas confront us regularly. Every time Tanner has a new birthday, it's the first time we've had a six-year old, a seven-year old, an eight-year old. We grab a new book on parenting, talk to friends who've got kids older than ours, and pray that we rise to the challenge. As our family grows, develops, progresses (choose your verb), so do we as parents. Our parenting is not static. In fact, sometimes we'll say that we feel "stuck in a rut," which is a sure sign that we need to move forward, to rethink things, to talk more openly about parenting. In that sense, our parenting is always temporary: a moment of action, based on the parenting theories we hold (as well as our intuitions), to confront a specific situation.

Julie and I sometimes look at our children and joke, "Can we laminate them so they'll just stay this size and never grow into unwieldy teenagers?" The very fact that we kid about such things is based on the premise that, indeed, we cannot. Kids are meant to grow. We can't hermetically seal them at eighteen months of age, no matter how cute we think they are. Neither can we hermetically seal God's ever-expanding Kingdom or our experiences of and articulations of that Kingdom.

SKIING THE SLIPPERY SLOPE

That theology is local, conversational, and temporary does not mean that we must hold our beliefs without conviction. This is a charge often thrown at emergent Christians, but it's false. As a society, we've been wrong about all sorts of things in the past, like slavery. And not letting women vote. And not letting nonwhites drink from the same water fountains as whites. I could go on and on. Our forebears held positions on these issues with deep conviction, but they were wrong. And I can say that unequivocally. At least, I can say that *from my vantage point*—as one who came after them—they were wrong. What I cannot say is which side of those issues I would have been on a century or two ago. Nor can I say which issues I'm mistaken on today.

Dispatch 11: Emergents believe that awareness of our relative position-to God, to one another, and to history-breeds biblical humility, not relativistic apathy.

Recently, I was a guest on the Albert Molher radio show with guest host Russell Moore, a dean at Southern Baptist Theological Seminary in Louisville, Kentucky. Moore repeatedly voiced his concern at the emergent movement on the show. At one point, I told him that I'd listened to his show a couple of days earlier and heard him tell a caller that nothing in the Bible prohibits interracial marriage. "Now there was a time," I said, "when the Southern Baptist Convention held it as true that an African American and a white should not get married." Our society—Southern Baptists included—have come to realize that we were wrong about that. I continued, "It's not relativism, it's not 'anything goes'; it's a deliberate process by which we listen to God's Spirit, we live together in communities of faith, and we have a different opinion about a particular item of truth than we did, say, one hundred years ago."

"It's not that we came to a different understanding about what human beings were," Moore responded. "It's that we recognized we were liars. We called ourselves to repentance on the basis of what we were already saying, what we have received from scripture that it is 'from one blood that God created all men.'"[15]

My only question for Moore—which I didn't get to ask—was, What are you and I liars about today?

What I can proclaim with confidence is that in a hundred years, the church will not be debating gay marriage anymore. We will have reached consensus and moved on. The issues of today will be resolved, one way or another. In a century, it might be genetic manipulation or colonization of the moon or cloning that we're debating. Should we let clones be pastors? Should they be allowed to have their own churches?

With that in mind, emergents are pretty humble about the positions we hold today and about the issues that we consider most important.

Atonement

The Christian doctrine that attempts to explain how human sins are forgiven by God, particularly in relation to the death and resurrection of Jesus Christ.

However, humility does not breed apathy. We have all sorts of strongly held positions about all sorts of things, and we'll be happy to debate anything from the atonement to national politics to bioethics. So it's simply not accurate to say (as many critics do), "Once the emergent Christians start talking about 'truth in context,' they relativize what Christians believe, and they're sliding down a slippery slope to meaninglessness. They can't say anything authoritative about anything. Therefore, anything goes."

Slippery Slope

In philosophy and rhetoric, the argument that one action will begin an inexorable chain of events, culminating in an undesirable conclusion.

Case in point: a few years ago, I was having a friendly public debate with an evangelical Christian college professor, Duffy Robbins, in front of a couple of hundred youth pastors. Duffy held up a book, *The Post-Evangelical*, by the Anglican priest Dave Tomlinson, which Emergent Village had just published in the United States. In the book, Tomlinson argues that the church has been co-opted by nation-state governments, particularly concerning their definition of "marriage." He goes on to explain that as an Anglican priest, he's worked with many unmarried couples in London who are actually living more Christ-glorifying lives than those who have been officially married in the Anglican Church.

Tomlinson then appeals to the German theologian Karl Barth to argue that the church should reconstitute marriage on biblical, theological, and covenantal grounds and not allow the government to dictate what is and is not a marriage—at least not for ecclesial purposes. Tomlinson is saying, in effect, that marriage isn't an objective fact in the world. Instead, we decide what it is (and it's been evolving in meaning since men and women started pairing up). In the current cultural debate over what is marriage and family, Tomlinson writes, the church should continue to have a strong voice.

Referring to this passage, Duffy held up Tomlinson's book and warned people not to buy it and not to read it. "It's dangerous," he said. "Don't buy it!" He went on to warn the crowd that Tomlinson perilously relativizes marriage. And then he came up with a real shocker: "If these Emergent guys get their way," he said, "pretty soon we'll be having sex with animals!"

What would cause someone to level the charge of interspecies intercourse against the emergents? Well, it's become clear that there are a couple of pressing concerns about the emergent church, and the primary concern for traditional evangelicals is the specter of *relativism*.

Bestiality aside, my response was "We're all relativists." Consider this: you go into you local Christian bookstore with the virtuous intent of purchasing a Bible. You get to the Bible aisle to find that there are as many versions and editions of the Bible as there are types of cereal at your supermarket. Which will you choose? Each version was translated by a team or an individual with a different theological disposition toward the Hebrew and Greek manuscripts. These manuscripts necessitate scores of interpretive choices for any Bible translator, choices that were built on the various choices of previous translators. Plus, each edition has study notes or call-outs—even headings—designed by human beings, not by God, which reflect the theological biases of the people who prepared them.

Consider, for instance, *revolve: The Complete New Testament*. This Bible[16] looks like a teen-girl magazine. Complete with laughing girls on the cover and big, bold call-outs like "200 + Blab Q&A's" and "Beauty Secrets You've Never Heard Before!" *revolve* is a glossy-paper version of God's Word that asks questions like "Do *revolve* girls call guys for dates?" (They don't.) It's chock full of advice to young girls about dating, beauty, and divorce, but all with a particular (and generally conservative) slant. One "blab" in the margin reads as follows:

> Q: What is God and the church's view on homosexuality and its place in our world?
>
> A: You want God's view, or the church's? Start with God. Romans chapter 1 says that it is impurity. It's a sin, just like gossiping about your best friend is a sin. You need to stop acting on your impulses. Sometimes the church's view can be a little harsher. Many people in the church see it like the worst of all evils. But they are looking at it through human eyes. God says it's a sin; it's not how He made you, so stop.[17]

Although gossip is indeed among the litany of sins that Paul lists in Romans 1, he's surely not equating human sexuality with gossip. Romans 1:18–32 is a particularly vituperative attack by Paul on the activities of those who know God's righteous decrees but continue practices to the contrary. The rest of Paul's magisterial treatise to the Roman churches is an explication of God's grace and God's call to righteousness. "It's not how he made you, so stop" is up there with "Just say no" in its naiveté.

The translation in *revolve* is the New Century Version—basically the work of Ervin Bishop of the World Bible Translation Center in Fort Worth, Texas. Originally translated as a Bible for the deaf, it became the Easy to Read Bible and then the New Century. It is translated so that the text is at a third-grade reading level.

My point is not to belittle *revolve* but to reveal its biases. For instance, this sentence appears in the introduction: "God never intended the Bible to be too difficult for his people." Now, making assertions about God's intentions is, obviously, a theologically weighty matter. A bit down the page, this paragraph, signed by the never-identified "Kate and Laurie," explains the translation:

> Translators kept sentences short and simple. They avoided difficult words and worked to make the text easier to read. They used modern terms and measurements. And they put figures of speech and idiomatic expressions ("he was gathered to his people") in language that even children understand ("he died").[18]

Now their biases become evident:

- The Bible is meant to be plain and simple, easy enough for a child to understand.

- What causes people to have difficulty in reading the Bible is not the theological concepts but the wording.

- The quality of the original phraseology should be sacrificed for modern clarity.

But one might counter those biases with some emergent biases:

- The Bible is an inescapably difficult text, meant to be lived into as a person matures and grows in wisdom.

- While some language and phrasing may be difficult for the modern reader, the real difficulties in reading the Bible have to do with theological concepts (like God dying on a cross and human suffering).

- To abandon the traditional phraseology of the Bible puts the modern reader at a distinct disadvantage, since historic cultural references, from Shakespeare to punk rock, depend on these very idioms. (Indeed, there are hundreds of biblical references in the Shakespearean corpus.)

Clearly, this particular packaging of the New Testament is brimming with bias. From the choice of translation to the glossy paper to the "blab" questions and answers, they all reveal the dispositions of "Kate," "Laurie," Ervin, and the rest of the team that produced *revolve*.

Consider another example: when our first child, Tanner, was born, we were given *The Rhyme Bible Storybook* by some well-meaning friends. Written by Linda Sattgast, a home-schooling mom in the Pacific Northwest, *The Rhyme Bible* refashions some of the best-known stories from the Bible into toddler-friendly verse, accompanied by colorful illustrations.

Here's a rhyme from the book, titled "Joshua 1–6: The Walls Fall Down." It begins:

> The Israelites came
> To the Promised Land.
> A man named Joshua
> Was in command.
> The first thing they saw
> In the valley below
> Was a pretty little town
> Called Jericho.

The illustration shows men in shepherd's clothing—and a camel—looking over a cliff at a high-walled city. Turn the page, and the rhyme continues:

> God told Joshua
> "There's something you should know.
> It's all about the city called Jericho.
> The people there are wicked,
> So I'm giving you their town,
> But you won't get in
> Till the walls come down."[19]

The accompanying picture shows a village of corruption: men arguing and gambling, there's lots of public drunkenness, a guy's getting pushed down some stairs, and others are being tossed out of windows. A man chases a woman through the streets, and bottles litter the town.

Herein lies the problem: when we go to the opening chapters of the book of Joshua in the Bible, there is nothing to indicate that the inhabitants of Jericho are wicked in any way. Instead, we read that God has told the Israelites that the land is theirs, regardless of who happens to currently reside there. After forty years of wandering in the wilderness, the Israelites are finally ready to enter the Promised Land, promised to them by God through Moses.

Joshua, the leader who succeeds Moses, sends spies across the Jordan River into the Promised Land with the instructions to do reconnaissance work, especially on Jericho. The spies wind up in the home of Rahab, a prostitute. The king of Jericho discovers that spies have infiltrated his town and, understandably, tries to find them. Through a series of deceits, Rahab gets the spies out of Jericho. They return to Joshua and tell him that the residents of Jericho are shaking in fear. Emboldened, Joshua leads his warriors across the (miraculously dry) Jordan River and marches around the city for seven days, at which point, the text reads:

> When the trumpets sounded, the army shouted, and at the sound of the trumpet, when the men gave a loud shout, the wall collapsed; so everyone charged straight in, and they took the city. They devoted the city to the LORD and destroyed with the sword every living thing in it – men and women, young and old, cattle, sheep and donkeys.[20]

Only Rahab, the lying prostitute, and her family were spared.

Now, one can see why Sattgast and the publishers of *The Rhyme Bible Storybook* would want to avoid all that messy business about a deceitful harlot. And one can even understand why they'd steer clear of the ritual that takes place just before the sack of Jericho: a mass circumcision at Gibeath Haaraloth (which means "Hill of the Foreskins")—that story doesn't make many children's Bibles. But it's downright dishonest to impugn the morals and motives of the seemingly innocent residents of Jericho. They were, by all accounts, just going about their lives in Jericho when, unbeknownst to them, God promised their acreage to the Israelites. Their only crime was being in the wrong place at the wrong time.

Sattgast, like many modern Christians, must blanch at the thought that God would wipe out a city of thousands for no good reason. But regardless of one's distaste for this kind of thing, one is not free to twist the story to make God more palatable. The biblical God is the instigator of all sorts of nasty incidents, especially in the Old Testament, that don't make for good children's stories. It might be easier to swallow if the Jerichoans were indeed "wicked," but we simply don't have any evidence that they were any more or less wicked than the Israelites themselves.

An emergent might say, if you can't handle all of the ambiguities of the story of Joshua and Jericho, then leave it out of your children's Bible. Don't revise the story to suit your own theology.

A few years ago, I read through the entire Bible in a year with a group of eighteen-year-olds. Upon reading the story of Joshua and Jericho, a girl named Carrie said, "At this point, God seems a lot like Hitler."

I swallowed hard and asked, "Why do you say that?"

"Well," she said, "he's just going around killing anyone who's not from the race of people that he likes best. Isn't that what Hitler did?"

Equating the God of the universe with Adolf Hitler is not something I commend, but I had to acknowledge Carrie's gut-level impression of this passage. God's actions at this and other points in the Bible are difficult to abide. And while we might be tempted to gloss over the unsavory parts or even to add bits to the story that make sense of the contradictions, to do so robs the biblical narrative of its raw beauty. It's these very moral ambiguities in Christianity's sacred text that speak to the ambiguities in our own lives and our own world. And it's unconscionable that the church wouldn't provide a place for questioners—adolescent or adult—to struggle through these ambiguities. Like myriad Christians through the ages, emergents are attempting to do just that, to figure out where God is in the world, what God is up to, and how the biblical narrative jibes with our own twenty-first-century lives.

So back to the local Christian bookstore, where we're standing in the Bible aisle, trying to make a choice. Whether it's *revolve* or *The Rhyme Bible Storybook* or the New International Version Study Bible or the Oxford Study Bible, we're making a choice—a selection that is *relative* to all of the other choices on the shelves. Is there a *better* choice in Bibles? Probably. Is there a *best* choice? Maybe—for you. Is there a *perfect* choice that everyone should use? Surely not.

But does the fact that we're making a *choice* that is *relative* to all of our other *choices* mean that we're on a slippery slope to all-out radical relativism? To sex with animals? Of course not, for we make the best choice that we can at a particular point in time, with all of the evidence we can muster, and we live into that choice.[21] That's the human condition. And indeed, the plurality of available translations surely bolsters our understanding of God's truth.

SO, A BIBLICIST AND A RELATIVIST WALK INTO A PASTORS' CONFERENCE...

Now that we've opened that Pandora's box of biblical interpretation, we might as well deal with the spirits that dwell therein. For it is the question of how we read the Bible—how we interpret it and how we apply those interpretations—that really separates Christians on the left and Christians on the right.

Often this becomes clear to me when I'm speaking at a conference. Having reached the end of my presentation, I'll finally have to call on the guy (it's invariably a guy) who's had his hand up for most of the previous hour. And the hand isn't just up—it's up and demanding to be seen. The hand gropes for an invisible lever; it waves slightly, and the fingers twitch. The hand is connected—by an arm that needs to be propped up by the other arm after fifteen minutes—to a body that leans forward in its chair. Atop that body is a Brain full of Bible trivia and minutiae. That Brain is most often connected to a mouth, and the mouth longs to speak.

When I point to the hand, the Brain unlooses the tongue. "Earlier you referred to a woman pastor that you work with. Isn't the Bible clear that women are not meant to be pastors?"

While here on paper that looks like a straightforward question, the aforementioned mouth has shaped it into a query laden with political ramifications—an attempt to unmask the heretic in the room ("But aren't you the grandson of the famous Victor Frankenstein?"). I say this because in my experience, this question is only the opening salvo. It's the precursor to the *real* question, because I know that when I answer that I think the Pauline prohibition of women teaching over men in 2 Timothy and 2 Corinthians was culturally relevant for the time but is now superseded by the Pauline exhortations that "in Christ there is no more male or female, Jew or Greek, slave or free, barbarian or Scythian,"[22] the Brain comes back at me with "So really, you're just picking and choosing which texts are cultural and which aren't? Who's to say that the resurrection isn't cultural too? So where do you draw the line? Aren't you on a slippery slope as soon as you start picking and choosing the scriptures that you like?"

While a less generous person might call this passive-aggressive behavior, the Brain isn't just out to undermine my credibility. Instead, he is earnest. He wants his own worldview confirmed. He believes that the trustworthiness of the entire Bible rests on its every jot and tittle being factually true and eternally applicable.

What the Brain really thinks is that I am a Relativist, someone who chooses to believe some things in the Bible but ignores other things. More precisely, a Relativist chooses to believe the "easy," "politically correct," or "culturally acceptable" parts of scripture. The Brain, on the other hand, considers himself an Absolutist or, better yet, a Biblicist.

A Biblicist claims to love and obey all portions of the Bible equally, not to live under a biblical hierarchy (wherein some sections of the Bible are more authoritative than others). Nor does a Biblicist give any ground to the culture as it demands supposedly "liberal" readings of the text. For instance, the Biblicist's compatriots recently built the $27 million Creation Museum near Cincinnati. Promoting a "literal" interpretation of the Bible, they believe that the reliability of the resurrection—the centerpiece of Christianity—hinges on the facticity of a seven-day "young earth" creationism. To heck with scientific consensus, they say, as they show visitors an animatronic exhibit with dinosaurs and humans cohabiting.

But the Brain is not really a Biblicist. The Brain is actually a Relativist of a different hue. This became clear when I overheard a conversation, once upon a time, between a Brain and a True Biblicist. It was taking place in a back hallway at a pastors' conference. As I walked up, the discussion was already heated:

Brain: What do you mean I'm a Relativist?!? Stop saying that! Why do you keep saying that?!?

True Biblicist: Calm down, man. It's not such a big deal. Only a few of us are really able to be of the true faith. It's a very high calling. The few, the proud. It's OK. You'll get over it.

Brain: No. Stop it. I'm serious. We're on the same team. I'm a card-carrying conservative. We believe in the Bible as it was originally written, every jot and tittle. Not like those Liberals.

True Biblicist: For instance?

Brain: For instance, we don't let women preach, as is made clear in certain foundational texts of our holy scripture. Everything in our culture pushes us toward egalitarian perspectives on women, but we have stayed true to the "complementarian" position that women and men have different roles in life. Egalitarianism is the relativist's position, but complementarianism is the true Biblical position.[23]

True Biblicist: Do you make your women cover their heads in church?

Brain: Um, no.

True Biblicist: Then you shave their heads? Because Paul is clear: "For if the woman be not covered, let her also be shorn."[24]

Brain: Well, that's a little extreme.

True Biblicist: How about stopping women with braided hair from coming into the church?

Brain: No, we don't stop them.

True Biblicist: Hmm. That's 1 Timothy 2:9. Gold?

Brain: We allow gold.

True Biblicist: Pearls?

Brain: Allow 'em.

True Biblicist: Expensive clothes?

Brain: What's your point?

True Biblicist: My point is that all of these things are prohibited by Paul within a breath or two of his command that women should keep silent in the assembly and not teach over a man.

Brain: But surely those are culturally bound prohibitions. They're not meant to be taken at face value. Paul didn't want women dressing like prostitutes in church, and neither do we!

True Biblicist: Neither do I! Have you been to my church?

Brain: No.

True Biblicist: Well, our women cover their heads, wear plain dresses, and have their hair unbraided. We're hardcore, man. Old-school. We take the Bible at face value, not like you. You're interpreting it. We don't interpret it. If it's not in there, we don't do it. That's why we don't drive cars, use electricity, or use shampoo. I mean, have you ever seen shampoo mentioned in the Bible?

Brain: Do you put homosexuals to death, as commanded in Leviticus 20:13?

True Biblicist: We would if we could find any.

Brain: Are you serious?!? That's outrageous! Jesus came to fulfill the law. There are all sorts of crazy laws in the Old Testament that I'm sure you ignore in your church.

True Biblicist: Actually, you're correct. We pretty much ignore the entire Old Testament, except for the Psalms. There's some crazy shit in there!

Brain: So you're not a true Biblicist either!

True Biblicist: Oh, didn't I tell you my full name? It's "New Testament Biblicist."

Brain: You just said the S-word. How can you swear if you're a Biblicist? Doesn't James say that boasting and cursing should not come out of the same mouth?

True Biblicist: You know Philippians 3:8?

Brain: Of course. "I consider everything a loss compared to the surpassing greatness of knowing Christ Jesus my Lord, for whose sake I have lost all things. I consider them rubbish, that I may gain Christ."

True Biblicist: "*Rubbish*"? That's rubbish! In Greek it's *skubalon*, which was common gutter talk in Paul's day for human excrement. So I figure that if Paul can say "shit," I can say "shit."

Brain: So let me get this straight: you make the women in your church take the braids out of their hair before they can worship, but you allow yourself to use curse words?

True Biblicist: Yup, you've pretty much got it. Except that we don't let our women curse, since there's no woman in the New Testament who curses.

In fact, there are very few passages in the New Testament in which women speak at all, so we just keep our women quiet all of the time.

Brain: This is just getting weirder and weirder.

True Biblicist: Hey, man, you wanna be a True Biblicist or not? If you do, you can't go around picking some passages to take literally and ignoring others. Then you're even worse than a Relativist.

Brain: How so?

True Biblicist: Because at least the Relativist is honest. You're disingenuous. You say you're a Biblicist, but you're not really.

This is about when an Emergent pastor joined the conversation.

Emergent: Hi. I'm a Relativist.

True Biblicist: Hello there!

Brain: Uh, hi.

Emergent: I couldn't help but overhearing your conversation. Say, True Biblicist, can I ask you a question?

True Biblicist: Shoot.

Emergent: What version of the Bible do you use?

True Biblicist: The King James, of course. Actually, we refer to it as the "Authorized Version."

Emergent: Why that version?

True Biblicist: Because it's the most literal. It's the most accurate translation from the Hebrew and Greek texts.

Emergent: Hmmm. I find it interesting that you would say "most accurate" rather than "perfectly accurate."

True Biblicist: Well, I guess I might say that it's perfect, since God guided and has blessed that translation.

Emergent: Why don't you read the Bible in its original languages?

True Biblicist: Well, I know a little Greek, but not well enough to read everything. And I don't know any Hebrew. What's your point?

Emergent: Well, I've talked to others who claim to be Biblicists, and they swear by—oops, bad choice of words—they claim that the New American Standard Version is the most accurate, on a word-for-word basis. Others claim that the English Standard Version is the most literal. And still others will read only the original languages.

True Biblicist: So?

Emergent: Even in the original languages, you've got competing texts to choose from. For the New Testament, you've got the Codex Vaticanus, the Codex Sinaiticus, and the Codex Alexandrius, all coming after the mid-fourth century. Those are just a few of the Greek versions. Then you've got all sorts of versions in Latin, some as early as A.D. 250. And every one of these versions is incomplete. What we've got is a hybrid New Testament, a cut-and-paste rendition of the best of these ancient fragments.

True Biblicist: What's your point, man?

Emergent: You're a Relativist.

True Biblicist: Bull!

Emergent: Sure you are. You choose the King James Version even though, I must say, it's not based on the oldest and most reliable manuscripts. You've made a choice, and that choice is relative to the other options you've got in choosing a Bible. Not surprisingly, you've chosen a version that tends to support your own view of scriptural interpretation.

True Biblicist: There you go, trying your liberal spin on me. Well, it's not going to work. I don't interpret the scriptures. I take them at face value.

Emergent: Do you think that in hell there will be an actual "lake of fire" as Jesus said?

True Biblicist: Right about now, I'm hoping there is, and I'm hoping that you know how to swim!

Emergent: Seriously.

True Biblicist: Seriously, I don't know. I think hell will be like a lake of fire.

Emergent: "Like"? So you think that Jesus was using a simile?

True Biblicist: Of course Jesus used similes. He said that the Kingdom of God is "like a mustard seed."

Emergent: Well, I'd say that as a figure of speech, a simile demands interpretation. I'd say that Jesus wants us to interpret his sayings about mustard seeds and yeast and hidden treasures because that's the only way that we can begin to get our minds around the reality of the Kingdom.

True Biblicist: Nope.

Emergent: What do you mean, "Nope"?

True Biblicist: I mean, I won't concede your point. We'll have to agree to disagree.

Emergent: Um, OK.

With that, the True Biblicist turned on his heel and walked away, leaving the Emergent alone with the Brain.

Emergent: How are you doing? Are you OK?

Brain: I'm a little discombobulated, to be honest. I feel a bit like the rug's been pulled out from under me. I mean, I really thought that I was a biblical literalist. But that guy's crazy! I mean, he wants homosexuals put to death! That's insane!

Emergent: Well, I think when you really run out the string on literalism, that's where you come out. At least he's consistent. But I'd argue that it's just not possible to be a true and perfect literalist when it comes to the Bible — or any book for that matter. God gave you a mind, brother; don't be afraid to use it! Interpretation is all we've got.

Brain: Why does that sound so scary to me?

With that, the Brain wandered back into the crowd of pastors, and his khaki Dockers and golf shirt quickly blended in with all the rest. And the Emergent was left wondering, why does interpretation thrill me and scare him?

THE EXPURGATED LECTIONARY

Lest I be considered unfair in my contrived dialogue between the Brain and the True Biblicist, let me rally to my defense a more famous inventor of dialogue, C. S. Lewis, who makes a similar point when discussing Christian pacifism:

> The whole Christian case for Pacifism rests, therefore, on certain dominical utterances, such as "Resist not evil: but whosoever shall smite thee on thy right cheek, turn to him the other also." I am now to deal with the Christian who says this is to be taken without qualification. I need to point out – for it has doubtless been pointed out to you before – that such a Christian is obliged to take all the other hard sayings of Our Lord in the same way. For the man who has done so, who has on every occasion given to all who ask him and has finally given all he has to the poor, no one will fail to feel respect. With such a man I must suppose myself to be arguing; for who would deem worth answering that inconsistent person who takes Our Lord's words *àla rigueur* when they dispense him from a possible obligation and takes them with latitude when they demand that he should become a pauper?[25]

Here Lewis is invoking the same challenge of pick-and-choose literalism against left-leaning pacifists. And it's not just regarding pacifism that the biblical nonliteralists hedge their bets on scripture. Their Sunday morning readings show a very similar posture toward the Bible as their conservative peers.

The lectionary is the three-year cycle of biblical passages used by many mainline churches. Oriented around the church year, the lectionary assigns four texts to each Sunday of the year: an Old Testament reading, a Psalm, a Gospel reading, and a reading from the Epistles. But as I was told recently by a frustrated young Episcopal priest, "The lectionary readings are full of ellipses!"

What she meant was that in many places, the lectionary replaces passages with points of ellipsis ("..."), and not coincidentally, these edits often coincide with the orthodoxies of the left. For instance, Psalm 104: 24–35 reads as follows:

> 24 How many are your works, LORD!
> In wisdom you made them all;
> the earth is full of your creatures.

25 There is the sea, vast and spacious,
   teeming with creatures beyond number—
   living things both large and small.

26 There the ships go to and fro,
   and the leviathan, which you formed to frolic there.

27 All creatures look to you
   to give them their food at the proper time.

28 When you give it to them,
   they gather it up;
   when you open your hand,
   they are satisfied with good things.

29 When you hide your face,
   they are terrified;
   when you take away their breath,
   they die and return to the dust.

30 When you send your Spirit,
   they are created,
   and you renew the face of the ground.

31 May the glory of the LORD endure forever;
   may the LORD rejoice in his works—

32 he who looks at the earth, and it trembles,
   who touches the mountains, and they smoke.

33 I will sing to the LORD all my life;
   I will sing praise to my God as long as I live.

34 May my meditation be pleasing to him,
   as I rejoice in the LORD.

35 But may sinners vanish from the earth
   and the wicked be no more.
   Praise the LORD, my soul.
   Praise the LORD.

A beautiful and provocative Psalm, to be sure, and a reading that's slated for one of the most important days in the church calendar, Pentecost, in all three years of the lectionary cycle. But strangely, the lectionary calls for this reading: "Psalm 104:24–34, 35b."[26] In other words, the preacher is instructed to excise the line, "But may sinners vanish from the earth and the wicked be no more."

This happens over and over in the lectionary: Sunday morning Bible readings are purged of their unsavory—some might say "politically incorrect"—content. This dubious practice raises the obvious question: How does censorship serve the faithful who sit in congregations across America? The answer: it doesn't. Instead, this practice is an injustice both to the Bible and to those who place their trust in the Bible's words. It assumes that average Christians can't handle all that the Bible has to offer, or worse, that preachers can't manage the prickly parts of the text.

This is the left's sin against the Bible. About a year ago, I subscribed to a verse-a-day e-mail from a well-known Christian justice ministry. But the verses that arrive in my inbox daily are not representative of the breadth of scripture. I'm reminded that Jesus said, "Turn the other cheek" in the Sermon on the Mount but not that when the disciples ended the Last Supper, they pointed to two swords, and Jesus said, "That is enough."[27] On both the left and right of modern American Christianity, the cut-and-paste approach to the Bible is a disservice to the people of God. Emergents, for their part, are trying to embrace the whole text.

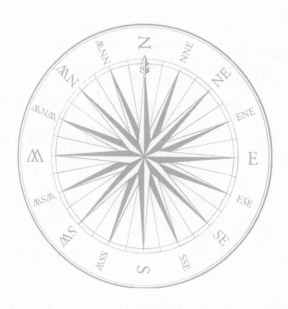

Dispatch from Seminary:
Legalisms of the Left

"The worst part of my current job," Bob told me, "is that twice a day I drive past the house we sold. It's a constant reminder of my mistake."

Bob's mistake? Going to seminary.

Bob grew up in Dallas. A cradle Episcopalian, he's never left the Anglican fold.

Anglican Communion

The wide array of churches under the Church of England. Begun with Henry VIII's break from Roman Catholicism in 1534, Anglicans are bound not by theology but by their hierarchical structure and by the liturgy, spelled out in the Book of Common Prayer. In the United States, most Anglicans are known as the Episcopal Church, but conservative parishes have recently been leaving that church and reorganizing under conservative bishops.

After a successful twenty-year career in marketing and consulting, he found himself at a crossroads. In Christian parlance, he felt called to full-time ministry. Bob's married, with a teenage daughter, and he lives in San Francisco, so dropping out of the workforce to attend seminary meant significant sacrifices.

He and his wife sold their home, and Bob started commuting to the closest Episcopal seminary, which also happens to be one of the stalwartly liberal seminaries within Anglicanism. He stayed two years, almost completing his degree before dropping out due to a nervous breakdown. When asked to sum up his two years at seminary, he calls it "soul-shattering."

"It's a conservative liberalism," Bob told me. "It was an orthodoxy that said, 'In the interest of maintaining our cohesiveness and our viability, here's the playbook, here's our position on these things.'" There was little wiggle room for a guy who didn't quite fit the mold, who wanted to question the status quo, and who didn't necessarily fit in all of the right theological, political, and gendered boxes.

As Bob continued to relate his story to me, he said that it was acceptable at his seminary to pity those who've been harmed by the past colonialisms of Christianity and to give the formerly marginalized a voice. But only to a point. For when the formerly marginalized turn out to have opinions that are deemed unsophisticated (in other words, conservative), they are re-silenced. "So it's entirely appropriate to assign a reading from an ecofeminist theologian from Africa," Bob said, "but a conservative Anglican bishop from Africa is excluded.

"The current way that the Episcopal Church is trying to explode itself is over the ordination of the first openly gay bishop," Bob told me, noting that gay men—just not openly gay—have, of course, been bishops in the past. "I've belonged to seven Episcopal churches in my life, three of which have already left the denomination over this issue. And I attended the seminary of which Katharine Jefferts Schori, the current presiding bishop of the Episcopal Church, is a graduate. So I have the unfortunate gift of having friends on—quote-unquote—both sides. And it broke my soul to try to contort myself to see the issue in the way it was framed."

As a man in the middle on that most contentious of issues, he was thrilled when the seminary hosted an "intercession," a three-day conference in which all sides—conservative, liberal, "low church," and "high church"—were represented. Afterward, he went up to the administrator who programmed the weekend and told him that it was the best three days he'd had on the campus. "Then I asked him," Bob said, "'why can't this happen in the curriculum on a regular basis?' And he said it never could, here or at a conservative campus, because this breadth of point of view puts the institution at risk. I realized that his job at the seminary was to hone the canon, to firm up the boundaries, not to expand the boundaries.

"The result of that posture," Bob continued, "is that it's easier to have an interfaith conversation with a Buddhist than it is to talk with another Christian from the opposing camp."

So it's a different kind of fundamentalism. Bob calls it "absoluteness, just poured in a different glass." So he would go to church history class and hear that to the victors—the educated, ecclesial elite—goes the ability to write history. This is a sin for which the church must repent, went the lecture, and the traditionally marginalized voices must be heard. He was encouraged to rethink his views on doctrine, to hold his images of God with ambiguity, to take the creedal statements of church councils with a grain of salt. "Ambiguity is fine when you're talking about images of God," he said. "But it is absolutely not OK on issues of social justice."

Then he'd go to into his liturgy class, where he was told, "Don't stray from the rubric of the liturgy by even a word." In other words, theological doctrine was slippery, squishy, but the words of the Book of Common Prayer were to be adhered to without modification when a priest was administering communion.

Liturgy

The regularized communal religious practices of a particular group. From the Greek leitorgia, meaning "public work" or "work of the people."

He started thinking of the irony that he had given up all his volunteer ministry at his church to make time for seminary. And he felt his marriage slipping away.

"Seventy thousand times, I told myself to drop out," he said. "But on so many different occasions, so many people I adore and still count as close, personal friends said, 'Your only option is to keep your mouth shut and get a pension, and by then you can get your own church and you can do whatever you want with it.' I wish I had listened to myself. I wish I hadn't bought into the allure that 'in twenty years, you'll have a nice pension to show for it.'"

Bob went on to compare that allure to a dysfunctional family. "It's like when Grandma is suffering from dementia and you tell the kids, 'Wait a couple of hours till the medicine kicks in; then she won't be cruel to you anymore.' All the while you're forgetting that the real sadness for the kids is that Grandma isn't a loving, vibrant person anymore. Your sadness isn't that she's mean to you; your sadness is that you can't even recognize her.

"It ended really, really badly," he said, with sadness in his voice. "In a peculiar way, the money I gave up was the easiest to replace. What I did to my marriage, the way I contorted myself to fit into it ... I'm less and less convinced that 'this is really what God wants for you.' I know that God can't want something like that.

"I finally realized that seminary was soul-shattering, and that was the *best* it was going to be."

Bob concluded with a strong caveat: "I was not a victim, and I left in a very bad way." He acknowledges that he hurt people and hurt the seminary when he left. He went down swinging, out of his own pain and frustration. He not only wishes he had listened to his own voice earlier; he wishes that he had left better.

But now, as he occasionally tells his story to people, to others in seminary, they resonate with it. "While it's uniquely my story," he says, "I'm not alone.

"When you run into three disgruntled Catholic nuns, you realize that you're drinking from the same cup. It's the institution of the church that's in its death throes, not the Christian faith itself. A series of institutions that were built for a different context are dying or else they died fifty years ago and they've been coasting ever since on palliative care."

Almost two years removed from his painful ending at seminary, Bob is back in ministry and back in business. He and his family have moved to Austin, Texas, and they're starting to look for a church.

> "It's the institution of the church that's in its death throes, not the Christian faith itself."

CHAPTER 5

AFTER OBJECTIVITY:
BEAUTIFUL TRUTH

A FRIEND TOLD ME THAT EMERGENT CHRISTIANITY WAS recently mentioned in a sermon by a conservative megachurch pastor just a couple of miles from my home in the Twin Cities. I went online and listened to the podcast of the sermon, which was on traits of leadership, and here's what he said:

> Friends, it's not an easy world in which to stand up for truth, is it? We're in a society that doesn't even believe that truth exists: "Ah, well, if it works for you, it's true for you; if it works for me, it's true for me. Let's just all find our own way." . . .
>
> Within Christianity today, there's a big movement — it has some good and some bad to it — called the emergent movement. One of the great dangers of this movement is what they call a "hermeneutic of humility." "Hermeneutics" is the science of interpreting scripture — and of course, the idea of humility. And the basic idea is, "Let's not be too clear, too dogmatic, too strong about what we believe. I mean, how

do we know we're really right, you know?" And in a sense, it's giving in to the conflict of society, giving in to the pressure of the culture to say, "Well, you know, absolute truth, we're not sure, so let's just be *really* humble about the way we communicate it."[1]

The pastor went on to compare an emergent Christian to a child who wants to eat Lucky Charms cereal for dinner in the place of spinach, and he concluded by telling his congregation, "If you want to be a person of influence, you've got to stand for something."

THE THRILL OF INTERPRETATION

Although his conclusion about emergents not eating their spinach is dubious, the pastor's assertion that emergents generally espouse a humble hermeneutic is accurate. Humility about what human beings can know, about the limits of human knowledge and our ability to accurately articulate that knowledge—what philosophers call *epistemic* humility—is a common trait among emergents.

Hermeneutics

The study of theories of interpretation.

This stems, in part, from the acute awareness among emergents that our ancestors were dead wrong about some things in the past. Ask an emergent, "Why so humble about making strong truth claims?" and you're likely to hear a response like this: "One hundred years ago, my great-grandfather thought that women shouldn't vote. He was absolutely certain about that, and I'm absolutely certain that he was wrong. Two hundred years ago, my great-great-great-great-grandfather believed that white men should own black men. He was absolutely certain about *that*, and I am quite certain that he was wrong.

"I'm humble," an emergent might tell you, "because I don't know what I'm wrong about today. I'll speak with confidence, and I'll speak with passion, but I won't speak with certainty."

So why does a "hermeneutic of humility" appeal to emergents but sound dangerous to this pastor? Based on his comments, he fears that humility—at least in the interpretation of the Bible—will lead to meaninglessness, to an inability to stand for something. If someone says, "I think the Bible is saying this, but faithful Christians through the years have disagreed with me," that's caving in to society's desire for ambivalence. Standing *for* something, for this pastor at least, means standing *on* something: a sure and indubitable foundation.

The emergents, however, claim just the opposite. They confidently stand for all sorts of thing—the twentieth-century theologian Lesslie Newbigin called it "proper confidence"—this, he said, is how one can be deeply Christian, even in a pluralistic world, without the imperialism that is necessarily engendered by certainty.[2] For if one has rock-solid certainty, it's only natural to suppose that all other viewpoints are wrong and therefore impose one's certainty on others. Proper confidence, by contrast, lends itself to persuasion, not imposition.

Emergents have also occasionally been mocked for promoting conversation and dialogue in the place of proclamation, propositions, and monologue. However, the desire for dialogue can be understood under this same rubric of interpretation. While an emphasis on interpretation does preclude the many propositions about eternally "right" and "wrong" answers, it doesn't mean that there's no truth. Instead, it means that there are inherently *better* interpretations—that one interpretation can trump another. For instance, the 1850 argument that human slavery was biblically permitted was eventually overcome by the interpretation that the Bible condemns practices such as slavery. Unfortunately, these differences of interpretation led to armed conflict and much bloodshed, but today we agree that the *better* interpretation won out.

How does one become a *better interpreter*? Through conversation. Emergents hold that by talking to others, they get closer to the truth. That's why emergents are virtually obsessed with dialogue—they talk to Christians of other stripes, to dead Christians (via books), to non-Christians, and to one another. They talk on the phone, attend conferences, frequent coffee shops, read and comment on blogs, and buy lots of books. For one does not become better at interpretation while sitting in an oven. One becomes a better interpreter sitting at a dinner party, engaging in a conversation.

To take this one step further, emergents believe that the conversational, interpretive quest for truth is an act of faithfulness. In fact, emergent Christians will argue that they're actually being faithful to the great theologians and pastors in the history of the church, for they're doing just what those predecessors did: actively working to understand God's ongoing work in the world. This accounts for the emergent attraction to the speculative, the adventurous, in theology. Emergents consider the faithfulness of saints like Francis of Assisi, Martin Luther, Dorothy Day, and Dietrich Bonhoeffer to be their bravery—they challenged the status quo and pushed the boundaries of the conventional—all, it must be said, to get the gospel right in their time and place.

Further, emergents are enamored of story, particularly of telling their own stories and listening to others' stories. The interest in story, too, stems from the desire for better interpretation. To better know one's own story means that one's own biases and prejudices are revealed, and when those are revealed, their implications on one's interpretations can be accounted for.

Here's an example. If your family has a history of mental illness—let's say obsessive-compulsive disorder (OCD)—most psychologists would tell you *not* to ignore that history. They'd say that you should understand OCD: study it, get to know it, and then you'll be able to look for indicators of OCD in your own life. The same goes for alcoholism and any number of other disorders, as well as more positive traits like musical talent. Indeed, if you ignore something like OCD in your family's history, you may be condemning yourself (or your children) to repeat the cycle, or in the case of a positive trait, of missing out on taking advantage of it.

In the same way, recognizing the opinions and angles that one brings to the biblical text aids in the interpretation of that text. If I can admit my position as a white man with a relatively great amount of power in the world, I can start to understand how that taints my reading of scripture. I can also discipline myself to listen to less powerful voices as they interpret the Bible. That's why so many emergents immerse themselves in a wide variety of conversations—they'll read an array of authors, regularly engaging the works of those with whom they disagree. Emergents from conservative backgrounds will read books they've been taught were off-limits, and emergents with liberal pedigrees will engage books deemed politically incorrect by their former tribe. While this practice is common in the academic world, it's been woefully lacking in the church world, where very many pastors and lay leaders read only those authors with whom they already agree. Emergents are bent on changing that rule.

READING THE *WHOLE* BIBLE

When I was a youth pastor, I began to notice something. The students came into our ministry when they were in sixth grade, which meant that most of them had at least ten years of Sunday school experience under their belts. As you might imagine, they were quite familiar with the story of Noah and the ark. In fact, they'd probably been taught that story a couple of dozen times—more if they attended vacation Bible school in the summers.

However, they'd been taught *part* of the story of Noah. They were well versed on the building of the ark, the two-by-two gathering of the animals, and the forty days and forty nights of rain. If they'd had a particularly honest Sunday school teacher, they'd even considered Noah's drowning neighbors.

But in all those years, I never met a student who was familiar with the story's ending:

To drunk!

> Noah, a man of the soil, proceeded to plant a vineyard. When he drank some of its wine, he became drunk and lay uncovered inside his tent. Ham, the father of Canaan, saw his father's nakedness and told his two brothers outside. But Shem and Japheth took a garment and laid it across their shoulders; then they walked in backward and covered their father's nakedness. Their faces were turned the other way so that they would not see their father's nakedness.
>
> When Noah awoke from his wine and found what his son had done to him, he said, "Cursed be Canaan! The lowest of the slaves will he be to his brothers."
>
> He also said, "Praise be to the Lord, the God of Shem! May Canaan be the slave of Shem. May God extend Japheth's territory; may Japheth live in the tents of Shem, and may Canaan be the slave of Japheth."[3]

Basically, one of Noah's sons walked in on the old man (he was 650 at the time), saw him drunk and naked, and for some strange reason Noah laid a curse on Ham's youngest son. The "curse of Canaan" has subsequently been used by many generations to biblically justify slavery, particularly of dark-skinned people. And this is just one of many examples of the seemingly arbitrary justice meted out by God and by the heroes of the Bible.[4]

One can see why Christians would be tempted to "clean up" the Bible. Whether it's *The Rhyme Bible* or the lectionary from Chapter Four or the myriad Sunday school teachers who end the story of Noah just after the successful docking of the ark on Mount Ararat, it would seem that the unsavory bits of the Bible are best ignored.

But emergents counter this trend. Maybe it's the legendary angst of Gen Xers or the success of postmodernist English professors, but whatever the reason, the trend among emergent churches is to use the *whole* Bible, even if that means that some passages are basically inexplicable.[5]

Dispatch 12: Emergents embrace the whole Bible, the glory and the pathos.

Other Christian churches don't ignore these passages; they do something even worse: they attempt to moralize them.

Take the story of Jephthah and his daughter. They're characters in the book of Judges (that's the time in Israel's history between the wanderings in the desert and the epoch of the kings). Jephthah was a warrior, and he wanted the Lord to know just how loyal he was. So as he was about to go and make war on some enemies of Israel, he made God a promise: "Lord, if you grant me victory in this battle, I will sacrifice to you the first beautiful thing that comes out of my door upon my return. In fact, I'll make it a burnt offering to you!" And off to battle he went.

Now Jephthah had a daughter, a beautiful virgin daughter. She was the love of his life. As you might guess, Jephthah defeated Israel's enemies; in fact, he destroyed twenty towns. Marching home triumphantly, he looked down the road and saw—you guessed it—his daughter dancing toward him, overjoyed to see her father.

What follows is possibly the least savory tale in the Bible. When Jephthah sees his daughter, he swallows hard and tells her about his vow to God. We can only imagine the look on her face as her beloved father broke the news that he'd have to kill her in order to keep his vow to God.

"You're kidding, right, Dad?"

"No, I'm afraid not, sweetheart."

"But . . . um . . . I don't want to die."

"Sorry, honey, I really am sorry. In fact, I feel sick to my stomach about this. But there's no going back on a promise to God. We can't break our vows to him – our entire system of religion is built on the premise that he keeps his word to us and we need to keep our word to him. And he granted me victory in battle, so I need to keep my vow to him."

"But, Dad, maybe you won the battle because you're a better warrior. Maybe the Lord had nothing to do with it."

"Don't say such things! Of course the Lord granted me the victory. We can do nothing without him!"

"But isn't he capable of all things?"

"Yes, of course, dear. You know that. You learned it in Sabbath school."

"Well, that's great, Dad! That means there's a loophole! If God can do *anything*, then he can release you from your vow!"

"I'm afraid it doesn't work like that, honey. The Lord can't go around releasing people from their vows. That would lead to anarchy. There have got to be certain laws, certainties, fundamentals that hold the whole thing together. Anyway, it would show weakness in God's character if he let me off the hook on this promise."

" 'Weakness in God's character'? How can anything we do affect God's character? Isn't the Lord completely sovereign? Isn't his reasoning far above ours? Isn't his wisdom beyond our grasp?"

"Well, yes, of course it is."

"Then maybe, in his infinite wisdom, he'll release you from your promise. Maybe that's his higher plan. Can't you at least ask?"

"No, dear, I can't ask. I've made my vow, and I'm sticking to it. I'll
give you a couple of weeks to grieve that you'll die a virgin before I
slit your throat and burn you on the altar."

My apologies for the contrived dialogue, but if I were Jephthah's daughter,
these are the kinds of questions that I'd be asking. Instead, the Bible records
that she said, "My father, you have given your word to the Lord. Do to me
just as you promised, now that the Lord has avenged you of your enemies,
the Ammonites. But grant me this one request: give me two months to roam
the hills and weep with my friends, because I will never marry." We then read
that the young girl went into the wilderness with her handmaidens for a few
weeks during which she grieved her fate, and then she returned and submitted
herself to her father's sword and a funeral pyre.

The very thought of a father murdering his own daughter turns my stomach,
as it probably does yours. The idea that this is God's sovereign plan is distasteful
to our intellect. And the fact that this story is recorded in the book that
Christians consider the sacred and inspired text of holy scripture is almost
enough to make one's spiritual life come unhinged.

Presenting on the intricacies of this passage at a conference recently, one
pastor raised his hand. "You're making the story of Jephthah much more
complicated than it needs to be," he said. "The point of the story is that we
should never make deals with God. And we should never make a vow to God
that we're not willing to keep."[6]

Emergents find this kind of moralization of scripture almost as distasteful
as they find the story of Jephthah. A friend of mine calls this the "Aesop's
fablization of the Bible"—that is, the tendency to find a moral at the end
of every passage.[7] This type of moralization belittles scripture, turning the
confounding and often frightening Bible into a pleasant bedtime story for
children.

I submit that *there is no moral in Jephthah's story*. There's only pathos and
tragedy, which raises all sorts of questions.

- *Psychological questions:* Was Jephthah mentally ill? How do we deal
  with passages in scripture that portray behavior that we today consider
  psychopathic?

- *Sociological questions:* Why did no one else step in and tell Jephthah just
  how insane this thinking really was?

- *Theological questions:* What is the nature of God's character? Does God hold us to our vows, even when they're stupid? Can human beings even make deals with God: If I do this, God will do that?[8] Why is this story in the Bible? Why did God stop Abraham's sacrifice of Isaac but not Jephthah's sacrifice of his daughter?

In the end, the way to approach this passage, as well as many others, is to allow it to infect us, to live inside of us, like a virus. That's easy with verses like "Love one another," but it's more difficult with a story like this. However, when a mother rolls her car into a lake with her toddlers strapped in the backseat (Union, South Carolina, 1994) or when another drowns her five children in the bathtub (Houston, Texas, 2001), Bible-believing Christians shouldn't be quite as shocked as the rest of the population. These horrific actions have been a part of human history as long as it's been recorded. Infanticide is part of our story, part of the human condition. Even our sacred Bible doesn't avoid the horror of parents who kill their children.

The question is not how someone could be capable of this. The question instead becomes, Where is God in this horror? And the answer is this: in the back of the car with those drowning children. In the bottom of the tub. On the funeral pyre.

Standing in a crowd being forced to watch the hanging of an angel-faced child at Auschwitz, Elie Wiesel heard someone ask, "For God's sake, where is God?" "And from within me, I heard a voice answer," Wiesel writes, " 'Where is He? This is where—hanging here from this gallows.' "[9] Reflecting on Weisel's writing, the Christian theologian Jürgen Moltmann writes:

> If that is to be taken seriously, it must also be said that, like the cross of Christ, even Auschwitz is in God himself. Even Auschwitz is taken up into the grief of the Father, the surrender of the Son and the power of the Spirit.... As Paul says in I Cor. 15, only with the resurrection of the dead, the murdered and the gassed, only with the healing of those in despair who bear lifelong wounds, only with the abolition of all rule and authority, only with the annihilation of death will the Son hand over the kingdom to the Father. Then God will turn his sorrow into eternal joy.... God in Auschwitz and Auschwitz in the crucified God – that is the basis for a real hope which both embraces

and overcomes the world, and the ground for a love which is stronger
than death and can sustain death.[10]

I have just as much confidence that God was with Jephthah's daughter as
she was burned in sacrifice to God. This does not particularly make Jephthah's
story easier to swallow, but it does bring it into our lives today with more
relevance. For whether it's Auschwitz or ancient Israel or Houston, Texas, or
Union, South Carolina, hell on earth is a reality for many people, even children.
The God we follow promises to be a God of presence, to be available to all
people, even to suffer with us. Indeed, this is an important way to understand
the cross of Christ, as the cosuffering of God with us.[11]

And it is, I think, the most honest way to come to terms with the story of
Jephthah and his daughter.

"SONNY, IT AIN'T NOTHING TILL I CALL IT"

For many years, I was an umpire. I started umpiring girls' softball when I was only
fourteen, and I had to ride my bike to every game. By age sixteen, I was working Little League baseball games; by twenty, it was high school; and by my
mid-twenties, I was umpiring college games. I retired from umpiring in 2001,
after the birth of our second child made the time away too difficult, but not
before I reached my goal: I worked an NCAA Division I baseball game (I was
the third-base umpire, and I made only one call all game).

When I started umpiring, I was by-the-book, as every novice umpire is.
I had to basically memorize the rule book in order to pass the annual rules
exam. And if you know anything about baseball, you know that the rule book
is treated like a sacred text more than in any other sport. I was, you might say,
a baseball fundamentalist.

The baseball rule book is quite specific about many things. The strike zone,
for instance. Here's how it's defined in Rule 2.00:

> The strike zone is that area over home plate the upper limit of which is
> a horizontal line at the midpoint between the top of the shoulders and
> the top of the uniform pants, and the lower level is a line at the hollow

beneath the knee cap. The Strike Zone shall be determined from the batter's stance as the batter is prepared to swing at a pitched ball.

From the "hollow beneath the kneecap" to the "batter's stance," this rule actually leaves a lot of room for interpretation.

You've only got to watch about an inning of a major league baseball game to see how liberally this very specific rule is applied. For instance, no umpire in the majors will call a strike above a player's belt, no matter what the rule says. On the other hand, balls just beneath the knee hollow (whatever that is) are routinely called strikes. This wasn't the case in Babe Ruth's day, but in the past few decades, the strike zone has gotten consistently smaller and lower. It's also moved outside by at least an inch.

Why has the strike zone changed? First of all, it's because umpires have switched from the old, external chest protectors to new, lightweight protectors that they wear under their shirts. As a result, they're able to crouch lower behind the catcher, and their line of sight has moved lower, thus causing them to call lower pitches strikes.

The zone has moved outside because as the strikes have gotten lower, batters have moved closer to the plate to reach those lower pitches, and baseball officials have been cracking down on "brush-back pitches." To give pitchers back some of the zone that they've lost on the inside, umps often give them pitches that are one or even two inches outside.

There's one more reason, and you won't hear many people in baseball talk about it. The manager of a baseball team stands in the dugout while his team is at bat; that is, he's at a 90-degree angle from the line on which the pitch approaches home plate, with his eyes at about the level of a batter's belt. If an umpire calls a strike on a pitch that's up at the letters, the manager is sure to start barking from the bench. However, the manager can't really tell if a pitch is an inch or two outside of the plate. So if any umpire is going to cheat in order to gain a few strikes, it'll likely be on the outside pitches (more strikes means fewer walks, which means a quicker game, and every ump wants quick games).

In 2001, major league baseball tried to get its umpires back to fundamentalism. Officials told the umps to call the strike zone as it was spelled out in the rule book, not as it has been traditionally interpreted and enforced. They even sent umps out to each team during spring training to explain the new interpretation. By the 2002 season, most baseball writers agreed that the zone had gone right back to the low, outside zone that it had become in the 1990s.

Currently, major league baseball is grading umps using a computer system called QuesTec and again trying to enforce the literal interpretation of the rule. Again, most baseball experts say that it's not working.

Stanley Fish, one of the preeminent postmodern thinkers alive today, was quoted a few years back in the *New Yorker*, telling a story of the legendary umpire Bill Klem:

> Klem's behind the plate.... The pitcher winds up, throws the ball. The pitch comes. The batter doesn't swing. Klem for an instant says nothing. The batter turns around and says, "OK, so what was it, a ball or a strike?" And Klem says, "Sonny, it ain't nothing till I call it." What the batter is assuming is that balls and strikes are facts in the world and that the umpire's job is to accurately say which one each pitch is. But in fact balls and strikes come into being only on the call of an umpire.[12]

Fish goes on to say that slow-motion replays—and I'm sure he would add QuesTec—do not supplant the role of the umpire as the authority on what is a strike and what is not. There is no objective thing, a strike, until it is named such by the one to whom the baseball community has granted authority. There is, instead, interpretation by the umpire, and the umpire, as interpreter, stands in the middle of the baseball community.

And the strike zone is just one of the hundreds of rules in the baseball rule book.

As a young umpire, I was, as I said, a baseball fundamentalist. I also became frustrated in my early twenties that it was taking me so long to reach the "big games." I wasn't assigned to a high school playoff game until I was twenty-four. I'd been an ump for years, and I knew that I was ready for a big game earlier than that. Well, I *thought* I was ready. That is, until I got to that game: it was the California high school state quarterfinals. The pitcher was a sixteen-year-old phenom, and a dozen major league scouts were camped in the bleachers, each with a radar gun to clock this kid's ninety-mile-per-hour fastball. I'd never stood behind a ninety-mile-an-hour fastball before, nor had I umpired in front of a dozen major league scouts. After about two innings, I was awfully grateful for the ten years of umpiring experience that I'd had—I'd come a long way from umpiring third-grade girls' softball, but I'd also seen thousands of balls and strikes in those years.

What had happened in the intervening years—and it happened still more before I got that NCAA Division I game—was that I became a *better interpreter* of the rules. I had to *live into* the rules of baseball, to umpire scores of games, to have coaches scream in my face, and to have veteran umps lecture me in the parking lot before I was ready for a really big-time game.

A person is not born a great umpire. And the legalist who merely memorizes the entire rule book is surely a terrible ump. What makes someone a good umpire is *experience*, and that experience caused me to realize that the rules of baseball are meant to be applied with *wise interpretation*. Be it a balk, a strike, or the infield fly rule, the rule as it's printed on the page is worthless without the interpretation of a good umpire, and the application of the rule by a bad ump can render the rule—and the game itself—meaningless or even disastrous.

The Bible is not so very different in Christian life. In the hands of a wise expert, it's a thing of beauty. In the hands of a cult leader like David Koresh, it's a thing of terror and oppression. And we all can, indeed, become *better interpreters* of it.

Christians and non-Christians alike choose all sorts of interpretive lenses through which they read the Bible. David Koresh saw it as a prophecy of his own messiahship. The televangelist Jack van Impe reads it as a book predicting the imminent apocalypse. Others read it through the Synod of Dordt or the Sermon on the Mount or Luther's Shorter Catechism or the Catechism of the Catholic Church. None of these interpretive lenses, in and of itself, is necessarily dangerous. But relying on one to the exclusion of all others fosters a kind of myopia that leaves out much of the richness and beauty of God's story. Myopia like this often becomes pathological. It's been said that heresy is the exclusive focus on one truth, at the expense of all other truth.

But such myopia has become a real problem in the church and in biblical interpretation today. If a baseball umpire became myopic, seeing only the strike zone without watching the rest of the game, he'd be a terrible failure. If he became an expert on only one rule, without studying the rest of the rule book, he'd not be allowed onto the field.

That's because being a baseball umpire is an *art*, not a science. Learning the rules and knowing how to apply them in specific instances does not take place in a sterile laboratory but on a dirt-covered field, in the complex mix of a couple of dozen human beings involved in the complex movements of a game.

Interpreting the Bible is no different. It's an art. And we hone our interpretive skills not only by studying the Bible but also by practicing it in the complex movements of life with fellow humans.

TRUTH (A.K.A. GOD)

Having already argued that emergents think objectivity is as real as a unicorn, they will also concur with this statement: *God is truth*. Though never directly quoted in scripture, I think we can safely say that this statement is a consensus opinion among Christians.

Most persons who follow God would without reluctance affirm the assertion that "all truth is God's truth." That is, whatever is true necessarily proceeded from God; truth doesn't come from anywhere else. So if it's true, it's definitely from God. Truth and God are somehow aligned, maybe even one and the same. You might even say, *God equals truth* and *truth equals God*. To those who affirm that statement, we might next ask, Can you describe God in words? Most emphatically and in all humility, most Christians would respond in chorus, "*No!*"—for human language is limited, finite, and altogether incapable of fully describing God. Few human beings would be so arrogant as to presume to have the ability to definitively sum up God. God's too big. We can't get our arms around God, so to speak. Indeed, to claim that we can fully sum up God is idolatry, if not outright blasphemy.

And yet, surprisingly, many people claim an ability to fully articulate truth, and when someone questions their ability to do so, they get rather feisty. But there's a disconnect here. The same one who claims that God is truth and that God cannot be fully described cannot go on to claim that truth *can* be fully described. What emergents claim is that *talk of truth* demands the same humility as *talk of God*.

But alas, we rarely hear Christians talk about truth with humility. Instead, we hear well-meaning Christians who would never say the same about God proclaiming that truth can be circumscribed, domesticated, and subsequently proclaimed to the unsuspecting masses.

```
Dispatch 13: Emergents believe that truth, like
God, cannot be definitively articulated by finite
human beings.
```

Another troubling trend, one that tells us a lot about the state of "truth" in American Christianity, is how many Christians resort to qualifiers before the words *true* and *truth*. Here are some of the phrases you may have heard:

> "Really true"
> "Objectively true"
> "Really, *really* true"
> "Absolute truth"
> And the real doozy (drum roll, please): "True truth."

It's telling that when we hear these phrases, all of the verbal emphasis is put on the *qualifier* of the truth. For example, I've had this shouted at me: "Sure, I understand what you're saying, but there is such a thing as *true* truth!"

But emergents propose that the word *true* cannot take a qualifier. It's like the word *unique*. *Unique* means "one of a kind"; nothing can be "really unique" because it's not possible to be more than one-of-a-kind. A thing either *is* one-of-a-kind or it *is not* one-of-a-kind.

It's the same with truth. That's why true-false tests have two options:

> _____ True _____ False

and not three:

> _____ True _____ False _____ Absolutely true

This desire to qualify truth, to bolster the concept of "truth" with an adjective, is a recent phenomenon.[13] It gives the verbal impression of someone who's trying to grasp at something that's slipping away, like sand that's slipping through your fingers, even though you're trying desperately to hang on to it.

Some people are convinced that the ways in which emergent Christianity is talking about truth (and God) is cutting the heart right out of it. But the ways in which emergents are talking about truth are not novel, nor should they be scary. What emergents say about truth is inherently more in keeping with a traditional and time-honored understanding of truth than those who talk about truth with utter certainty.

Why talk of truth at all? Is "truth" a central tenet of Christianity? Indeed, it was a term both used by Jesus and thrust on him as a question by Pontius Pilate. Yet "truth" is not the hinge on which the biblical narrative turns. The narrative turns, instead, on a way of life into which Yahweh in the Old Testament and Jesus in the New calls us.

The preoccupation with "truth" among emergents has often been pushed on them by their conservative critics, primarily because truth is a central concern of theirs. And their preoccupation with truth is a symptom of their modernism. They want the Bible to be unswervingly factual (here, *truth* equals *fact*), for if it is, then its claims about eternal salvation cannot be ignored. So they publish books against emergents titled *Truth and the New Kind of Christian* and *The Truth War*, and blogs excoriate the emergents on the issue of truth.

To the left, there is also talk of "truth." Liberal brothers and sisters care about truth too, though they sometimes seem squeamish about the truth of the biblical narrative. I had the pleasure of hearing the biblical scholar Marcus Borg speak recently, and in the question-and-answer session after his address, he was asked a question he's surely been asked hundreds of times: "Professor Borg, what about the empty tomb on Easter morning?" After a bit of theological hemming and hawing, Borg responded, "If I were a betting man, I'd bet—my life or one dollar—that the tomb was not empty. Or that there was no tomb."

Why would the resurrection seem unbelievable to Borg? It's because he is beholden to a certain framework for historical truth: if it violates physical laws, it's probably not "true" (at least not in a factual, historical sense; he still considers it "true" in a literary, metaphorical, even spiritual sense). He is unwilling to entertain two mutually contradictory ideas simultaneously: (1) that the physical laws by which the universe operates hold unremittingly and (2) that events that break those laws—such as resurrection, miraculous healings, and transfigurations—*really* did happen. In his talk, Borg referred to those who hold the latter as "fideists," people who allow faith to trump reason.

But Borg has fallen into the other gutter of the bowling alley, allowing reason to trump faith—his, we might say, is a "faith in reason." But the problem with reason is that what we human beings have considered "reasonable" (a geocentric universe, slavery, healing with leeches) has often been overturned.

John Piper, who stands on the opposite end of the theological spectrum, is beholden to a similarly modern framework. After the Interstate 35 bridge collapse in August 2007, Piper wrote about the tragedy, which happened just a mile from his church in Minneapolis. "The meaning of the collapse of this bridge," he wrote, "is that John Piper is a sinner and should repent or forfeit his life forever." He went on to explain that God (seemingly not beams and girders) holds up every bridge in the world, and if one ever falls, God has a perfect reason for it.[14]

What's ironic is that both Borg and Piper want an airtight understanding of God, a God that makes perfect sense. For Borg, it's a God who does not defy the physical laws of the universe. For Piper, it's a God whose sovereignty requires his personal responsibility for all calamities. Each man is constricting God by forcing God to play by certain rules: the rules of physics or the rules of sovereignty. And each is attempting to squeeze all of the paradox out of God.

But emergents don't fear paradox; they embrace it. God can be the creator of the universe *and* the breaker of the rules of physics. God can be sovereign *yet* not the author of evil.

So, again, the emergents are left to chart a middle course, one between the fideism (in human reason) of the left and the fideism (in the supernatural) of the right. As is so often the case, the "truth" lies in between, in a person (Jesus the Christ) who was *truly* human and *truly* divine—in *faith*, not fideism.

AFTER OBJECTIVITY: DIALOGUE

In the aftermath of the myth of objectivity, of fideisms and airtight systems, we're left to embrace our subjectivity, to revel in it, for it's only when we accept our own biases that we allow them to be shaped by contrary opinions and biases. One place where this is most poignant is interreligious dialogue.

In late 2005, some of us emergent Christians were invited to meet with a group of young and innovative rabbis. Meetings between Jewish and Christian leaders are nothing new, and a lot of us, on both sides, had been involved in previous meetings (though not with each other). However, we were committed to making this meeting different. In the blogosphere, we began taking heat for even announcing the meeting, especially my quote in the press release that I was excited to meet with the rabbis to "talk about the future and God's Kingdom." Some of my Christian friends made it clear that Jews could not possibly be involved in Kingdom of God work because they did not profess belief in Jesus. To emergents, this kind of thinking binds God's work to the church and implies that outside the lives of professed Christians, God is handicapped.

Rejecting this belief, I set to work with Shawn Landres, the director of research at Synagogue 3000, the group that convened the meeting. In the past, Shawn and I have each been involved with interreligious dialogues that were based on a kind of lowest-common-denominator spirituality. That is, the parties present predetermine what they can agree on and then talk only of those things. That usually leads to lots of discussion about peace or social justice but very little robust theological conversation about what leads religious people to hold the beliefs they hold. Senator Barack Obama fell into this same kind of thinking when he proposed that "democracy demands that the religiously motivated translate their concerns into universal, rather than religion-specific, values."[15] While I agree with much of what Obama says about the intersection of religion and public life, this universalizing tendency is exactly what has crippled liberal churches across America. By looking for what can bring everyone together, they've too often lost what it means to be who we are as followers of Jesus.

We've got to figure out a way to be *robustly and distinctly who we are* yet *authentically open to and respectful of the other*. This is a truly emergent sensibility, premised on the idea that a postmodern, globalized world demands just such a posture. For me, that means being truly Christian, yet profoundly open to the rabbis.

So Shawn and I set out to bring together the emergent Christian leaders and the emergent Jewish leaders. We decided that we would ask no one to leave anything at the door—who you were in your synagogue or church is who we wanted you to be at this meeting. To that end, Shawn began our meeting. We were all sitting in a circle—about two dozen of us—and Shawn said, "To my fellow Jews, I want to let you know that these emergent Christians are going to talk openly about Jesus and the Bible. This may make you uncomfortable at first, but that's what they believe, so that's what they're going to talk about." I went on to say something similar to my Christian peers about the rabbis talking about the Torah.

The resulting conversation was a thing of beauty. Though occasionally awkward, those moments were far outweighed by times of great poignancy.

I led a meditation on a story of Jesus, and Troy Bronsink led songs he has written about Jesus. The rabbis taught from Torah, and the cantors led us in songs of Jewish faith. No one held back, which ultimately led to more candor and openness about what we really believe. And that, in turn, led to deeper friendships, since openness and authenticity are such important qualities in making friends. One instance from the gathering represents this best. In one small group, the question was raised about whether rabbis from older, established synagogues might bless and assist young rabbis who are attempting to start something new. After some discussion among the Jewish members of the small group, Tim Keel, pastor of Jacob's Well in Kansas City, spoke up. He told the story of Eli and Samuel, found at the beginning of 1 Samuel, and of how the very old prophet, Eli, and the young boy and prophet-to-be, Samuel, formed a mutually beneficial and nonhierarchical relationship.

When Tim finished, silence ensued. Then a rabbi quietly said, "*Yasher koach.*" Shawn told me later that's a Yiddish version of the Hebrew *yishar kochachah*, which means, "More strength to you." He also told me that it's a traditional expression of appreciation and respect for an interpretation of Torah.

It was a moment of beautiful truth.

Beautiful moments like this are not exclusive to the emergent way of being faithful, but they are more likely due to the emergent commitment to conversation under the auspices of self-identity and respect of the other. I am confident that alongside the rabbis, we entered into such helpful times of conversation and poignant times of worship because we each owned up to our biases. We did not attempt to downplay them or hide them. We confessed our joint belief in God, and we differed on the details. We didn't try to expunge the awkward conflicts of belief but instead let ourselves stew in them. And we did give up a bit of ourselves—our confidence, our "lingo"—for the sake of each other, but that's what true friends do.

BEAUTIFUL, MESSY, INCARNATIONAL TRUTH

Is truth a question to be answered, or is it beauty to be sought? The last two centuries of science have taught us the value of the former, but it's possible that we've lost our acquaintance with the latter. For when it comes to designing a space shuttle that will get off of the launching pad or a heart bypass machine that will keep a patient alive during transplant surgery, technical precision is vital, and truth looks a lot like science. But when it comes to convincing someone to join a fight against hunger or to stop beating his children, truth looks more like persuasion. How do you change someone's mind using statistics or arguments? It's hard, I can tell you, because I spent many years as a guest speaker in my local public high school, recommending abstinence to sophomores in health class. All of the statistics on sexually transmitted diseases, unwanted pregnancies, and date rape did little to convince those sixteen-year-olds that they might be too young to be sleeping with one another. The only thing that seemed to make a difference, albeit small, was when I used narrative and humor and whimsy—including my own story—to get them to consider abstinence as an option.

So often we attempt to remove all of the nonscientific components of something in our quest to get at that thing's true essence. Science, it seems, is above the prejudices inherent in stories and art and music—those things whose beauty lies in the eye (or ear or nose) of the beholder. But it has become clear that even the way that science progresses is just as much a result of politics and infighting as any other field.

Take the field of medicine. Obviously, here, scientific accuracy is key. You can't fight a virus with an antibiotic. And you can't replace a kidney with a liver. But we all know that medicine is an art as much as it is a science. That's why some doctors are better than others. If doctors were automatons without art or creativity, every hospital would be the same. But people fly in from all over the world to visit the Mayo Clinic in Rochester, Minnesota, because it has assembled arguably the best team of physicians and most advanced technology on the planet.

And if we can stick with the medicine thread for a moment more, consider the operating room as a metaphor of our quest for truth. My brother, who's a surgeon, wants an OR to be as sterile as possible when he walks in. "Sterile" means free of living microorganisms and germs, and to that end, every surface in the OR is scrubbed with antiseptic, all of the instruments are run through the autoclave, and every human being in the room is scrubbed down and gowned up. But the room is not perfectly sterile—there are still germs in there—because there's no such thing as a perfectly sterile room. So what's my brother to do? Should he wait outside, refusing to operate until every germ is removed from the environment? Of course not. When the room is as sterile as possible—or, you might say, *relatively* sterile—he enters and operates.

He does the best he can with what's available to him.

So it is with us when we quest after truth. We are not able to excise all of our biases and prejudices, so we work with them, we acknowledge them, and we quest nonetheless.

And now, in an act of literary bravery (or stupidity), let me extend the metaphor to the breaking point. Many emergent Christians have developed an appreciation for what is called alternative medicine (a.k.a. naturopathy). My friend Shelley Pagitt has become a natural health coach because she found great relief from her own medical predicaments in chiropractics, organic eating and gardening, and other natural remedies. This doesn't mean that she refuses to take her kids to the physician when they're sick. But she will use all of the means available to her, both traditional and nontraditional, to heal them. And why wouldn't she use all of the means available to find a remedy?

Similarly, emergents will use all of the means available to them to quest after this truth we call God. They'll use their rational intellects, for they are a significant aspect of how we make our way in this world. But they'll also use media of beauty, like art, music, and poetry. They'll quest after God using the tools of the medieval mystics and the ancient monastics, since they clearly discovered truth about God that escapes modern scientific rationalism. And some will even be open to sources of truth that are external to traditional Christianity, be it philosophy or another religious system. This does not mean that another truth claim will trump that of the Christian faith but that the two can be put in conversation with one another—just as you might if you had back pain and went to see an orthopedic surgeon, a chiropractor, *and* a massage therapist.

It requires a change of mind to think of truth as *beautiful*. Considering truth beautiful can be quite difficult for someone who thinks of truth as verbal statements that correspond to reality.

But consider standing before Caravaggio's majestic painting *The Raising of Lazarus* at the Museo Regionale in Messina, Italy. At twelve-and-a-half feet tall, it's breathtaking. Lazarus, stiff, colorless, and naked but for a loincloth, is being pulled from an open sepulcher. His eyes are closed, but his hands seem to be coming to life. Jesus, standing to the left, points forcefully at the lifeless body of his friend as a frenzied crowd, including Lazarus's sisters, Mary and Martha, lift the dead man from the tomb.

It may sound strange to look at such a painting and declare, "This is true." But I defy you to stand before that magnificent painting and say, "This is not true." For truth, in fact, comes in all sorts of forms. It might take the form of statement: "The Holocaust actually happened" or "The earth is not flat." Those propositions, though dismissed by some, are generally thought to be in accord with reality. But is a painting of Lazarus's resurrection in some sense "true"? Is any painting "true"? Is a song or a poem or a sculpture? Is a conversation between two people "true"? In what sense could any of them be thought to be "true"?

A quick look at a dictionary of philosophy will show that conceptions and definitions of truth have been debated since Aristotle, and what human beings have long understood as true extends well beyond propositions and statements about "what really is." I say that because we know that what really is, sometimes *isn't*. I might slam my hand on a table and say that I'm hitting the table. But someone who knows physics will tell me that my hand isn't *actually* hitting the table. In fact, the electrons in my hand are being repelled by the electrons in the table. At the nuclear level, no contact is made.

So, is it "true" to say that I've *hit the table*? Well, yes and no.

But I'll still go on living my life as though my hand is hitting the table. I'll still drive carefully, lest the electrons in my car get repelled by the electrons in the approaching train! In the realm of "physical contact," *truth* means at least a couple of different things, and they both correspond to reality.

But just as representations of reality are in accord with truth, so is beauty. Beauty, you might say, is a delivery mechanism for truth. My friend Phyllis Tickle tells of a time when she was speaking to a big crowd at a church and kept fielding questions about the "truth" of the virgin birth of Jesus. This was a fairly liberal crowd, and some found the virgin birth dubious, bordering on myth. But after her presentation, a young boy approached her and said, "Ms. Tickle, I believe that Mary was a virgin."

"Why's that?" Phyllis asked.

"Because it's too beautiful not to be true."

Indeed, the Christian gospel is just that kind of truth. The beautiful truth that a young woman who'd never slept with a man would bear a son in a stable. The truth that that boy would be proclaimed the messiah by prophetess, priest, shepherds, and magi from his earliest days. And the strange truth that that boy would grow into manhood and announce, "I am . . . the truth."[16]

But that leads us to a dilemma even trickier than saying that a work of art is "true." Can we say that a *person* is true? Namely, can we say that Jesus of Nazareth is true? He claimed to be, but can we affirm that?

It seems incumbent on the Christian faith to affirm that Jesus is, indeed, true. In theological terms, we might claim that Jesus of Nazareth was the ultimate revelation of God in the world—we claim that the Word (*logos*) of God somehow inhabited that human being who was known as Jesus of Nazareth and walked around on this planet from about 4 B.C. to about A.D. 29.

If we affirm this about Jesus, then we must at least admit that truth can be concretely represented at a certain place and time. If truth is timeless and transcendent, then it is also time-bound and immanent.

Though that may not be too much of a leap, how about this: if we affirm that "Jesus is truth," then truth had lice, toe jam, smelly armpits, and a daily bowel movement. It is unquestionably more difficult to think of truth in these terms. Too often, when we consider truth, it's as an ethereal concept that hovers somewhere above the earthly realm, untouched by the messiness of human existence. But the beauty of the Christian faith is that truth is just the opposite: it's incarnate (made flesh) in an actual human being—a human being who happened to live before the era of advanced personal hygiene.

Is it disrespectful, even blasphemous, to consider Jesus' bodily habits? No. To the contrary, it's bad theology and possibly even unchristian to avoid the realities of God's incarnation in Jesus of Nazareth. Ours is not a spit-shined God who, as a "human," walked a couple inches off the ground so that his feet never got dirty. No, he had smelly feet and, I imagine, even stubbed his toe on occasion.

But contemporary North American version of Christianity rarely reflects these aspects of the truth-God. The statements of faith that populate church Web sites truck almost exclusively in theory, making unembodied statements about God, the Bible, and church government. You'll find declarations like "We believe that the Bible is the inspired word of God, without error in its original manuscripts" and "The Lord Jesus Christ is both true God and perfect man, a unique, supernatural manifestation of God in the flesh." All theoretical, impersonal statements. On the contrary, you aren't likely to find something like this on a church Web site:

Statement of Faith

We at First Christian Church acknowledge that God's coming to earth in the person of Jesus Christ and recounted in the Gospels turns upside down what we used to think about concepts like "truth." For in him, "truth" walked around, talked to people, and even cried and bled. We're left with a faith that, while deep, is also paradoxical and difficult. As a result, we've committed to leaning on each other as we collectively try to follow Jesus. We're confident about some things: Jesus' coming to earth was good news, it's still good news, and there's more good news to come. You're welcome to join us anytime.

PARADOXES

So a divine human being (Jesus) is truth. God is transcendent and immanent. Truth is both reliable and contextual. Relativism is relatively absolute.

Paradoxes abound in the Christian faith.

About a year ago, I spent a day at a church speaking to about two dozen youth pastors. I spoke quite a bit about the paradoxes inherent to Christianity; some of them appreciated what I had to say, and others were troubled. But something interesting happened at the end of the day. I was walking out the church doors with my laptop and some other stuff under my arms when an older man held the door open for me. I recognized him, for he'd been in the seminar I'd led.

"Thanks for what you presented today," he said. "I really appreciated it."

"My pleasure," I responded. "I'm glad you liked it."

"Yeah," he continued. "I wasn't supposed to be in there. You see, I was just going to drop in for a few minutes before I went off to some other meetings I was supposed to attend. But I liked the material so much that I asked my wife to go to the other meetings so that I could stay."

"That's great," I told him.

"There's just one thing," he said, with a look of consternation. "I just don't know why some of these young guys have such a hard time when you talk about paradox in the Christian faith. I mean, in my job, we deal with paradox every day."

"Oh?" I said. "What do you do?"

"I'm a physicist," he answered, presenting me with a business card that identified him as a physics professor at a major university.

Now I was hooked. "Tell me more about that."

"Well, very early in your education in physics, a professor tells you, 'An electron behaves as if it's a particle and a wave.' You respond by saying, 'That's impossible. Those two are mutually exclusive. An electron has to be either a particle or a wave!' 'Nope,' you're told, 'it's both. In the world of the very tiny, like electrons and atoms, things act as though they are both waves and particles.'

> "I just think, if there are paradoxes in physics, then why shouldn't there be paradoxes in theology, too?"

"And if you can't get over it," my new friend told me, "you can't be a physicist. You see, to be a physicist, you have to live with that paradox and many other paradoxes. And I just think, if there are paradoxes in physics, then why shouldn't there be paradoxes in theology, too?"

Dispatch 14: Emergents embrace paradox, especially those that are core components of the Christian story.

If paradoxes in theology are unavoidable, two are central to Christianity and have serious implications for emergent forms of faith.

Paradox 1: God Is Three in One   The first paradox has to do with the nature of God, and it's summed up in a tricky little word: Trinity. The article in the *Oxford Dictionary of the Christian Church* begins with a nod to the importance of the doctrine of the Trinity but with little acknowledgment of its paradoxical nature:

> **Trinity, doctrine of the.** The central dogma of Christian theology, that the one God exists in three Persons and one substance, Father, Son, and Holy Spirit. God is one, yet self-differentiated; the God who reveals Himself to mankind is one God equally in three distinct modes of existence, yet remains one through all eternity.[17]

The article then goes on to describe the theological gymnastics that have taken place over two millennia as Christians have attempted to make sense of this doctrine. You might remember from history class some of these names: Arianism, Adoptionism, Docetism, Sabellianism, Montanism, and Modalism. All of these formulations of the Trinity, deemed heretical in the early church, occasionally reappear.

But the explicit concept of the Trinity is virtually absent from the Bible. Jesus' final words in Matthew's Gospel contain the only overt reference: "Therefore go and make disciples of all nations, baptizing them in the name of the Father and of the Son and of the Holy Spirit."[18] Otherwise, the three-in-oneness of God can only be inferred by references to God's Spirit (active in both Old and New Testaments), the "Word" of God (explicit in John's Gospel), and the Father (to whom Jesus often prays).[19] The word *Trinity* made its first appearance around A.D. 200 in the writings of a theologian named Tertullian (c. 155–230), who contracted two Latin words, *tri* (three) and *unitas* (one).[20]

From there, the theologians were off to the races. What does it mean to be of one essence (*homoousias*) but three persons (*hypostases*)? Plato's shadow loomed large in the early church's debates about God's trinitarian nature—this is seen especially in Augustine (354–430), the pillar of Western theology, who wrote, "Let us believe that Father, Son, and Holy Spirit are one God, maker and ruler of the whole creation: that Father is not Son, nor Holy Spirit Father or Son; but a Trinity of mutually related Persons, and unity of equal essence."[21]

The trick here is the balance of oneness and threeness. If either gets emphasized even a bit, the scales tip into heresy. For instance, each of the aforementioned heresies attempted to make the doctrine of the Trinity more sensible and less paradoxical. In so doing, each failed to hold these two characteristics—threeness and oneness—in balance.

Not surprisingly, human beings have scratched and clawed our way toward understanding this paradox, often by using analogies. Augustine compared the Trinity to a lover (God), a beloved (Jesus), and the love between them (Holy Spirit), but this depersonifies the Spirit. More recent theologians have talked about the Trinity as liquid, ice, and vapor or as a baseball manager, pitcher, and catcher. These both fall short, the former because of the error that there is just one person in God but we experience that person differently as God performs different tasks (a heresy known as Modalism), and the latter borders on tritheism because there is really nothing more than a cloth uniform and game that unites the three.

My own attempts at analogizing the Trinity are twofold. When I was a pastor, I tried to explain the Trinity to middle school students by lighting a single candle that had three wicks—the problem here is that the three flames have no relationship with one another. Then, just last summer, I was lying on my daughter's bed, confronted with the challenge of explaining the Trinity to a five-year-old. I looked up and saw the three-bladed ceiling fan. It was on, and I asked her, "How many blades are on that fan?"

"Three."

"How do you know that? You can only see a blur and feel a breeze."

"I just know there are three," Lily emphatically stated, "because I've seen it turned off and there are three!"

"OK," I said, "you know there are three, even though when it's on, you can only see one constant blur. That's what the Trinity is like."

Now I was really proud of myself. I'd found an analogy for the Trinity that I'd never heard before. And it had the added bonus of an allusion to Jesus' description of a life in the Spirit: "The wind blows wherever it pleases. You hear its sound, but you cannot tell where it comes from or where it is going. So it is with everyone born of the Spirit."[22]

But I was humbled when I was out to lunch a week later with LeRon *Note!* Shults, a theologian of the highest pedigree. "You can't analogize God. You can't compare God to something," LeRon told me. "You can't say what God is, only what God is not." I was making the mistake of comparing God to a ceiling fan, a great insult indeed to the creator of the universe.

As you might guess, I was crestfallen. But I was also challenged. In LeRon's own writings, he challenges us to consider the Trinity from a different angle. Instead of looking at the three persons per se, LeRon asks us to look at the relationships between them. God is, he says, ultimately, a "Being-in-relation," and we humans are "beings-in-relation." It's the relationships that define us. In the case of the Trinity, divine love is the relational bond that unites Father, Son, and Holy Spirit. "We cannot prove the doctrine of the Trinity," he writes, "or secure our knowledge of the trinitarian God on the foundation of any finite analogy. However, we may identify ways in which the biblical experience of the trinitarian God illuminates the human experience of longing for truth, goodness, and beauty."[23] I might say it this way: the Trinity is too beautiful *not* to be true.

LeRon is far from the first to point to the relationships between Father, Son, and Spirit as the key to understanding the Trinity. Hilary of Poitiers (c. 300–367) reflected on Jesus' affirmation that "I am in the Father and the Father is in me."[24] It seems incomprehensible to us that "one should permanently envelope, and also be permanently enveloped by, the Other, whom yet He envelopes," writes Hilary,[25] and yet this is exactly the key to understanding God's existence. And along with LeRon and Hilary is a long tradition in the Eastern church of emphasizing the mutual indwelling, the eternal interpenetration of Father, Son, and Spirit. The Eastern Orthodox call it *perichoresis*, which means "going around" or "envelopment," and again, it emphasizes *relationality* (since something can only be enveloped by something else) as the starting point for understanding God.

In emergent Christianity, there is a strong affinity for these relational articulations of God, since emergent Christians are convinced of the priority of relationship for understanding ourselves. Like many postmoderns, emergent Christians consider the individualism of the modern era a blight that eventually led to holocausts and pogroms. The emergent impulse toward small house churches and new monastic communities exhibits this return to relationality. A church with couches in a circle is not pandering to Gen X informality but a nod to the open relationships demanded by Jesus' gospel of reconciliation.

Paradox 2: Jesus Was Both Fully Human and Fully Divine

Jesus himself had little to say about his own nature. He did make unique claims: that he was the promised messiah[26] and that he had a unique relationship with God.[27] But neither of these necessarily implies that he was God-in-the-flesh.

Looking back on the life, death, and resurrection of Jesus, the Apostle Paul took on the ambitious work of theologizing just who Jesus was, particularly in light of the Jewish understanding of the messiah. What Paul argues, and what was accepted in the first century of the church, was that Jesus of Nazareth was the most complete self-expression of God ever seen on earth and that he inaugurated the kingdom reign of God in a new and better way.[28] Already by A.D. 150, a consensus had developed that Jesus was somehow both divine and human.

But by the middle of the second century, a protracted battle over the nature of Jesus broke out, and it wasn't to be settled until the Council of Chalcedon (held in present-day Istanbul) in 451. At issue was both how much of God's power inhabited the human form of Jesus and to what extent Jesus was really human. Christianity had spread quite rapidly from its initial location in the seat of Judaism to the far reaches of the Roman Empire, and many of the converts had previously been schooled in the Greek philosophy of Socrates and Plato. But while the Hebraic concept of God had always been somewhat earthy (hadn't Yahweh walked with Adam in the garden, come to Israel in the form of a cloud, and even shown his backside to Moses?), the Hellenstic understanding of God was just the opposite: God was the Supreme Mind—an immaterial, transcendent, divine spirit. That made it difficult for many of the Hellenistic converts to Christianity to imagine that God would actually besmirch himself by being squeezed into human skin. Some argued that Jesus' human body was only an illusion. Others, who couldn't conceive of God undergoing crucifixion, taught that his divinity was snatched away just before the moment of Jesus' death. Still others believed that within Jesus were two distinct persons, one divine and one human.[29]

Back in the first millennium, when confronted with a sticky problem like the nature of Jesus, the leaders of the church could all gather for a few weeks, as they did in 451 in Chalcedon. As one might guess, the meeting was laced with politics, hidden agendas, and axes to grind, but in the end, the gathered bishops came out with a statement about the nature of Jesus that was definitively paradoxical:

> Following the holy Fathers, we unanimously teach and confess one and the same Son, our Lord Jesus Christ: the same perfect in divinity and perfect in humanity, the same truly God and truly man, composed of rational soul and body; consubstantial with the Father as to his divinity and consubstantial with us as to his humanity; "like us in all things but sin." He was begotten from the Father before all ages as to his divinity and in these last days, for us and for our salvation, was born as to his humanity of the virgin Mary, the Mother of God.
>
> We confess that one and the same Christ, Lord, and only-begotten Son, is to be acknowledged in two natures without confusion, change, division, or separation. The distinction between natures was never

abolished by their union, but rather the character proper to each of the two natures was preserved as they came together in one person and one hypostasis.

So these two paradoxes lie at the very heart of Christianity, and we (Christian) humans want to break the tension and fall on one side or the other. That's the natural, human inclination: solve the paradox. With the Trinity, the temptation is to emphasize the threeness or the oneness; with Jesus, it's the divinity or the humanity. And those temptations are just as strong today as they were in the second century.

Surely, the Christian faith is a rational endeavor; we want things to make sense. But to appreciate rationality does not mean to abjure paradox. If a physics professor can ask first-year students to live into a paradox, it seems perfectly reasonable that we as Christ followers would be asked to submit ourselves to paradox as well.

We are asked to submit to paradox in both individual and corporate iterations of our faith. If you ask an emergent Christian a question about a matter that has traditionally been considered a slam dunk for Christians, you're just as likely to get a quizzical look in return, an ambiguous response, or an invitation to sit down for a conversation. As Brian McLaren has said, "The moment that we have all the bolts screwed in tight and all the nails hammered in, it's at precisely that moment that we *cease* being faithful." The constant desire for more dialogue is not a cop-out, either, because the Christian faith is a journey—a Way—not a destination. We're faithful in pursuit of Jesus only so long as we are actually pursuing him.

> "The moment that we have all the bolts screwed in tight and all the nails hammered in, it's at precisely that moment that we cease being faithful."

This "spirituality of paradox" comes as a great relief to a great many people, in large part because it jibes with our experience of this ambiguous world. While some look for a firm foundation in a world of change, emergents grab on to a God who *is* the change. Prayer is a conversation with the Lord, not a quest for answers or a therapeutic practice. The Bible is a companion on the faith journey, not a textbook of proofs or a compendium of inspirational sayings. Emergent churches are full of persons who faithfully follow Jesus but do not fear paradox.

And consequently, emergent churches often have the look and feel of paradoxical places. Songs that end in minor-suspended chords and sermons that end with question marks are common, and that is a break from the tone of certainty with which many of their predecessors preached. The church may meet in a pub or a rundown abandoned church, in a warehouse or a basement. It's likely that handmade art will grace the walls, and songs will be made up on the spot.

But alongside this paradoxical messiness exists a deep desire that the church itself be a reflection of the Trinity. That is, the church would be, at its essence, *relationship*.

DISPATCH FROM THE END OF A THREE-MILE DIRT ROAD: RECOVERING "CHURCH"

"I hate church."

That my new friend, Brett Watson, said these words didn't shock me. It was the utter flatness with which he uttered them that caught my attention. I heard no irony in his voice, no anger, no bitterness. He said these words with no contempt. What sounded to me like the blaring alarm of a submarine that's been hit by a torpedo was to him as plain as announcing that tomorrow it will be partly cloudy.

Brett's in his mid-thirties, a man of slight build with a trim red beard and a winter cap pulled low on his forehead. But you can't help but notice his right hand, which is covered with scar tissue and poised in an awkward position. When asked, he offers this story: a year ago, while working as the shop foreman at a Northern California logging company, he was moving some items with a forklift. "I must have forgotten to put the forks down," he told me. "Even though I always set the forks down. Well," he continued, "my leg hit the down pressure lever while my hand was where it shouldn't have been. I tried to lower the forks more to release my hand, but that only made it worse. So I had to call to the kid who works in the office to come out and start up the forklift and raise the forks.

"My hand was a mangled mess. All the bones in my wrist were completely crushed and dislocated, and my hand was nearly severed from my wrist. I was sure I would lose it, but they flew me down to a hospital in San Francisco, where it was surgically repaired." Brett went on to tell me that the one broken bone pressing against his artery probably saved his life. The bones in his hand are now fused so that his thumb is immobile and his four fingers have some movement. His surgeon hopes to relocate his thumb so that he can at least use it as an opposable grip for his other fingers.

But here's where the "hating church" part comes in. For months in the winter of 2006, Brett had to sit at home with his arm held aloft, above his head. His wife was at work, and he was at home with their young daughter at the end of a three-mile dirt road, outside of Redding, California. Geographically and psychologically, he was at the end of the world.

"Those days were very dark," Brett said quietly, "and only two things kept me alive. Without those two things, I wouldn't be here today, and the two things weren't Jesus and the Bible." Brett's working assumption is that "church people," as he calls them, have a particular set of prescribed answers to the existential questions and crises common to the human condition. Somewhere along the line, Brett heard from the church that with enough faith in Jesus and confidence in the Bible, God will magically alleviate the symptoms of life-crushing depression. Maybe he'd heard that explicitly from pastors in the past, or maybe he'd read it between the lines, but in either case, the message was clear: you'll overcome your depression by a witches' brew of personal faith and supernatural intervention.

"The two things that kept me alive," Brett said, his jaw set, "were my relationship with my eight-month-old daughter and Prozac. Church people don't want to hear about that, but the Prozac kept me alive."

The dock on which Brett told me his story juts into the duck pond at Glorieta Conference Center, a Christian camp outside of Santa Fe, New Mexico, and the site of an annual event called the Emergent Gathering. A family reunion of sorts, the Gathering is a collection of misfits and dropouts and ragamuffins, all of whom are on a quest to live in the way of Jesus in the world. At first blush, it

> "Church people don't want to hear about that, but the Prozac kept me alive."

might look like a church conference: several dozen "professional Christians" mix with laypeople for the better part of a week, and they all share in worship, meals, and seminars. But there's no speaker, no worship band, and no brochures or tote bags. It's a truly open-source event, built by all of the participants. For instance, each morning, people have a chance to stand up and announce the seminars for the day:

"I'll be leading a discussion about the atonement at 2 P.M."

"Anyone who wants to do yoga, join me on the dock at 11 o'clock."

"I've got some questions about church planting. If you do too, meet me on the patio at 3:30."

Meanwhile, meals are made together, morning and evening prayer services are coordinated, and most significant of all, many life-changing conversations take place.

So what would bring Brett—a guy who "hates church"—to a conference for church people? Somewhere along the line, though he'd given up on church, Brett had not given up on Jesus. And even at the end of the three-mile dirt road, Brett had Internet access. In this sense, the World Wide Web lives up to its name: Brett got caught in the new media web of blogs and Web sites, social networks and mobile phone numbers that's been spun by emergent Christians over the past decade. But as opposed to sucking the spiritual blood from his veins, the emergent web gave him hope that a new kind of Christianity exists, one that reflects his own experience of life as a complex mix of joy and sorrow, success and defeat, love and Prozac.

CHAPTER 6

INSIDE THE EMERGENT CHURCH

THERE'S NO WAY OF KNOWING JUST HOW MANY EMERGENT churches there are or necessarily of quantifying just what constitutes an emergent church. They come in all shapes and sizes, from all denominational backgrounds, and in all geographical locales. The four churches profiled here are not necessarily exemplars of anything except an effort to be particularly faithful in their own time and place. They do lack many of the encumbrances of conventional churches—both theologically and structurally—which allows them freedom to explore new ways of faithfulness and to retrieve traditional modes of faithfulness as well. My words will not do them justice—each is a place of great beauty.

IT'S A GREAT DAY AT JACOB'S WELL!

If there's one element of Jacob's Well Church that represents its life as a church, it's the sidewalks. "JW" is housed in a former Presbyterian building, an early-twentieth-century brick edifice complete with a steeple, in the Westport neighborhood of Kansas City, Missouri. Westport is a hip neighborhood of coffee shops and eateries. A mix of residential and commercial, the neighborhood has a visible gay, lesbian, bisexual, and transgender (GLBT) presence. Throughout the neighborhood, bordering the bungalows and cafés, is a checkerboard of sidewalks from a bygone era when everyone went to church and everyone walked.

Every time I've visited JW, the sidewalks that frame the church have been decorated, festooned with chalk adornments: flowers and vines and happy faces and slogans: "SMILE, GOD LOVES YOU!" "IT'S A BEAUTIFUL DAY!" Their witness to the neighborhood is clear, as is their commitment to the binding glue of the emergent church movement: a hope-filled orientation toward the future. This is no doomsday Christianity, nor even a community filled with evangelical ambivalence about residing among Kansas City's GLBT community. It is a church whose members are filled with hope, with an iconic smile on the sidewalk beneath their feet.

Dispatch 15: Emergents hold to a hope-filled eschatology: it was good news when Jesus came the first time, and it will be good news when he returns.

Jacob's Well purchased the building from the Presbyterians a couple of years ago after cohabiting for several years before that. They've made a point to leave up the old softball tournament trophies and other reminders of the previous church's life, for they consider themselves a continuation of the Christian presence in the neighborhood. On one of the weekends I visited, Tim Keel, the pastor, took me over to the church on Saturday night.

"A lot of Africans have been moving into our neighborhood," he explains to me, "and we felt that we didn't know enough about them. You know, we tend to think that Africa is one, big, monolithic country, but, of course, it's a continent filled with many countries, each with its own culture, food, and music. So we're having a dinner tonight for our African neighbors, and so our Jacob's Well people can become more aware of their different African cultures."

In the basement of the church, the fellowship hall is abuzz with activity. Around a large map of Africa, immigrant children color in the countries from which their families hail. Music indigenous to several African countries emanates from the four corners of the room, and pans of exotic-smelling food are uncovered on a couple of long tables. Whites and blacks mix freely around food and song, and Tim practically floats around the room with exuberance at the scene.

Sunday morning, worship begins just after 10:30 with a couple of songs. To the classic Presbyterian sanctuary with dark-stained pews and a choir loft, JW has added the requisite video screens and replaced the pulpit with a band. All of the speaking takes place at the floor level—only the musicians are on stage. After a couple of opening songs, a young woman with a handheld microphone welcomes everyone to Palm Sunday worship and reads a selection from Henri Nouwen, a Roman Catholic writer. The congregants are then asked to welcome the people around them and then brought back together with a unison reading from Zechariah. The second set of songs is louder and more upbeat, and half a dozen people sway with hands raised as they sing. Another reading, this one from the Psalms, is led as a call-and-response with piano in the background.

The crowd is overwhelmingly white, and while many shaved heads, goatees, and tattoos are in evidence, there's also a healthy percentage of older folks and children. The sanctuary is packed—JW has recently moved to three services every Sunday. The Sunday school rooms are similarly at capacity, JW hosting hundreds of children every Sunday. Those rooms would be the envy of many a church, beautifully decorated as they are. Tim's wife, Mimi, oversees the children's ministry, and she coordinated an event, "Extreme Makeover: Church Edition," during which JW members overhauled each of the classrooms in the aging building. Bright paint, window treatments, and new furniture now greet the children each week.

Across the hall, the former church library is a gathering room for adults, particularly newcomers. A couple of coffeepots and a plate of scones sit on a table, and a quote from the obituary for Anabaptist theologian John Howard Yoder adorns the wall:

The work of Jesus was not a new set of ideals or principles for reforming or even revolutionizing society, but the establishment of a new community, a people that embodied forgiveness, sharing, and self-sacrificing love in its rituals and discipline. In that sense, the visible church is not to be the bearer of Christ's message, but to be the message.[1]

Back in the sanctuary's balcony, I lean over to introduce myself to the man next to me, who's in his mid-thirties and sitting with his three daughters. He wonders aloud why I was typing on a laptop during church, so I explain to him my project on the emergent church.

"Emergent church?" he asks.

"Yes," I explain, "this church is actually a part of a nationwide movement of churches like this." He's unaware of any broader movement to which JW is connected.

To my question of how he arrived at JW, he says, "My wife and I had made a list of churches to visit to get our girls involved a couple years ago, and there was an article in the *Kansas City Star* about this church. This was the first one that we visited, and we've never gone to another one. We came for the girls, but I come back because of the way that Tim gives so much of the history behind the Bible. Like the story of the fishermen that Jesus called. I mean, I had heard that story a thousand times in Catholic church growing up, but I always assumed that they were just a couple of guys out to fish on a Saturday afternoon. I had no idea how much they had to give up to follow Jesus. That's what I mean by Tim giving the history behind the Bible."

Down on the main floor, Tim is about five minutes into the sermon. He reads the Palm Sunday passage from Mark's Gospel, then invites the congregants to describe how they had "sensually experienced" the passage—he has them close their eyes during his reading and try to "sense" the passage as they hear it. Moderating the feedback for almost ten minutes, Tim calls on every commenter by name. He then passionately takes up the preaching again, unpacking the idea of pilgrimage and introducing the Stations of the Cross.

A traditionally Roman Catholic practice, the Stations trace Jesus' Good Friday journey from his condemnation at Pilate's house to his crucifixion and finally to his entombment. Visual artists from the Jacob's Well community had been commissioned to depict each of the fourteen stations, and their artistic representations hang throughout the building. Tim invites everyone to visit the Stations exhibition sometime during Holy Week, setting the experience in a communal framework: "This pilgrimage is what we're on as a community.

"The pilgrimage from Jericho to Jerusalem is a journey to freedom," Tim continues. Going on to unpack a complex message about freedom from tyranny and power, he shows the image of the man in front of the tanks in Tiananmen Square, quotes Henri Nouwen, and alludes to *National Lampoon's Vacation*, all the while weaving in and out of many passages of scripture. The sermon is over forty-five minutes long, and it is, by any measurement, masterful.

The sermon is followed by communion, a weekly occurrence at JW. Tim moves behind the communion table and invites everyone forward; however, he says, if you don't feel comfortable participating in the Lord's Supper, you can hang back and meditate. "As you come forward," Tim announces kindly, "I want you to consider what's covering you, what's *protecting* you. People spread their palm branches and coats at Jesus' feet. There are purple cards in your pew. I invite you to write down something you'd like to lay down at Jesus' feet and drop it in the aisle as you come forward." Over the next ten minutes, virtually everyone comes forward to receive communion, and the center aisle is a blanket of purple paper.

After communion, everyone stands to sing "Wonderful Cross" in full voice. Again, several hands are raised, but they are still in the minority. At 12:10, Tim speaks a benediction and then makes a few announcements. Then everyone joins hands, creating an unbroken sea of humanity as seen from the balcony, and they sing an upbeat benediction song that everyone seems to know, since the words are not on the screens. The band keeps playing for a few minutes longer, and there is a buzz of activity as the service ends.

After the worship, I ask a young man who's a leader in the congregation, "What's the secret to Jacob's Well?"

He smiles and says, "I like when Tim says, 'People experience God emotionally, intellectually, relationally, and aesthetically,' and this church aims to make every one of those experiences available to people."

> "I like when Tim says, 'People experience God emotionally, intellectually, relationally, and aesthetically,' and this church aims to make every one of those experiences available to people."

WIKICHURCH

Leon Trotsky once said, "Bureaucracy and social harmony are inversely proportional to each other."[2] Many emergents will echo that claim, substituting *church* or *Christianity* for *social harmony*.

Hierarchies and bureaucracies are not necessarily bad in and of themselves. Some things need centralized leadership, organization, and administration. For example, in my work as a police chaplain, I appreciate that the Minnesota Department of Motor Vehicles is a bureaucracy. Most assuredly, it's a pain to go to the DMV, stand in line, and renew your license with a crabby desk jockey. But sitting in a squad car after a traffic stop, a cop can get a host of information about the car and the driver that we're about to approach by punching six keys on the in-car computer. If there's a felony warrant on the driver, we'll come up to the driver's side window much more cautiously than on a nonfelony stop. So that's a bureaucratic system that we can all be fond of.

But not all human enterprises are hierarchical, nor do they necessarily devolve into bureaucracy. Recently, there's been a spate of interest in organizations and movements that develop along more egalitarian lines.

Dispatch 16: Emergents believe that church should function more like an open-source network and less like a hierarchy or a bureaucracy.

The Internet is an example. There is no Internet headquarters. You can't drive to an office building, park in the parking lot, and walk in the front door of Internet, Inc. When it comes to the Internet, there's no *there* there.

Of course, there *is* an Internet. It's just not centralized; instead, it has developed along the lines of what theorists call a "scale-free network." Certain "hubs" contain more information than other locations on the Internet, but no one hub controls the whole thing. Further, each hub is linked to other hubs via an intricate web of connections. Viruses, like AIDS, spread around the globe in a similar fashion: certain locales (Malawi) have a higher infection rate than other locales (Iowa), but that doesn't mean that Malawi controls the virus or that Iowa is unaffected by it. Al-Qaeda is another example of a scale-free network: it's a loosely affiliated system of semiautonomous cells.

One of the real struggles for journalists has been to discern the contours and boundaries of the emergent phenomenon. How big is it? How many churches? Who is the spokesperson? Who's in and who's out? The difficulty of answering these questions stems from the open-source nature of the movement thus far. The emergent church just doesn't act like previous ecclesial movements.

Three related terms are common parlance today, and each sheds some light on the phenomenon of decentralization that emergent Christianity exhibits.

- *Scale-Free Network.* In 1999, some researchers at Notre Dame used a Web crawler to map the connectivity in the World Wide Web. They'd expected to find a relatively flat structure—that is, they assumed that the connectedness in the Web was random. But they instead found that various "nodes," called "hubs," attract and generate the highest number of links to other nodes. So through the seemingly random connections of nodes, hubs are linked to one another, causing a weblike relationship of coherence. Somewhere between hierarchy and randomness, scale-free networks spread quickly and powerfully.

- *Open-Source Software.* By making their production materials freely available, open-source software developers allow individual users to adapt software (or an entire platform) to their own ends. The term was coined in 1998 by software pioneers who wanted to make their products accessible and flexible, but they felt that the phrase "free software" didn't quite fit. Linus Torvalds, the hero of this movement, created the Linux Kernel, an operating system. Whereas Apple kept its operating system completely proprietary for years (almost leading to the company's collapse), and Microsoft makes the Windows operating system available only to those who can afford hefty licensing fees, the underlying source code in Linux is available to one and all to adapt to their own needs. As a result, many large corporations (Sun Microsystems, Hewlett-Packard, and IBM) have adopted Linux for their own internal use. Torvalds has said, "The future is open-source everything."

- *Wiki.* The term *wiki* has come to refer to an Internet technology that allows any user to modify the content in a database, with few or no restrictions. The original and best-known wiki is Wikipedia, an online encyclopedia with over two million articles in English and over three million in other languages. Founded by Jimmy Wales and Larry Sanger in 2001, Wikipedia has quickly become the most accessible treasury of human knowledge in the world. *Wiki* is a Hawaiian word meaning "quick," and wikis are developed to be quickly and easily accessible.

The ways that emergent Christians gather in communities have a lot in common with the traits of scale-free networks, open-source software, and wikis. While many open-source innovations—like Linux—are still relatively unknown, Wikipedia is extraordinarily successful and popular. With millions of visitors each day, Wikipedia often ranks in the top ten most trafficked Internet sites. One can look at the qualities of Wikipedia and analogize them to many other scale-free networks, including the emergent church.

Six characteristics of Wikipedia can shed additional light on what emergent Christianity is—especially at the church level—and how it operates.

Open Access Wikipedia allows *anyone* to edit an entry. So if you don't like the paragraph in the entry for "Jesus Christ" that gives the date of Jesus' birth as "8–2 B.C.," change it! You don't need a Ph.D. in New Testament studies; you don't need to be a believer in Jesus; you don't even need a screen name or a password. You can go and change it to "Jesus was never born!" if you want. But just expect it to be changed back to "8–2 B.C.," probably within seconds, by one of the twenty-five thousand users who continually edit articles.

Open access is the guiding principle of Wikipedia. ("Open content" is the official phrase among Wikipedians, a deliberate parallel to open-source software.) Uninhibited access to content—and to changing that content—is a deliberate subversion of the academic and governmental structures that have traditionally controlled intellectual content. Although some problems with Wikipedia are developing—open access is not unequivocal, and some vandals have been banned from the site—it is based on the theory that more knowledge in the hands of more people will be better for humankind.

Similarly, emergent churches are questioning, subverting, and even disposing of the leadership structures common in churches. While in many mainline churches, robes and seminary degrees separate the clergy from the laity (as do terms like *clergy* and *laity*!), and other churches go so far as to erect "altar rails" to distinguish the classes of people in the sanctuary—only pastors and priests can stand behind the physical barricade—emergent churches are doing away with these class distinctions.

In evangelical churches, it's jeans and open collars for everyone, but the all-important "pastor-teacher" is still head and shoulders above the rest: spotlights, microphones, and JumboTrons have replaced the altar rail as the physical expressions of hierarchy. Emergent churches, on the other hand, are experimenting with no microphones, circular seating patterns, and more intimate settings for worship. Instead of theater seating in a "worship center," many churches are opting for meetings in coffee shops, pubs, and living rooms.

Trust   "Wikipedia is built on the expectation that collaboration among users will improve articles over time. . . . Some of Wikipedia's editors have explained its editing process as a 'socially Darwinian evolutionary process.'" So says the Wikipedia entry on "Wikipedia." [3]

The assumption of a wiki is that people, collectively, will create a database of content more accurate than one person or a select team of persons ever could. If you bought the *Encyclopaedia Britannica* from the door-to-door salesman years ago, you had to assume that the author of the article on the Vietnam War and the editor who approved that article were unbiased. But of course, they weren't. Try as they might to avoid it, their prejudices about that highly controversial war played out in their entry. On Wikipedia, however, the "Vietnam War" entry begins with a large caveat stating that claims in the article have been tagged as unverified or unduly biased, which in turn links to an extended discussion among editors and readers about the various sections of the article.

You might think of this as an inherent trust in human nature, the opposite of the Augustinian doctrine of Original Sin (which says that we're all inherently tainted with a sinful nature). In some ways, that's correct. A wiki does rely on human goodness or at least on the assumption that the good people will always outnumber the devious. The supposition that the Wikipedia community will root out undue bias seems to bear out: a study in the journal *Nature* found roughly the same level of errors and omissions in scientific articles on Wikipedia as in the *Encyclopaedia Britannica*.[4] Weaknesses exist, to be sure, and entries have been vandalized, but the open-source aphorism, "Given enough eyeballs, all errors are shallow," seems to hold. The bigger Wikipedia gets, and the more ownership people take of it, the better it is as an encyclopedia.

Many emergent churches work on the same assumption that when people get together and "edit" one another's beliefs, all are better for it. Whereas the vast majority of modern churches practice a unilateral form of communication, from pulpit to pew, emergent churches are innovating new forms of preaching that include communally written sermons, teaching that is primarily dialogue, and online discussion forums regarding past and future sermon topics. The content is not learned in seminary and then disseminated over a career of sermons and Sunday school classes but developed communally and shared among people who trust one another. The seminary-trained pastor brings expertise to the community, as does the quantum physicist and the lawn mower repairman. None claims to be an expert in all fields, but all realize that by pooling their expertise, the whole community is better. For while a seminary degree surely helps the community understand the Bible, so does some quantum physics and a dash of lawn mower repair: the physicist can open up some of the mysteries of God's universe, and the repairman can describe the conditions of manual labor that many a pastor has never experienced. If anything, the pastor in this scenario is a broker of conversation—*that's* how she teaches.

When I visit my children's elementary school, the same one in which I was educated, the classrooms look nothing like they did when I was a student there thirty years ago. My kindergarten teacher stood at the blackboard with a stern look while we pupils sat in straight rows practicing our penmanship. My kids' teacher spends more time on her knees than on her feet most days. She is down on the floor, at the kids' eye level. She rarely stands by the whiteboard because, truth be told, there's really no "front" of the room. In fact, if you asked my daughter, Lily, "Where's the front of the room?" she'd look at you incredulously, for you'd have just asked a nonsensical question. The students sit around tables (called "centers") and move around throughout the day. And instead of a class, it's called a "family."

Is their teacher less of a teacher than mine was simply because she uses a more communal pedagogy? No. Instead, my children's teachers are more aware of the different ways that different children learn (aurally, visually, spatially, kinesthetically, and so on), and they've adjusted their teaching methods accordingly. Brain research has shown conclusively that children learn better when they are engaged as cooperators in the learning process.

Center-based classrooms are not the encroachment of touchy-feely political correctness but a forward-thinking didactic innovation that is better preparing kids for a world that demands participation.

But how much has the church changed in those same thirty years? Maybe the pews have been replaced by theater seating, the organ by a guitar, and the robe by a Hawaiian shirt, but the content delivery mechanism has remained the same. Whether it's a lack of imagination or a lack of trust, the vast majority of churches in America have been unwilling to open-source their biblical and theological content.

Some people will worry, What about heresy? It'll just become a mad free-for-all without any baseline of sound doctrine!

To the contrary, nothing roots out heresy better than a group. As the literary critic Stanley Fish has argued, we derive our interpretive authority in the midst of communities.[5] (David Koresh wasn't looking around the room at the end of a sermon, asking, "So what did y'all think about that? Did I get anything wrong?")

Add to the already powerful group dynamic the Christian conviction that the church is guided by God's Spirit, and the Christian community acts like the gutter bumpers that you see in bowling alleys when children go bumper bowling. The ball may veer off to one side or another, but it keeps making progress down the lane, kept in line by the bumpers. It's the community in which we place ourselves that keeps the ball out of the gutter as it rolls down the alley. The collection of Christ followers called "church" should act in just this way.

This, then, is a high view of the church: the collected people of God, in community with God's Spirit, will stay on track and engaged with God's work in the world. That is, if they stick together.

Mutual Accountability Wikipedia isn't a willy-nilly affair. Multiple structures have been built into the system just for it to work, and most of it is retrofitted. First of all, there is the "wiki engine," the collaborative software that runs the site. It didn't appear out of nowhere—a team of engineers built it and maintains it in Saint Petersburg, Florida. In the case of Wikipedia, there is a *there* there.

An additional team of people around the globe maintains the massive site:

• *Developers* write the software and maintain the site.

• *Stewards* can grant and take away access to the site.

- *Bureaucrats* can promote users within the system and rename user accounts. They also control the *bots*, highly repetitive processes (like editing) that have been automated.

- *Administrators* (a.k.a. "sysops," for system operators) are regular contributors who have access to some of the technical features of the site. They can lock and delete pages and block others editors' access.

- *Overseers* can revert articles to earlier versions after vandalism.

- *Checkusers* can see the Internet provider address of someone who has made a revision to an article, in order to guard against "sock puppets" (banned users who log in under a different user name).

And founder Jimmy Wales has unparalleled access to the users and content on Wikipedia. Only he can ban a user for life.

It looks at first blush like a hierarchy, not unlike any corporation or denomination. But in fact, the personnel at Wikipedia serve more as sentries of a sort. They safeguard the content and the community from the minority of users with nefarious motives. By offering these strictures to Wikipedians, the vast majority of the Wikipedia community can safely collaborate on articles.

Similarly, emergent churches do not forsake structure. Most have pastors, a leadership team, a person in charge of the children's ministry, and someone to coordinate the music for worship. Other people are engaged in other tasks, some temporarily and some indefinitely. But these roles are seen as paving the way for others to contribute to the process of "being church," not to mitigate their contributions by predetermining what the church will do, what congregants will believe, or anything else.

Max Weber (1864–1920), the founder of modern sociology, famously wrote that the success of capitalism was due in large part to its partnership with Calvinist theology: the strict modesty of Calvinism provided a moral curb to the relentless growth impulse of a free market. Weber, who also wrote extensively about religion, said that religious movements founded initially on the charisma of a leader or leaders will inevitably settle into routine patterns of administration and bureaucracy. The intense fervor exhibited at the genesis of a movement cannot hold for long—soon people want to make a living off of this new way of being religious. They do so by turning religious items into commodities (for example, "sacraments") and then afford themselves a salary to administer those commodities. Weber called this the "routinization of the charisma."[6] His words have proved prophetic in every modern religious movement, all revivals and reformations of Christianity included. The question for emergent Christianity is whether the temptation of routinization can be avoided or whether it's inevitable.[7]

Agility   Wikipedia has an extraordinary ability to respond to the events of the day. Within minutes of his execution, the entry for "Saddam Hussein" reflected that fact. The same goes for any number of recent events. If Rosie O'Donnell and Donald Trump get in another spat, it's sure to show up in their Wikipedia biographies. No team of editors needs to vet the information, and there are no constraints as to the word count for The Donald's entry, or anyone else's.

Rapid access to information is one of the hallmarks of postmodern life. In general, the so-called new media have made a name for themselves by beating the traditional media on stories. The latter are restrained by their self-imposed need to have multiple sources on every story, whereas there's no such system of checks and balances on the Drudge Report or the Huffington Post. And when the traditional media have attempted to keep up with the new media, they often get burned, as they did when they reported that the West Virginia miners buried in a mine collapse had been found alive in 2006—that was the headline in the Minneapolis *StarTribune*—when in fact all but one had perished.

A whole host of problems comes with agile new media, the most glaring being the frequency of mistakes. However, mistakes in an electronic format can be corrected just as quickly as they were made. And further, we as readers are becoming more cognizant of the higher frequency of errors. We're being socialized to expect some errors, just as we were socialized to believe that newspapers are trustworthy and unbiased.

Emergent churches, in part because of their smaller size and relatively egalitarian leadership structures, demonstrate similar agility. Often large, bureaucratic, conventional churches have taken too long to respond to crises in the world. They've taken action against the Iraq War, for instance, by having committee meetings, passing resolutions, and sending letters to the president—letters which have been unremittingly ignored. But this is how big bureaucracies work; they lumber along and take action that will ultimately offend no one and affect few.

Rethinking the church as an essentially *activist* organization means fundamental changes in the way that church is run. For the church to be responsive to the rapidly changing world, it must be light and quick on its feet. The local church will be relatively small and relatively autonomous. Then the assembled people can discern God's Spirit on a matter (however they happen to do that), make decisions, and act on them as they deem appropriate. The American government may have to wait until all the facts are in and then follow the protocols of diplomatic engagement in responding to the most pressing genocide in Africa, but the church is not bound by those strictures. The church can act immediately, especially when the mandate of God in a matter is clear (as it is during a genocide; God's mandate: "Stop the genocide!").

Connectivity Alice in Wonderland or Morpheus in *The Matrix* might have compared an hour or two lost in Wikipedia to a journey down the rabbit hole. Wikipedia articles are laden with hyperlinks, underlined words and phrases that beckon you, with the click of your mouse, to another article: while I was reading an article on the Vietnam War, a link took me to the article on President Lyndon B. Johnson, in which I read that he appeared on national television on March 31, 1968, to announce, "I will not seek, nor will I accept, my party's nomination for President of the United States." Well, that's my very birthday—I was born at 6:50 P.M. Central Time, and LBJ began his speech just ten minutes later—so I clicked on March 31 to see what else historic happened on my birthday. There I discovered that the very first Wrestlemania took place on that date in 1985, René Descartes shares my birthday, and it's the Feast of Saint Amos.

Wikipedia makes the linkages in human knowledge prominent. Some of the connections are profound (is the War in Iraq really parallel to Vietnam?), while others are mundane or even trivial (like the game Six Degrees of Kevin Bacon). But there, in glimmering blue words, Wikipedia exemplifies the thesis of the Harvard philosopher W.V.O. Quine, who argued in the 1950s that human knowledge did not function hierarchically (as posited by Descartes and his followers) but instead like a web: "The totality of our so-called knowledge or beliefs, from the most casual matters of geography and history to the profoundest laws of atomic physics or even pure mathematics and logic, is a man-made fabric which impinges on experience only along the edges." [8] Wikipedia trumps other media (like this book) in its weblike ability to link bits of knowledge with myriad other bits of knowledge.

The emergent church has serendipitously pioneered a new ecumenical connectivity simply by virtue of the fact that it showed up at the advent of the Internet. First by e-mail and cell phones, then via Web pages, then through blogs, and now by instant messaging and, increasingly, live Webcams, emergents connect with their friends around the globe daily. By staying in frequent contact with one another, they're able to engage one another's lives and ministries in ways previously unheard of. Sivin Kit, an emergent Lutheran pastor in Kuala Lumpur, Malaysia, is one of my constant companions via instant messaging. We'd been friends for two years before we met face to face, and we continue to bounce ideas off each other weekly. I consider über-blogger Bob Carlton of San Francisco one of my closest friends, although we've never been in the same room. He's constantly plying me with links to articles that he knows I'll find interesting; some of those articles, which I doubt I would have found on my own, have informed various chapters of this book.

But the connections between emergents aren't exclusively Internet-based. Travel is easier today than ever before, meaning they can conveniently visit one another's churches or conferences. Thus one of the suggested practices listed on the Emergent Village Web site under "Value 4: Commitment to One Another," reads, "To make an annual pilgrimage to an Emergent Village gathering; to give one another the gift of our presence at annual gatherings whenever possible." (See Appendix A for a complete list of Emergent Village's Values and Practices.) Even the ubiquity of the English language has begun to reverse the curse of Babel, bringing together Christians who previously wouldn't have been able to communicate.

And when you mix the power of the new media with the generous orthodoxy of the emergent church, you have a potent porridge called *change*. As noted in Chapter One, Christians no longer communicate only with others in their own tribe. More Lutherans are talking to Episcopalians, and those Episcopalians are sometimes playing in the sandbox with Pentecostals, and the Pentecostals are discovering their similarities with Nazarenes and Methodists, and so on. Denominations used to act as the primary, if not exclusive, hub for Christian communication. That is no longer the case. Most Christians realize that we've got a lot to learn from each other. Like the old saw about the six blind men who are touching and describing different parts of an elephant, each of our traditions gets a bit of God right, but we've got to follow the links into other traditions to get the bigger picture.[9]

Messiness Wikipedia isn't without its warts. Jimmy Wales and Larry Sanger have parted ways. Sanger (who has a Ph.D.) has accused Wikipedia entries of an anti-intellectual bias. Wales (who does not) disagrees. Sanger, in turn, has begun a new venture called Citizendium, which takes Wikipedia entries and allows experts in various fields to vet them for accuracy and then lock them against future revisions. Meanwhile, Wales has been caught editing his own Wikipedia biography (which is contrary to Wikipedia guidelines) to expunge his connections to a now-defunct pornography Web site.

Vandalism has also been an issue, most notoriously when the entry for the Nashville-based journalist John Siegenthaler Sr. (father of the NBC anchor) was changed to indicate that he'd been linked to JFK's assassination. Though completely spurious and written as a joke, the entry stayed on Wikipedia for nearly four months before it was revised. Since 2005, Siegenthaler has been an outspoken critic of Wikipedia, and Wales instituted many of the accountability structures as a result of this incident.

So Wikipedia's dominance on the Internet has not come without mistakes—even embarrassments—and adjustments. But the open-source world is built on the assumption that the users will break the tool; in the breaking, the weak points become known and can be repaired. And though the failures of the program take place on a public stage, what is a humiliation for Microsoft Vista is a badge of honor for Linux. Wikipedia is built to be broken.

Already some critical voices have risen against the emergent church for not being "effective" or "efficient" or not growing fast enough. "Where's the success?" they've been asked. "Where's the growth?" First of all, the metrics of growth that are used to judge most American churches don't apply to emergent churches. "Church growth" implies numerical growth, a concept in line with capitalism, to be sure: corporate growth means more widgets sold, a larger market share, and a better return on investment for shareholders. But that's not how one measures growth in one's family. A couple might stop procreating after three children because two adults, three kids, a dog, and a cat seem like a sustainable way of life; eighteen children and thirty-two cats does not. But of course, that family is still *growing* in various ways, many of which cannot be numerically quantified. So it is with emergent churches, many of which have reached a size—be it a living room filled with a dozen people or a church building filled with hundreds—that they consider the limit of a sustainable way of life for their community.

The "sustainability movement" has many advocates in the emergent church. Gro Harlem Brundtland, a founder of the movement, described sustainable development as development that "meets the needs of the present without compromising the ability of future generations to meet their own needs."[10] Proponents of sustainability look for continuity between human and nonhuman inhabitants of this planet and sensible economic, social, and institutional growth that will harm neither. Similarly, emergent churches value "growth," but it is growth differently conceived. To put it conversely, what good is a church that makes scores of converts but cannot offer them a habitat for long-term spiritual growth? Or a massive church with an egomaniacal senior pastor? Emergents want a Christianity that will meet current spiritual and theological needs but will also be around to sate the spiritual longings of their children and grandchildren.

Further, like Wikipedia, emergent churches harbor no great fear of failure. In fact, failures are a natural consequence of innovation and adventure. If you play it safe, you can be assured of few failures; if you're trying new things all the time, failures are assured. And if you let people get their fingerprints all over the church, those failures will be public. A church that vets every potential speaker before handing over the microphone probably won't have many verbal miscues in the worship setting, but they'll also keep hearing from the same sort of (confident, articulate) people every week. However, when emergent churches open-source their worship environments, all sorts of people make themselves heard, leading to a richer experience for all, albeit one with some serious misfires.

Emergents, by their nature, embrace the messiness of human life. And the church, as a reflection of the human life in relationship with God, is in no way immune to this messiness.

Jesus famously promised that "where two or three are gathered in my name, I am there among them."[11] Since he uttered those words, Christians have, in principle, claimed that nothing more is required to constitute a church than a couple of believers on a park bench. Yet the vines of bureaucracy and hierarchy have snaked their way around God's people for centuries, often choking out innovation and progress.

Churches inevitably grow, build infrastructure, and then add scaffolding to support that infrastructure. Bureaucracies are meant to ensure the sustainability of the church organism by providing items like health insurance and pension plans to clergy, land for local churches to build on, centralized financing for mission operations, and theological training for leaders. In theory, the bureaucracy of a denomination or a megachurch frees up the people of God to do God's work without having to worry about things like liability insurance or criminal background checks; the bureaucracy will dispassionately take care of those mundane details. But a bureaucracy is never satisfied in a merely supportive role. Invariably, the scaffolding morphs into an exoskeleton, sealing off the life within, for bureaucracies are bent on one thing: their own self-preservation. And all of the well-meaning individuals within cannot overwhelm the evils of bureaucracy once that bureaucracy has taken on a life of its own.

Many people hope that the end of bureaucratic Christianity is nigh and that emergent churches will be able to avoid the temptation to develop bureaucracies and hierarchies. The twentieth-century American church reflected prevailing culture by matching the rise of corporations and institutions with its own large, bureaucratic structures. Maybe the postmodern church will take a cue from the open-source movement about structuring in a way that affords authorship and opportunity to all.

TIGHTLY KNIT: JOURNEY

In the landmark Supreme Court case of 1819, *Dartmouth College* v. *New Hampshire*, Daniel Webster famously said of Dartmouth, "It is, Sir, as I have said, a small college. And yet there are those who love it." He could have said something similar about Journey, a small band of emergent renegades meeting in the shadows of Dallas's tall steeples.

On the second floor of Gaston Oaks Baptist Church at the north end of the Dallas "Loop," in a room shrouded in black and lit with candles, young adults wander in casually. The band is small, using a track in lieu of drums. Six or seven televisions project the words to songs.

About fifty people are in attendance, most in their twenties, and dress is extremely casual. The furniture is a mixture of pews, lounge chairs, and small tables with Bibles and literature about the church on them. Art hangs on the walls, and a bar in the back is stocked with sodas. The stage and two sections of seating form a triangle, with a lectern in the middle. I see two children.

The worship gathering, at 5:30 P.M. on Sunday, opens with an audio recording of a monologue by the atheist comedian Julia Sweeney. It's from Sweeny's show *And God Said, Ha!* and it's completely irreverent. Alex, a dark-haired young man in jeans and a collared shirt, stands. (He's also wearing a blazer, I discover, because it is "Bad Blazer Night" at Journey.) He welcomes everyone and leads a liturgical prayer that appears on the screens.

The band opens with four songs written by the evangelical recording artists Robbie Seay and David Crowder. A woman leads the singing and takes center stage, with men playing guitars and bass. As the songs go on, some remain standing while others sit.

After the singing, trance music begins playing in the background. A young woman reads from the Old Testament book of Ezra in a dramatic and engaging way, with a handheld mike behind a small lectern. Pieces of abstract visual art appear on the screens.

When Danielle Shroyer gets up to preach, it's 6:30. Danielle is Journey's second pastor. Scott Gornto, the founder, was asked by Gaston Oaks to start a young adult ministry in the traditional Texas Baptist Church. But under Gornto's leadership, Journey went in its own direction (in what Journeyers call "the Divorce") and has had an awkward relationship with Gaston Oaks ever since.[12] Danielle landed at Journey via a circuitous route. As an undergrad at Baylor, she was involved with the genesis of University Baptist Church-Waco, planted by emergent church celebrities Chris Seay and David Crowder. She then interned at Journey before leaving Texas for Princeton Theological Seminary. There she worked part time at a conservative evangelical church that tried, unsuccessfully, to begin a postmodern outreach service. Upon graduation from Princeton, she became a chaplain at a nursing home, where she served until she was beckoned back to Journey in 2005.

Danielle opens the sermon by talking about how important stories are in her family and about how they sit around the Christmas dinner table and tell stories for hours. She reflects on Christians being "people of the Book" in her church as she was growing up. But she quickly transitions to theologian Miroslav Volf's work on memory, and she quotes him as saying that Americans are quick to put up memorials—like the one to the victims of 9/11—so that they can move on and let the memorial do the remembering. Danielle then invites others to tell about important stories that they remember.

A man talks about his dad bouncing him on his knee and reading *Where the Wild Things Are*. Another man remembers reading *The Catcher in the Rye* in high school, and then he confesses how much he hates that book now, for it reminds him of how stupid he was in his teens. A woman talks about seeing *Schindler's List* and *Dances with Wolves* and how those films caused her to confront the pain of others for the first time. Another woman tells about reading *Sadako and the Thousand Paper Cranes*—she was so moved by the story that she folded a thousand paper cranes in response.

A half dozen more people respond before Danielle asks them to speak of their fondest memories of Journey. One man tells about the pranks of the "Man Group"—a kind of spoof of the men's ministry common in evangelical churches—which leads several people to contribute their own memories of that group. The discussion gets somewhat boisterous before Danielle shifts the focus again, asking people to talk about their favorite stories from the Bible. One woman says that she liked the stories of the plagues on the Egyptians as a kid, and a man talks about Mephibosheth—he refers to him as "the gimpy kid in the Old Testament." Another man talks for a time about the Tower of Babel.

Danielle shares her own favorites and then talks about the overall story of the text from Ezra—"It's telling us to remember, remember, remember," she preaches. "We want scripture to be central to our life of faith because the story is formative for us. At Journey, we center our lives on the grand narrative of scripture—and I love that we put *grand* in front of *narrative!* We don't want to be the type of community that just lets the Bible do the remembering for us. We want to do the remembering. We don't want to slip into amnesia, to forget where we've come from."

After Danielle leads a prayer, the offering is introduced by a young woman who also makes some announcements in a friendly, lighthearted way. There's a book club, she says, and an opportunity to lead worship at a home for mentally challenged adults. She invites everyone to dinner after worship, and all stand and recite a benediction in unison.

Then no one leaves.

After the gathering, people stand and talk and laugh until Danielle finally says she's got to lock up the building. The majority of the group reconvenes at a Mexican restaurant a couple of miles away. Over margaritas and burritos, I get the sense that this group of people is really connected. Let me put that more boldly: these people are more committed to one another than people in any other church I've ever visited. Indeed, sitting at the end of a long table of

Journeyers, I feel tears welling in my eyes as I watch them enjoy one another. This, I think, is what church is meant to be.

In Robert Putnam's *Bowling Alone*—an article in 1995 that he turned into a book in 2000—he predicated the breakdown in American democracy based on the declining commitment of Americans to civic and community organizations.[13] Since the 1950s, he showed, participation in PTAs, church groups, and bowling leagues has shrunk precipitously. As a result, people feel less connected to one another, and this is especially acute in megalopolises like Dallas. In that environment, Journey is something of a throwback. Not that the congregants hold potluck suppers in the church basement, but they are fulfilling a need in one another's lives not unlike a small-town church of a half-century ago. And a similar commitment to deep, relational connection can be found across the emergent church landscape.

The next day, I gathered with a dozen Journeyers to ask them about their experiences of Journey. It's a young group—the average participant at Journey might be twenty-five years old. What I had observed the night before immediately comes out in their comments. They are uniquely committed to one another, they say. This is especially true in the wake of the last year: Scott Gornto, the founding pastor, left, and the community was led by committee for nearly a year before Danielle was hired. Some of the folks around the circle talk wistfully about those times of self-leadership; although they all wholeheartedly affirm Danielle's leadership, they know that their time "in the wilderness" made them closer as a community. It also thinned their ranks—about half of the congregation left when Scott left, and most of those were the folks about Scott's age, in their thirties, and with kids.

Left were, primarily, people in their twenties: Luke, Winston, and Z; Lindsay, Courtney, and Jen. They and a few others are sitting on couches, behind a curtain in the modified Sunday school classrooms that house Journey. When I ask what brought them to Journey in the first place, Winston leads off the conversation:

> I came to the "Theology for Skeptics" discussion group, which Danielle was leading. She said, "We're going to talk about the Trinity," and I just started laughing a lot, and I said, "What can you say about the Trinity that isn't some heresy or anthropomorphic?" you know, and

laughed it off – I was kind of venting a little bit. But everybody was like, "Yeah, that's a really good point. Let's talk about that." And I was struck by how open the dialogue was through the rest of the time I was there, and it was something that I've always wanted to find in a church. I wanted to go to church, but I wanted to go to a church in a place where I could have an open dialogue and be up-front about who I am, which I failed to be able to do at every other church I that I attended in Dallas.

This sentiment eventually gets reiterated by everyone in the group:

Jen: "The thing that I always tell people about Journey is it was the place where I could truly be myself and not worry about what other people thought or if they agreed with me or anything like that."

Dale: "I realized that it was more of a real place as opposed to some of the fakeness that I saw with the other church I was working in and at other churches I had worked at." By "real," he goes on to explain, he means that people at Journey don't put on airs or act like they've got all the answers.

Lindsay: "I'm free to think how I think, and somebody will challenge me on that or I can talk. I can at least be myself and say what I think and why I think it, and everybody may go, yeah, we completely agree, or no, we absolutely disagree, but nobody's going to ostracize me or ask me to leave the church."

"I was struck by how open the dialogue was through the rest of the time I was there, and it was something that I've always wanted to find in a church."

Michael even tells a funny story that some in the group hadn't heard before: when he first visited Journey, he was sure that everyone was going to hell. He was so convinced, in fact, that he went home that night and wrote a song, "Journey Is Going to Hell." Now, five years later, he's a musician in the church.

But what led Michael to that initial impression is an interesting question. Danielle calls Dallas a land of "doctrinal cleansing," and it's true: many of these Journeyers come from conservative church backgrounds. Danielle herself was brought up in a church that didn't allow women to preach. Michael was leading music at a conservative Methodist church when he first visited Journey. And the evangelical megachurch known as Watermark™, which meets nearby, comes up several times in the course of our conversation.[14] So Journey feels a bit like a group of friends who've gathered in a foxhole—Dallas is the home of many enormous megachurches and several conservative seminaries, and Journey is a little band of renegades that sometimes nips at the heels of the giants.

Dispatch 17: Emergents start new churches to save their own faith, not necessarily as an outreach strategy.

Two particular characteristics stand out in the course of our conversation. One, the *progressive* nature of Journey is illuminated by the homemade T-shirt worn by Courtney, a twenty-five-year-old freelance photographer. It is inscribed:

Straight Christians for Gay Rights
(My Bible Teaches Social Justice)

When I ask how Journey's brand of progressivism is different from other liberals, Lindsay says:

> I've never gone to a really liberal church, and so I don't know for sure, but the impression in my head would be that a liberal church actually thinks that everything that I do is OK. But an emergent church, a church like this, may disagree with me and think it's not OK, but that's a discussion for the two of us to have, maybe, or that's something to bring up and discuss. I would think people in a liberal church may have the same viewpoint on, who knows, any of the hot topics that are [out there] – divorce or gays or whatever it may be – and we have those same topics. It's just that we don't have a unified view of how we feel about that, but it's still OK.

And then Darrell, the forty-year-old "old-timer" in the group, chimes in: "There isn't really any push to create a unified way of thinking. It's OK to bring whatever you have to the table. Valid or invalid is always up for debate, and that's one thing that has not changed through the course of everything that has happened over the five years that I've been here."

So Journey's progressivism isn't conventional—several people there express to me their disaffection with Jim Wallis and Sojourners, for instance. (They consider Sojo too "inside the Beltway" and too bent on selling books and coffee mugs.) Courtney is outspoken about her convictions, but she's well aware that many in the church don't agree with her. Journey doesn't have an "official statement" about homosexuality, but there's obviously enough freedom in the community for Courtney to wear her beliefs on her shirt. To this point in Journey's history, conversation is still the end, not just the means.

The other characteristic that stands out to me about Journey is the *irreverence*. Whether it is the Julia Sweeny recording or the liberal use of swear words, these people are clearly trying to shake free from the pietism that defines much Dallas-style evangelicalism.

Pietism

A Christian movement of the seventeenth and eighteenth centuries that combined the Lutheran reverence for biblical doctrine with the Puritan commitment to a vigorous Christian life. Pietism lives on today in evangelicalism that joins conservative theology with "clean living."

Winston tells another story to this end:

> [From the beginning,] I really enjoyed the aesthetic of the service. It was really beautiful and weird. The group was weird. The service was quirky. It had this real nice beauty and realness to it. I remember the first time I was there – there was some couple that was pregnant and they had made a plaster cast of her naked upper torso and brought it to Journey and donated it to be used as a chip bowl. I thought this was just one of the greatest things ever – that was just awesome!

This irreverence is part of the ethos that makes another woman comfortable at Journey. She tells her story of getting married young, to a man who became abusive toward her. She approached the pastors of her conservative Bible church, and they told her to stick with her husband. "I told them, 'He's crazy!'" she says, "but they just kept after me with really threatening phone calls when I started talking about divorce. It freaked me out so much that I never wanted to go to church again." Then she spoke about arriving at Journey:

> I thought I had this huge black cloud over my head and that everybody was going to judge me for the rest of my life. And people were like, "Oh, yeah, so I like that shirt you're wearing." I mean, [my divorce] was just a nonissue, . . . and that so shocked me. That alone was enough to make me keep coming, just to figure out what is it about these people that they do Christianity so differently than everybody else.

As you might guess, it takes an extraordinary person to pastor this unusual group, and Danielle Shroyer is indeed extraordinary. First off, she's juggling the demands of Journey with being a mom—she is employed half time at Journey, which means, she tells me, that either Journey or the family gets short shrift each week. She simply looks at her calendar at the beginning of the week and decides which it will have to be.

If it seems unlikely that a suburban mom would be the pastor of this motley band of twenty-somethings, it is. They ride her about living outside the Loop (in Plano), about not having a blog, and about the fact that a Google search of her name reveals connections between her family and that of George W. Bush. Danielle admits to some ambivalence about not being able to join the Journeyers as they gather three or four nights a week for movies, poker, and the "theology pub."

But to my mind, Danielle is the perfect fit. She is not a mother to the group—she's seen as a peer—but she does have a certain maturity that acts as glue in a group that could easily fragment. Part of her maturity is a true lack of ego—or, I should say, a rightly chastened ego. When Danielle became Journey's pastor, this band of ecclesial dissidents had been holding the church together for nine months. Had she come in with a desire to control, it would have surely proved disastrous. Instead, Danielle leads quietly, from the midst of the group, and they love her and trust her for it. That is, they trust her because she first trusted them.

Danielle jokes about the process that brought her to Journey. The search committee, dubbed the "pastor search posse," was as unconventional as the church itself. She explains, "The questions they asked on the questionnaire were really funny because you could tell none of them were really professionals, because they didn't ask, 'What do you think about the doctrine of the Holy Spirit?' I mean, there were no doctrinal-type questions on this. It was like, 'What are your favorite movies? What kind of music do you listen to?'"

Far more important, she goes on to say, they really pressed her on how she was going to pastor and live a holistic life. And here her brilliance shines, for she immediately looked to the small band of leaders who had seen the church through its pastorless months:

> I just don't really care. I don't care if I don't get credit. I don't want all the spotlight to be on me. I don't want this to be a Danielle-centered church, at all. So from the beginning, I just kind of said, "You guys, I know you need a break because you've been working your tails off for the last nine months, so take your break and then get your butts back in here, because this isn't just about what I'm going to do. I literally am not going to do this without you, and I can't on twenty hours a week, [not] with two kids. So take your break and then get on back."

Due in large part to Danielle's commitment to shared leadership, the magic of Journey that started under Scott and held the group together through transition has continued. The future is uncertain. Journey has moved twice to new locations since my visit, and the transitory nature of single young adults who live in a metropolitan area has taken its toll. Danielle wonders, and worries, about whether this church will last. At forty to fifty people, it's too big to qualify as a house church but not quite big enough to be sustainable on its own. But like her favorite theologian, Jürgen Moltmann, Danielle is a Christian who is guided primarily by hope. So when she looks into that uncertain future, her smile trumps her worry.

BINITARIANS

Allow me a bold indictment: most American Christians don't *really* believe in the Holy Spirit.

Now, most would *say* they believe in all three persons of the Trinity, but we should in this instance look at action as a reflection of belief. Many Christians grew up hearing the phrase "It's God, not us, who does the saving," the point being that it's not really up to us whether someone comes to a saving relationship with Jesus; it's ultimately up to God. This was meant, of course, to take some of the pressure off of us, the young evangelists, and to avoid the insidious problem of idolatry—if we think that we're the agents of our own salvation, then we've really confused ourselves with God.

And the same thing goes in church. I've sat in many staff meetings, at several churches, in which protracted discussions have asked: How do we get more people to come to our church? Should we have a better band? Throw the organ in the dumpster? Landscape the entryway? Serve better coffee?

A friend of mine recently told me about that very discussion on her church staff. The ubiquitous whiteboard was rolled into the staff meeting, and the senior pastor said, "Let's have a brainstorming session. How can we get more young adults to come to this church?" Then he went to the board and wrote "Hooks" at the top (meaning, what can we do to snag eighteen-to-thirty-five-year-olds and get them in the door?).

A rather pathetic discussion ensued, leaving my friend disheartened. She asked my advice, and I said, "Does your church believe in the Holy Spirit?"

"Of course," she replied.

"Then why in the world would you think that you can do *anything* to get people to come to church? Instead, why don't you worry about being faithful—living out a beautiful Christianity—and see what the Spirit does in your midst? I think that people will be more attracted to the Spirit than to anything you could ever do to 'hook' them."

But my friend is not alone. All of us who care about God's Kingdom have been tempted to think that the advancement of that Kingdom is up to us. Almost every pastor has sat in his office on the eve of an important event and wondered, "Will anyone come?" And almost everyone has convened an activity to which only one or two people came and wondered, "What have I done wrong?"

What we do in these situations is disregard Jesus' promise that the Holy Spirit will be our constant counselor and comforter, that our power will result from the release of God's Spirit.[15]

Indeed, the same Spirit who invested Jesus with his power is the Spirit who descended on the apostles on Pentecost and is now working in the world. But in truth, our reliance on the Spirit is negligible. Think of the last time you heard a sermon or read a book on the Spirit; sermons abound on Jesus and the Father, but there's a paucity of sermons on the Holy Spirit.[16]

Dispatch 18: Emergents firmly hold that God's Spirit-not their own efforts-is responsible for good in the world. The human task is to cooperate with God in what God is already doing.

This "binitarian" (as opposed to trinitarian) Christianity is what Parker Palmer calls "functional atheism,"

the belief that ultimate responsibility for everything rests with us. This is the unconscious, unexamined conviction that if anything decent is going to happen here, we are the ones who must make it happen – a conviction held even by people who talk a good game about God.

This shadow causes pathology on every level of our lives. It leads us to impose our will on others … stressing our relationships, sometimes to the point of breaking. It often eventuates in burnout, depression, and despair, as we learn the world will not bend to our will and we become embittered about that fact. Functional atheism is the shadow that drives collective frenzy as well. It explains why the average group can tolerate no more than fifteen seconds of silence:

if we are not making noise, we believe, nothing good is happening and something must be dying.[17]

Now, it's one thing for me as an individual to think, It's up to me. That's forgivable, for it seems inherent to human nature that I would struggle with self-centeredness. It's a far greater sin when that self-centeredness expands via institutionalization. The church should be a place where individuals who struggle with self-centeredness get reminded that our calling is to be God-centered and other-centered. When "It's up to us" is the subconscious mantra of the church, the church has lost its way. That's why Brad Cecil, pastor of Axxess in Arlington, Texas, and his elder board occasionally wear T-shirts to worship that read "IT'S NOT ABOUT YOU."

Idolatry is the next link on this dangerous chain. When a church places undue emphasis on its programs, buildings, staffing, or other human inventions, reliance on the Holy Spirit has most likely been lost. Past success can be the forbidden fruit here, as can the envy of another church's success. In any case, some little success breeds a desire for more success, and as self-centered as we are, we tend to imagine that our own efforts have been the key.

A return to true trinitarianism in the American church is desperately needed. That will entail, first, a commitment to the doctrine, and second, behavior that reflects a true reliance on God's Spirit.

THE PEOPLE'S LITURGY: CHURCH OF THE APOSTLES

On a gray, unspectacular March night in Seattle, a somewhat bedraggled group of young adults gathers quietly in a Lutheran-Episcopal church. In the heart of the trendy Fremont neighborhood, the formerly abandoned church has been populated by the people of Church of the Apostles.

Videos flicker across the screen, and techno-trance music pumps from the venerable speakers. An unassuming African American woman, her straightened hair falling in front of her face, sits behind a Mac G4 at the sound board. From the rear of the sanctuary, she's "VJ-ing" the worship service. Her name is Karen Ward, and she's the pastor-priest of Church of the Apostles, a thriving community of about one hundred faithful in what is arguably Seattle's least churched neighborhood.

Ward doesn't call herself an Episcopal priest or a Lutheran pastor, both of which she is. "Abbess in training" is her preferred appellation. She does not speak for the first hour of the worship, leaving that to an assortment of others. She finally rises, dressed in jeans and a wool sweater, and leads the community in the Eucharist.

Dispatch 19: Emergents downplay-or outright reject-the differences between clergy and laity.

After the service, an openly gay man sits next to a Moody Bible Institute graduate in a group that discusses the church's future. They lovingly refer to Church of the Apostles as "COTA" and to themselves as "Cotans," and they passionately (and somewhat worriedly) wonder aloud about how long this communal equilibrium can hold. How long, they ask, can this little band of renegade Christians avoid being co-opted by the political and marketing forces of institutional American Christianity? One young man responds that other churches like this are springing up around the United States, and he's right.

The COTA building still smells like the homeless shelter that it was for the previous four years. Folding chairs and a few couches face the front of the old church sanctuary. A sheet is stretched artistically across the front wall, and a cartoon of Jesus' life is projected onto it. The band—bass, piano, percussion, xylophone—plays a repetitive jazz riff in a minor key, and Father Ryan, the youngish Episcopal priest, invites people to begin the service with "open space." Light comes through alabaster windows, and people paint, pray, and talk quietly.

At 5:15, people are invited to stand (if they are able). Guitar music begins, and the song "Forty Days" is led ("Forty days to wander . . ."), a song about Jesus' days in the wilderness. The words are in purple, the color of Lent, on the screen.

Aside from Karen, the crowd is all white, with only a couple of children in attendance. The room is casual and dark, and everyone is in their twenties or thirties.

From the back, Father Ryan says, "Welcome to Lent" into a handheld mike. "It's day eighteen of the Lenten journey, and Jesus is tired and hungry...." He moves into a reflection on the Ten Commandments. "Decalogue: The Ten Words" fills the screen, and an intentionally out-of-focus video loops as Ryan asks a series of questions about why God would give a list of rules and laws.

The band leads the congregation in "Kyrie Eleison, Christe Eleison" to a techno-trance beat, broken up by the chant of a cantor. It's a mash-up of ancient and future, and this is the brilliance of Ward's leadership. She is an indefinable commodity—a black woman ministering to whites, an aficionado of Belgian beers and techno-trance music, and a darling among the well-heeled mainline set who'd like to revive traditional Protestantism. (The church has financial backing from the old-guard Trinity Church-Wall Street, across the country in Manhattan.) She's a walking, talking mash-up. "They're my tribe," Ward says unapologetically when asked why she continues to hang out with the robe-and-liturgy crowd of Lutherans and Anglicans.

As worship continues, a young woman named Rachel stands up to share her story. She describes being motivated to stand up and advocate for those who need advocacy: the blind, the autistic, and so on. But tonight she wants to talk about a failure. She tells of two instances when, as a youth pastor, she failed to advocate for those who desperately needed it. At the end of her story, she says, "This is my story," and the congregation responds, "Thank you, Rachel." It is obviously a common call-and-response element in their worship—more intimate than a traditional church service, but not as reminiscent of Alcoholics Anonymous as one might imagine.

Next, the song "Invocation" is led by the band ("Today when we hear your voice, we won't harden our hearts; Heaven and earth meet here, and we will hear your voice"). The Gospel lesson is introduced with the invitation, "Please rise for a story from the journey." The bass player tells a narrative version of the cleansing of the Temple.[18] It's long, dramatic, and almost shockingly contemporary.

Tim, the seminary intern, stands up under the heading (on the screen) "Reverberations." People are asked to reflect with the person next to them. Tim then delivers the sermon—it's intense and whispery, interpreting the cleansing of the Temple to be an example of Jesus' compassion for the oppressed and for all of us.

The band leads a mournful and minor-key version of the traditional Lenten hymn "O Sacred Head, Now Wounded." Prayers that were written down during "open space" are prayed, and people are asked to share the peace of Christ with one another.

Only now does Karen appear, inviting the congregation to give their offerings and reminding them that their church is growing in its connection to God. The band sings, "God is good," as the offering is taken, and the bread and wine of the Eucharist are then brought forward in traditional Catholic-Episcopal fashion. Karen prepares the communion table as the band continues to play. Everyone stands as Karen leads a communion liturgy, and everyone sits and then proceeds forward individually to take wine or grape juice from the common cup.

At the end of communion, Karen invites Father Travis, another Episcopal priest, forward as hip-hop music plays. He leads announcements and invites all to the "Sanctorum" service on Sunday night, a "Goth Mass." Travis uses the traditional poem "St. Patrick's Breastplate" as the closing benediction.

After the service, I sit down with a dozen Cotans, and there's a palpable concern in the air. These people love COTA with such vigor that it's difficult for them to articulate. But they worry—they worry that it's too good to be true.

What brought them to COTA varies widely among them. One woman came thinking that since the priest is a single woman, it must be a progay church. But a guy in his twenties counters that on his first visit, "It was like sort of evangelical—like, it felt sort of Assembly of God–ish. I felt like, yeah, I can raise my hands and not feel like a freak." A married couple first visited for the "Dr. Seuss Liturgy"—a postmodern twist on the Book of Common Prayer—and another man came because it seemed like a church he could invite his friends to without being embarrassed. James, a guy in his early thirties, speaks next:

> I have the biggest risk in telling this story in that I'm openly gay. It was really important for me to find a place where I didn't necessarily have to be accepted for being gay – whatever gay means and how they look at me – but at least to be a part of the discussion and still feel welcome to be a part and not looked down on, like, "You're in but still on the outskirts." I'm not on the elder board, but since close to COTA's inception, I've been in so many types of leadership positions and roles, and I'm always challenged. I have the most amazing friendships here, and that's what keeps me.

Another guy grew up Southern Baptist, and his wife comes from the similarly conservative Missouri Synod Lutheran Church. Jerry, a mid-twenties software designer, converted to evangelicalism in college and then "jumped ship" and became a conservative Roman Catholic. "I was totally in line with absolutely every syllable or sneeze that came out of the Vatican," he says. "But

> "I have the most amazing friendships here, and that's what keeps me."

I discovered that that didn't make my Christian life simpler or happier or easier, and I started searching a lot after that. That's pretty much how I came here to COTA. I'm here to just kind of explore other ways of being Christian, I guess."

Surely, many of these folks have been burned by the church in the past. James and the Moody grads both have amends to make to one another, and they have a great sense of peace at being able to sit next to one another and to serve as leaders in this community. Here it's the liturgy that unites. Those who hold degrees from Moody Bible Institute (fundamentalist) and Seattle Pacific University (evangelical) are allowed to hold their final verdict on homosexuality in abeyance because the church's position on sexuality is not central to their identity, nor is Karen going to let either of her denominations thrust that issue to the forefront of her congregation. (For that matter, the gay members of the church are allowed to hold their opinions of the Moody and SPU grads in abeyance as well!)

But really, they wonder aloud, is this possible to sustain? How long until politics or gender issues or something else tears COTA apart? These are people who have obviously witnessed the tearing apart of many churches. And what's more, they live in the shadow of an eight hundred–pound gorilla: Mars Hill Fellowship, an emerging church pastored by the self-described "Bible-thumping fundamentalist" Mark Driscoll. Mark and Mars Hill come up in almost every conversation I have at COTA. Driscoll himself has distanced himself from "emergent" and claimed the title "emerging" for Mars Hill. He gets a lot of press, has a column in the Seattle newspaper, and has a rising profile nationwide.[19] But the very attributes of emergent Christianity—humility regarding interpretation, nonpropositional appreciation of truth—Driscoll rejects outright. He's not-so-subtly criticized Karen for replacing the proclamation of doctrine with finger painting. With Driscoll's three thousand–member megachurch claiming "emerging" status, the Cotans understandably wonder about the future of their emergent tribe.

The Cotans also worry about overload on the staff. Several paid staff members work a lot, paid in part by the beneficence of Trinity Church-Wall Street. What happens when that money runs out? Can the assortment of young adults pay for a church building and staff, not to mention realize their dreams of a brew pub and restaurant in the building? I sense that they ask these questions not so much because they're pessimistic but because they love COTA so much, and they're afraid that it might go away someday. If it does, many of them doubt they'd join another church.

When I ask what's the core of their loyalty, twenty-four-year-old Gary gives the credit to the Anglican liturgy. Unlike the conservative caricatures of Episcopal "liberalism," he says that the liturgy is founded on scripture but does not espouse one particular doctrinal viewpoint. "It provides a safe space for us to step into relationships with people who are different from us," he says. Every week, the creative team gathers to plan the worship around the liturgy, making a special effort to create open space for new people. "It's not an evangelistic moment where we're trying to get people to make a decision," Gary continues. "Rather we're trying to get people to know each other, and every new person at COTA necessarily changes the community and takes it in a different direction, I think."

The word *liturgy* comes from the Greek *leitourgia*, which literally translates to "work of the people." This probably comes as a surprise to some readers who think it would be more accurate to say that the liturgy is the "work of the priest" while the congregation just sits passively and listens. But a sign of emergence at COTA is that the liturgy is truly the glue that binds the community. At the end of our conversation, I ask what concrete practices make COTA what it is. "The liturgy" is the first response. "It initiates individuals into community—brings one context into another." There's a rhythm in COTA's liturgy, says someone else, that moves from communal singing into "open space" in which individuals get to "work out what's between them and God."

"But there will also be a communal dinner tonight," says Mary, "which is a natural outgrowth of the liturgy." Gary nods in agreement: "I think that a big part of what makes up COTA is that we're not just a church that meets once a week; we're a church outside of church. We have community and we have church with each other in smaller groups or bigger groups in a variety of settings, doing a variety of different things. And most of it's disorganized." But, he reiterates, for them it all flows outward from the liturgy.

TIME TO RETHINK SEMINARY

Around emergent Christians, you're just as likely to have a conversation about seminary as anything else. Since it's the professional training ground for pastors, it's easy to see why emergents—prone to rethink most things—are quick to question seminary education.

Modern seminaries were first instituted in the Roman Catholic Church as part of the Counter-Reformation of the sixteenth and seventeenth centuries. Protestant seminaries and divinity schools, however, are more beholden to the German and French university model of the eighteenth and nineteenth centuries. With the rise of science and empiricism, the modern university was founded as a center for the study of the sciences and the humanities. While theologians held university chairs at first, by the turn of the twentieth century, they were a vanishing commodity. Often the theologians crossed the street and founded a seminary, the religious equivalent of a university.

From an emergent perspective, two problems stand out with modern seminary education. The first is that there's nothing particularly theological about the structure of the seminary institution. Instead of reflecting some theological convictions or virtues, seminaries are entirely reflective of secular universities. The schools are run by presidents, provosts, and deans. Professors (stratified into adjunct, assistant, associate, and full) compete for tenure by writing abstruse monographs for their own guilds. And students are run through the gauntlet of papers, exams, and the compulsory—if marginalized—field education. At some seminaries—particularly those that share a name with a nearby institution—the desire of the administration to earn the respect of the university across the street is palpable.

Second, emergents are often troubled by the fact that most seminaries are residential. Thus prospective pastors are required to leave their communities of faith for three or four years to learn the theory and practice of parish ministry. To many emergent leaders, the sacrifice of one's rootedness in community for the temporary "community" of a residential seminary is too high a price.

So conversations have been taking place among emergents for several years now regarding the future of theological education and pastoral training. One model that consistently comes up is the monastic model. For centuries prior to the Council of Trent (1545–1563), clergy were trained in small communities bound together by a "rule of life." A rule is a set of practices by which the men in a monastery or the women in a convent order their lives. The most influential is the Rule of Saint Benedict, which has been guiding the lives of Benedictine monastics—both Catholic and Protestant—since the sixth century. Benedict's Rule prescribes everything in the day of a monastery, from prayer times to who should wash the dishes.

Theological education in a monastic setting is more like apprenticeship than like a traditional university education. While Catholic monastic communities are known for their scholarship, they also inculcate spiritual discipline—an especially valuable trait in a pastor. A combination of work, reading, silence, prayer, and teaching makes up the life of a monastic in community. As these conversations evolve, emergents will surely adapt these historical monastic practices to present situations, but it's already taking place in "new monastic communities" like Rutba House in Durham, North Carolina, The Simple Way in Philadelphia, and Communality in Lexington, Kentucky. In these places and others, Protestants and Catholics, married and single, have committed to life together, binding themselves with vows. How theological education will begin to take place in these communities remains to be seen, but it is inevitable.

MYCHURCH: A PAEAN TO SOLOMON'S PORCH

A couple of weeks ago, two of my friends from South Africa were in Minnesota for the weekend. They wanted to visit our church, Solomon's Porch. During the five o'clock worship gathering, Doug (the "pastor") invited Deon and Eugene to the center of the room. They sat on stools, and Doug asked them to talk a bit about what they do and why they were touring emergent churches in the United States. After a few minutes, Doug asked how Solomon's Porch could support them and pray for them.

Deon said that one of the things he's trying to do is buy bicycles for kids who live in townships. "One boy I know wants to go to art school," Deon told us, "but it's five miles each way, and he has to walk with art supplies. I'd love to get him a bike."

My wife, Julie, punched me in the arm. "Let's buy a bike."

"You mean, us?" I asked.

But as I was asking, she was pulling the stocking cap off her head. "Doug," she said above the crowd as people were gathering to lay hands on Deon and

Eugene and pray for them, "I'm going to pass my hat to raise money for a bike for that boy."

Doug looked at her quizzically. "You mean you're literally going to *pass a hat?*"

"Yeah," she said as she dropped in a twenty-dollar bill.

As the hat was going around, Julie leaned over and whispered to me, "A bicycle *is* childhood. I can just see that kid bumping down a dirt road with his feet sticking out and a smile on his face."

Meanwhile, I was thinking how truly odd this was. Never, I thought, have I been part of a church where *anyone* can stand up in the middle of a service and pass the hat for something. Julie would have gotten tossed out of some churches for that behavior, or at least received a reprimand that all fundraising efforts must be approved in triplicate by the missions committee—because if any old person with a pet project gets up and asks for money, the wheels will come off! Not to mention that it might adversely affect the weekly offering!

But no one—not even the pastor—batted an eye when Julie passed the hat. It seemed not a bit unusual. And ten minutes later, when the hat got back to Julie, the 150 or so people in the room had contributed $307. Deon told us that would buy bikes for two or three children. At the 7:00 gathering, no one had a hat, so they passed a cowboy boot. And they raised even more.

So two South African pastors went home with enough cash to buy half a dozen bicycles.

Some will call us naive: what if they spend the money on themselves, not the bikes? Where are the receipts for charitable giving? Who's to say that the neediest kids will get the help they need? Indeed, if the kids do get the bikes, who's going to make sure that they don't turn around and sell them for cash?

But we're all cynical enough to know that checks and balances do not really curb corruption all that much. If people want to misuse money, or other people, they will. The underlying assumption at Solomon's Porch on a night like this was trust: trust in one another at the Porch; trust in Deon and Eugene; trust in God's Spirit.

This is a paean, a love song to Solomon's Porch. It's not a perfect church, but it's a beautiful and messy church. It's a church in which my wife can pass a hat, Trucker Frank can interpret the Bible, and a person I've never met can hold out a loaf of communion bread, look me in the eyes, and say, "May the life of Jesus be within you."

I was a bit nervous when my parents first came with us to Solomon's Porch. They're in their mid-sixties and have spent their adult lives committed to the very mainline Congregational church that I once served as a youth pastor. That's a church of robes and red carpeting and a booming organ.

The Porch, in stark contrast, is a collection of fairly ragged people and even more ragged couches. We meet in a church owned by the local district of the United Methodist Church—there used to be five UMC churches in South Minneapolis, but there are now only two in operation, and those two will likely merge in the near future.

In the winter of 2006, we had been moved out of our second building when it was sold, and we were temporarily meeting in a small Presbyterian church. Doug, the pastor, was looking around Minneapolis for available meeting places when he heard about this building, the former Hobart Methodist Church—the congregation had disbanded about a year earlier. He was on a tour of the building with the caretaker when she asked him if there was anything he wanted to know about it.

"Well," Doug said, "we'll probably remove these pews since the way we meet doesn't really work with them."

"Oh, you can't remove the pews," she said to him without pause.

"We can't?" Doug was puzzled. "I didn't know that would be a problem."

"It's not a problem," she countered. "It can't be done. The pews can't be moved. They're part of the floor. They've been here since the church was built in 1933."

Doug saw his opening. "Do you have a screwdriver?"

She rounded one up, and six screws later, Doug was sliding a pew across the floor.

"Omigosh! I had no idea that pews could be moved."

This little story packs a powerful metaphor for so much of life at Solomon's Porch as person after person has a paradigm-shifting experience of "church as they didn't know it could be."

Hence my hesitancy at inviting my parents. I'd already had a few friends visit and tell me that the Porch was just "too weird" for them.

Dispatch 20: Emergents believe that church should
be just as beautiful and messy as life.

The worship gathering is scheduled to start at 5:00 P.M., but it usually starts to roll ten or fifteen minutes after that. That's when the music begins—music and words that are composed exclusively by members of the Solomon's Porch community. In other words, you won't hear any cover tunes or hymns at the Porch. Not only that, but the music you'll hear is executed with an authentic intensity that I've rarely heard in church. (The two main vocalists, Ben and Corey, are trained opera singers, adding to the intensity.) Deeply meaningful lyrics are paired with soaring melodies of the rock opera variety. Here's one of the most poignant songs, written by Corey Carlson.

> *God of Rage*
> Close the window now
> To the logic in your brain
> You've heard the stories told
> I know it sounds insane
> The anger he unfolds
> In the hallmarks of our faith
> Of flooded earth and burned-down cities
> A request to kill the son of Abraham
>
> What kind of god is this?
> He seems to have a vengeance and a rage.
> To find a truth that holds
> Is a pursuit of rarity
> A story that's not whole
> Can't be seen with clarity
> A god who creates man
> And a woman as his own

An image he has made
So he's a god who can be known
A god who loved so much
That he gave his son
To save the ones of Abraham.

He's a god of rage all right
Of raging compassion and thunder in his steps
Of raging hearts and a raging quest to win them
Of raging seas and miracles
He's a god of rage all right
Of a raging love that is never hidden.
Never hidden far
Though we seek as though it were

One scrapes through shallow faith
To find haze beyond the blur
You shout and plead for us
Through a storm of selfless grace
To cloud our skies with you
Block the lovers that we chase
We always chase too far
And forget the one
Whose only son we ran from.

He holds us in his eyes
As one would hold his bride
He's jealous of our desires
And he wants us to see
His tireless pursuit
His unending love
His unbridled, wild
Unrelenting attempts
To capture us
To bring us back to his arms.
He's a god of rage all right
Of raging compassion and thunder in his steps
Of raging hearts and a raging quest to win them

Of raging seas and miracles
He's a god of rage all right
Of a raging love that is never hidden.[20]

We sit on couches that are arranged in a roughly concentric fashion. The point of the interior design of couches, floor lamps, and coffee tables is twofold. First, it encourages conversation—those of us who've grown up in church have been socialized to respond to pew-sitting in a certain way: sit down and shut up; we stand and sit at the appropriate times, always facing forward; and we briefly and somewhat awkwardly break the forward-facing

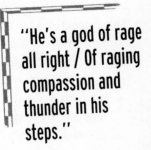

"He's a god of rage all right / Of raging compassion and thunder in his steps."

stance to welcome one another or pass the peace to those sitting around us (we may have to briefly acknowledge their existence again at the passing of the offering plate or the communion elements).

But we're socialized into an entirely different behavior when sitting on living room furniture: we know that we're expected to talk to one another, to look at one another, even to touch one another. As a result, you'll hear lots of conversation at the Porch, and you'll see lots of babies crawling over the laps of adults and teens.

And the reason for the concentric arrangement is to encourage the practice of openness and hospitality with one another. Whereas I grew up accustomed to looking at the backs of heads in church, wherever you sit at Solomon's Porch, you'll be looking into someone else's face. There's really no place to hide in the worship space (which we call the "living room").

If all of this seems a bit contrived, I can understand. Many people wonder why we call it a "living room" instead of a sanctuary, a "worship gathering" as opposed to a worship service, and a "holistic, missional, Christian community" rather than a church. Though it may seem faddish, it's actually a nod to a postmodern understanding of language. In that view, language doesn't just point to things; language *does* things. It makes things happen, particularly in the minds of those who are using the language. Language creates reality (as any politician who's buying advertising time will tell you). Words like *church* and *pew* conjure up thoughts for people that quickly translate into reality—a kind of self-fulfilling prophecy. So if we want to develop new mental frameworks for how we understand the relationships between God and human beings, we've got to find language that is unencumbered by much of the old baggage.

After a couple of songs, Michelle, a twenty-three-year-old artist, stands up and says, "Here at Solomon's Porch, we begin our worship gatherings with an invocation; that's a prayer that recognizes that God is in this place and involved with our lives, and it is a reflection of who we want to be as the people of God." The invocation is a call and response between a member of the community and the rest of the congregation, and it might be an ancient or traditional prayer or one that was written last week.

After another song, one of any number of elements is introduced, depending on the week. It might be a baby baptism or dedication; one week there was a wedding of a couple of street youth who attend the Porch (including bridesmaids that were dogs—and by that I mean canines); or some weeks there is a "body prayer" in which we're led to engage our bodies and our spirits in a posture of prayerfulness.[21] We've taken the pose of a parent cradling a baby to pray for AIDS orphans in Africa, and we've sheltered our heads with our arms to pray for people being bombed in Baghdad. Then we're asked to mingle with one another and offer a blessing, along the lines of "May the Spirit of God be visible in your life."

We're all called back together with another song, and the "sermon time" begins. Sitting on a stool in the middle of the community, Doug or another member of the Porch leads a combination of traditional sermon, reportage from the Tuesday night Bible discussion group, line-by-line explication of a chapter of the Bible, and discussion with the entire crowd. It can be disjointed, to be sure. The point is to jettison the magisterial sermon that has ruled over much of Protestantism for five hundred years. Here the sermon is deconstructed, turned on its head. The Bible is referred to as a "member of the community" with whom we are in conversation, and the communal interpretation of a text bubbles up from the life of the community.

That's not to say that it doesn't get ugly sometimes. Recently, we've had a spate of first-time visitors who've felt comfortable enough to stand up during the discussion time and challenge the faith of the stool-dweller and, by proxy, the entire community. "If we're just all 'figuring it out together,' how do we know what rock-solid foundations we can stand on?" begins a familiar line of questioning. That kind of question is dealt with head-on, sometimes by the preacher and at other times by someone on the next couch. One night a couple of years ago was particularly painful when a committed participant decided that sermon time would be a good time to announce that he and his family were leaving the church because it "wasn't meeting our spiritual needs." Like any church, the way that we as a community deal with these hiccups in the sermon discussion says a lot about who we are.

There's another song after the sermon, and then someone from the community gets up to introduce communion. A strange pastiche of traditions, communion at the Porch combines many elements including intinction (the communicant tears a piece from a loaf of bread and dips it in the cup), a common cup (shared by several persons), grape juice and wine, a loud party atmosphere, and an optional quiet meditation room. What's exceptionally rare among churches, however, is that this aspect of the worship is not guided by a clergyperson. In most Protestant and all Catholic churches, the sacrament of communion is considered the holiest part of the church's activity, so it is guarded by an ordained holy person. At the Porch, we too consider it holy, but we believe that the holiness resides not in the one who administers the sacrament but in the God who gifted it to us and in the community in which God's Spirit dwells.

As such, communion is introduced by a variety of persons—one week it will be with a poem, another week with a testimony about "what the Lord's Supper means to me," and another week with the traditional "Words of Institution" from the Book of Common Prayer ("On the night that the Lord Jesus was betrayed, he took bread and broke it and said..."). Together, we recite a short reading about the unity of the body and the purpose of communing, and then the party begins! While the band plays, people move about the room, serving one another bread and wine—adults, children, single, married, young, old, black, white. After about seven or eight minutes of this pandemonium, someone will shout, "May the life of Jesus be in you!" And we all respond, "And also in you!" Then, holding hands, we recite the blessing from Jude 24–25:

> Now to him who is able to keep you from falling and to present you before his glorious presence without fault and with great joy – to the only God our Savior be glory, majesty, power, and authority, through Jesus Christ our Lord, before all ages, now and forevermore! Amen.

We sit down again for announcements, and the kids then begin to fight over the leftover communion bread, since it's usually cinnamon raisin or chocolate chip or cheddar jalapeño sourdough. Announcements aren't an afterthought at the Porch, because we make a big deal of the fact that the Sunday evening gathering is only one of the many things we do as a community each week. So from artists' collaborations to men's breakfasts to women's retreats to pickup softball games, we meet throughout the week.

Finally, we stand and sing a doxology written by one of the musicians.

It's truly frustrating to attempt to put down on paper a weekly experience that is so beautiful and messy. Reading this chapter may be for you something like reading about a work of art. My hope is that it provokes in you the desire to experience the messy art of worship at the Porch. At worst, you're just as frustrated reading about it as I am writing about it.

But true worship of God is a messy endeavor. I make no bones about that. It's not meant to be done "decently and in order," but messily and with only a semblance of order, and with a great deal of joy.

P.S. We received photographs from Deon in South Africa about a month later, showing the kids with their bikes.

P.P.S. My parents loved it!

⋞ Epilogue:
Feral Christians ⋟

Across Australia, three hundred thousand feral camels roam the countryside. Arabian camels were brought to Australia in the 1890s to work in the gold mines, but by 1930, they'd been replaced by motorized vehicles. So the camels were abandoned, released into the wild, presumably to die. However, remarkably well-suited to the desert climate, the camels adapted quickly to the wilds of central Australia and have since reproduced with abundance.

Feral

Describing an animal that has left a domesticated state and returned to the wild. Alley cats and pigeons are two examples of feral animals.

Like other feral animals, the camels of Australia cannot be redomesticated. They live at the margins of civilization, stealing food from cattle and even behaving aggressively toward domesticated animals during times of drought. But after getting the food and water they need, they return to the desert.

And they're a nuisance. As reported by the Department of Agriculture of Western Australia, "The main problem caused by feral camels is destruction of fences. Camels pass through fences by leaning on them until they collapse, and will often demolish long lines of fence for no apparent reason."[1]

Emergent Christians, too, are pushing over fences and roaming around at the margins of the church in America. Once domesticated in conventional churches and traditional seminaries, more and more Christians are moving into the wilderness. They occasionally wander back, feeding off the structures and theologies of traditional Christianity, but they never stick around long.

Attempts to redomesticate them will fail.

They've gone feral.

⫷ APPENDICES ⫸

Albeit young, the emergent Christian movement has carved out a place at the table of twenty-first-century American Christianity. The following three documents represent some of the ferment around the emergent conversation in the last several years. Intriguingly, none has appeared in a published work before now; instead, each was posted on various Web sites and blogs. Here they are, in ink-on-paper, to preserve some of the early history of the emergent phenomenon.

APPENDIX A: "EMERGENT VILLAGE VALUES AND PRACTICES"

First posted on emergentvillage.org in 2001, and revised in 2006, these "Values and Practices" are an attempt to articulate the relational network that is Emergent Village. Primarily composed by Tim Keel, pastor of Jacob's Well in Kansas City and author of *Intuitive Leadership*,[1] they were vetted and edited by a couple dozen others within Emergent Village.

Members of Emergent Village hold in common four values and several practices that flow from them. In the language of a religious order, we call these four values our "order and rule":

1. COMMITMENT TO GOD IN THE WAY OF JESUS

We are committed to doing justice, loving kindness, and walking humbly with God. In the words of Jesus, we seek to live by the Great Commandment: loving God and loving our neighbors—including those who might be considered "the least of these" or enemies. We understand the gospel to be centered in Jesus and his message of the Kingdom of God, a message offering reconciliation with God, humanity, creation, and self.

We are committed to a "generous orthodoxy" in faith and practice—affirming the historic Christian faith and the biblical injunction to love one another even when we disagree. We embrace many historic spiritual practices, including prayer, meditation, contemplation, study, solitude, silence, service, and fellowship, believing that healthy theology cannot be separated from healthy spirituality.

Practices

As Christ-centered people, to understand the gospel in terms of Jesus' radical, profound, and expansive message of the Kingdom of God.

As people seeking to be formed spiritually in the way of Christ, to learn historic Christian spiritual practices (disciplines), and to use them for the development of character, integrity, and virtue which flow from true communion with God.

As participants in the historic Christian faith, to be humble learners, to stimulate learning in others, and to give priority to love over knowledge, while still valuing knowledge.

As lovers of God and God's truth, to seek wisdom and understanding, which are the true goal of theology, and to engage in respectful, thoughtful, sacred conversation about God, world, and church.

2. COMMITMENT TO THE CHURCH IN ALL ITS FORMS

We are committed to honor and serve the church in all its forms—Orthodox, Roman Catholic, Protestant, Pentecostal, Anabaptist. We practice "deep ecclesiology"—rather than favoring some forms of the church and critiquing or rejecting others, we see that every form of the church has both weaknesses and strengths, both liabilities and potential.

We believe the rampant injustice and sin in our world requires the sincere, collaborative, and whole-hearted response of all Christians in all denominations, from the most historic and hierarchical, through the mid-range of local and congregational churches, to the most spontaneous and informal expressions. We affirm both the value of strengthening, renewing, and transitioning existing churches and organizations, and the need for planting, resourcing, and coaching new ones of many kinds.

We seek to be irenic and inclusive of all our Christian sisters and brothers, rather than elitist and critical. We own the many failures of the church as our failures, which humbles us and calls us to repentance, and we also celebrate the many heroes and virtues of the church, which inspires us and gives us hope.

Practices

To be actively and positively involved in a local congregation, while maintaining open definitions of "church" and "congregation." We work in and with churches, seeking to live out authentic Christian faith in authentic Christian community.

To seek peace among followers of Christ, and to offer critique only prayerfully and when necessary, with grace, and without judgment, avoiding rash statements, and repenting when harsh statements are made. To speak positively of fellow Christians whenever possible, especially those with whom we may disagree.

To build sincere friendship with Christians from other traditions.

3. COMMITMENT TO GOD'S WORLD

We practice our faith missionally—that is, we do not isolate ourselves from this world, but rather, we follow Christ into the world.

We seek to fulfill the mission of God in our generations, and then to pass the baton faithfully to the next generations as well.

We believe the church exists for the benefit and blessing of the world at large; we seek therefore not to be blessed to the exclusion of everyone else, but rather for the benefit of everyone else.

We see the earth and all it contains as God's beloved creation, and so we join God in seeking its good, its healing, and its blessing.

Practices

To build relationships with neighbors and to seek the good of our neighborhoods and cities.

To seek reconciliation with enemies and make peace.

To encourage and cherish younger people and to honor and learn from older people.

To honor creation and to cherish and heal it.

To build friendships across gender, racial, ethnic, economic and other boundaries.

To be involved at all times in at least one issue or cause of peace and justice.

4. COMMITMENT TO ONE ANOTHER

In order to strengthen our shared faith and resolve, and in order to encourage and learn from one another in our diversity through respectful, sacred conversation, we value time and interaction with other friends who share this rule and its practices.

We identify ourselves as members of this growing, global, generative, and non-exclusive friendship.

We welcome others into this friendship as well.

We bring whatever resources we can to enrich this shared faith and resolve.

Practices

To make an annual pilgrimage to an Emergent Village gathering; to give one another the gift of our presence at annual gatherings whenever possible.

To publicly self-identify with Emergent Village where appropriate and to represent Emergent Village well whenever we can; to exemplify the best of what Emergent Village strives to be and do.

To invite others to participate and welcome new participants.

To seek to be positive and constructive in caring for the Emergent Village friendship. To find some specific ways we can help the circle of friends in Emergent Village.

To stay reconciled to one another. To give one another the gift of commitment not to give up on, betray, or reject one another, but instead, to encourage, honor, and care for one another.

To stay informed about emergent locally and globally via the website and email updates.

ACTION

We live out the four values of our rule through four lines of action:

1. We explore and develop ideas, theology, practices, and connections ... through conversations, conferences, think-tanks, gatherings, retreats, publications, learning cohorts, online resources, and other means.

2. We resource individuals, leaders, and organizations—funding their imaginations, stimulating their thinking, providing examples, events, literature, and other resources to assist them in their lives and mission.

3. We communicate our calling, vision, learning, and activities to the growing Emergent Village community, and to other interested people around the world.

4. We provide ways for people to belong, identify with, and participate in this community, conversation, and mission at varying levels. We encourage the development of generative friendships, collaborations, and partnerships.

APPENDIX B: "A RESPONSE TO OUR CRITICS"

In 2005, criticism of emergent Christian leaders was increasing. The blogosphere hosted many critics, and the first book-length critique appeared, D. A. Carson's *Becoming Conversant with the Emerging Church*. Caricatures and misrepresentations abounded, so seven of us wrote a response to these criticisms. It was authored primarily by Brian McLaren—the target of the most vitriolic denouncements—and edited by the rest of us. It was published online in June, 2005.

RESPONSE TO RECENT CRITICISMS

By Tony Jones, Doug Pagitt, Spencer Burke, Brian McLaren, Dan Kimball, Andrew Jones, and Chris Seay

We continue to be amazed by the enthusiastic interest in the work of Emergent, a conversation and friendship of which we are a small part. This conversation is bringing together a wide range of committed Christians and those exploring the Christian faith in wonderful ways, and many of us sense that God is at work among us. As would be expected, there have also been criticisms. A number of people have asked us to respond to these criticisms. These ten brief responses will, we hope, serve to clarify our position and suggest ways for the conversation to continue constructively for participants and critics alike. It is our hope and prayer that even our disagreements can bring us together in respectful dialogue as Christians, resulting in growth for all concerned.

First, we wish to say thanks to our critics for their honest feedback on our books, articles, speeches, blogs, events, and churches. We readily acknowledge that like all human endeavors, our work, even at its best, is still flawed and partial, and at its worst, deserves critique. We are grateful to those who help us see things we may not have seen without the benefit of their perspective. We welcome their input.

Second, we have much to learn from every criticism—whether it is fair or unfair, kindly or unkindly articulated. We pray for the humility to receive all critique with thoughtful consideration. Where we think we have been unfairly treated, we hope not to react defensively or to respond in kind, and where we have been helpfully corrected, we will move forward with gratitude to our critics for their instruction and correction. We especially thank those who seek to help us through cordial, respectful, face-to-face, brotherly/sisterly dialogue. As we have always said, we hope to stimulate constructive conversation, which involves point and counterpoint, honest speaking and open-minded listening. As a sign of good faith in this regard, we have invited and included the voices of our critics in some of our books, and as far as we know, have always treated these conversation partners with respect.[2] We have also attempted to make personal contact with our critics for Christian dialogue. Even though most of these invitations have not been accepted, we hope that the friendly gesture is appreciated.

Third, we regretfully acknowledge that in our thought, writing, and speech, we have at times been less charitable or wise than we wish we would have been. Whenever possible we will seek to correct past errors in future editions of our books; when that is impossible, we will make other forms of public correction.

Fourth, we respect the desire and responsibility of our critics to warn those under their care about ideas that they consider wrong or dangerous, and to keep clear boundaries to declare who is "in" and "out" of their circles. These boundary-keepers have an important role which we understand and respect. If one of your trusted spiritual leaders has criticized our work, we encourage you, in respect for their leadership, not to buy or read our work, but rather to ignore it and consider it unworthy of further consideration. We would only ask, if you accept our critics' evaluation of our work, that in fairness you abstain from adding your critique to theirs unless you have actually read our books, heard us speak, and engaged with us in dialogue for yourself. Second-hand critique can easily become a kind of gossip that drifts from the truth and causes needless division.

Fifth, because most of us write as local church practitioners rather than professional scholars, and because the professional scholars who criticize our work may find it hard to be convinced by people outside their guild, we feel it wisest at this juncture to ask those in the academy to respond to their peers about our work. We hope to generate fruitful conversations at several levels, including both the academic and ecclesial realms. If few in the academy come to our defense in the coming years, then we will have more reason to believe we are mistaken in our thinking and that our critics are correct in their unchallenged analyses.[3]

Sixth, we would like to clarify, contrary to statements and inferences made by some, that yes, we truly believe there is such a thing as truth and truth matters—if we did not believe this, we would have no good reason to write or speak; no, we are not moral or epistemological relativists any more than anyone or any community is who takes hermeneutical positions—we believe that radical relativism is absurd and dangerous, as is arrogant absolutism; yes, we affirm the historic Trinitarian Christian faith and the ancient creeds, and seek to learn from *all* of church history—and we honor the church's great teachers and leaders from East and West, North and South; yes, we believe that Jesus is the crucified and risen Savior of the cosmos and no one comes to the Father except through Jesus; no, we do not pit reason against experience but seek to use all our God-given faculties to love and serve God and our neighbors; no, we do not endorse false dichotomies—and we regret any false dichotomies unintentionally made by or about us (even in this paragraph!); and yes, we affirm that we love, have confidence in, seek to obey, and strive accurately to teach the sacred scriptures, because our greatest desire is to be followers and servants of the Word of God, Jesus Christ. We regret that we have either been unclear or misinterpreted in these and other areas.

But we also acknowledge that we each find great joy and promise in dialogue and conversation, even about the items noted in the previous paragraph. Throughout the history of the church, followers of Jesus have come to know what they believe and how they believe it by being open to the honest critique and varied perspectives of others. We are radically open to the possibility that our hermeneutic stance will be greatly enriched in conversation with others. In other words, we value dialogue very highly, and we are convinced that open and generous dialogue—rather than chilling criticism and censorship—offers the greatest hope for the future of the church in the world.

We regret that some of our critics have made hasty generalizations and drawn erroneous conclusions based on limited and selective data. We would welcome future critics to converse with us directly and to visit our churches as part of their research. Of course, they would find weaknesses among us, as they would among any group of Christians, including their own. But we believe that they would also find much to celebrate and find many of their suspicions relieved when they see our high regard for the scriptures, for truth, for worship, for evangelism, for spiritual formation, and for our fellow Christians—including our critics themselves.

Seventh, we have repeatedly affirmed, contrary to what some have said, that there is no single theologian or spokesperson for the emergent conversation. We each speak for ourselves and are not official representatives of anyone else, nor do we necessarily endorse everything said or written by one another. We have repeatedly defined emergent as a conversation and friendship, and neither implies unanimity—nor even necessarily consensus—of opinion. We ask our critics to remember that we cannot be held responsible for everything said and done by people using the terms "emergent" or "emerging church," any more than our critics would like to be held responsible for everything said or done by those claiming to be "evangelical" or "born again." Nobody who is a friend or acquaintance of ours, or who agrees with one of us in some points, should be assumed to agree with any of us on all points. Nobody should be held "guilty by association" for reading or conversing with us. Also, contrary to some uninformed reports, this conversation is increasingly global and cross-cultural, and because North Americans are only a small part of it, we urge people to avoid underestimating the importance of Latin American, African, Asian, European, and First Nations voices among us.

Eighth, we are aware that there is some debate about whether we should be considered *evangelical*. This is a cherished part of our heritage, but we understand that some people define this term more narrowly than we and in such a way that it applies to them but not to us. We will not quarrel over this term, and we will continue to love and respect evangelical Christians whether or not we are accepted by them as *evangelicals* ourselves. However others include or exclude us, we will continue to affirm an evangelical spirit and faith by cultivating a wholehearted devotion to Christ and his gospel, by seeking to join in the mission of God in our time, by calling people to follow God in the way of Jesus, and by doing so in an irenic spirit of love for all our brothers and sisters.

(We hope that those who would like to disassociate us from the term *evangelical* will be aware of the tendency of some in their ranks toward narrowing and politicizing the term so that it only applies to strict Calvinists, conservative Republicans, people with specific views on U.S. domestic, foreign, military, or economic policy, single-issue voters, or some other subgroup. We pose no threat to these sincere people, nor do we wish to attack or discredit anyone, even though we do not wish to constrict our circle of fellowship to the parameters they propose.)

Ninth, we felt we should offer this encouragement to those who, like us, do not feel capable of living or explaining our faith in ways that would please all of our critics: if our work has been helpful to you, please join us in seeking to preserve the unity of the Spirit in the bond of peace by not becoming quarrelsome or defensive or disrespectful to anyone—especially those who you feel have misrepresented or misunderstood you or us. As Paul said to Timothy, "The Lord's servant must not be quarrelsome but must be kind to everyone, able to teach, patient when wronged." In addition he warned Timothy not to develop "an unhealthy interest in controversies and quarrels about words that result in envy, strife, malicious talk, evil suspicions, and constant friction." The Apostle James also wrote, "the wisdom that comes from heaven is first of all pure; then peace-loving, considerate, submissive, full of mercy and good fruit, impartial and sincere. Peacemakers who sow in peace reap a harvest of righteousness." We believe it is better to be wronged than to wrong someone else; the Lord we follow was gentle and meek, and when he was reviled, he didn't respond in kind.

Instead of engaging in fruitless quarrels with our critics, we urge those who find our work helpful to pursue spiritual formation in the way of Christ, to worship God in spirit and truth, to seek to plant or serve in healthy and fruitful churches, to make disciples—especially among the irreligious and unchurched, to serve those in need, to be at peace with everyone as far as is possible, and to show a special concern for orphans and widows in their distress. We should keep careful control of our tongues (and pens or keyboards), and seek to be pure in heart and life, since this is "religion that God our Father accepts as pure and faultless."

With millions suffering from hunger, disease, and injustice around the world, we hope that all of us—including our critics—can renew our commitment to "remember the poor" (Galatians 2:10) rather than invest excessive energy in "controversies about words." "They will know you are my disciples," Jesus said, not by our excessive disputation, but by our love. Words and ideas are essential, for they often set the course for thought and action, and constructive dialogue is needed and worthwhile, but we cannot let less productive internal debates preoccupy us at the expense of caring for those in need.

Tenth, we should say that along with a few critiques, we are receiving many grateful and affirming responses to our work. Respected theologians and other leaders have told us, either in private or in public, that they are grateful for the emergent conversation and that they stand with us and support us. We are frequently told that people sense God graciously at work in the emergent community. We hope that those who see problems will not overlook the signs of God's presence and activity among us, just as we do not overlook our many faults, including those pointed out by our critics. Only time will tell what the full outcome will be, but in the meantime, we welcome the prayers of both friends and critics.

We must once more thank both our critics and those who affirm our work, because we know that both are trying to help us in their respective ways, and both are trying to do the right thing before God—as we are. At the risk of redundancy, let us state once again that we welcome conversation with all who desire sincere and civil engagement over ideas that matter.

If you would like to be involved in the emergent conversation and friendship, we warmly invite you to visit emergentvillage.com. And feel free to pass this response on to others for whom it may be helpful.

APPENDIX C: "DISASTROUS STATEMENTS"

For some time, pressure has been mounting on the leaders of the emergent movement to make some definitive statements about what we believe. Where do they stand on the ordination of gays? What's their position on the inerrancy of scripture? What do they believe about the doctrine of hell? But within emergent Christianity, there's been a reticence to make statements. Although statements of doctrine and affirmations of ideological positions abound on church and denominational Web sites, it seems to many emergent leaders a modern enterprise, especially when these statements serve a "gatekeeper" function, determining who is saved, who can be a member of a church, or who can be part of a conversation. The feeling among emergent Christians is that these determinations are best left to God alone. Thus, theologian LeRon Shults,[1] penned the following anti-statement of faith (irony noted), which was posted on the Emergent Village website in May, 2006.

DOCTRINAL STATEMENT(?)

The coordinators of Emergent have often been asked (usually by their critics) to proffer a doctrinal statement that lays out clearly what they believe. I am merely a participant in the conversation who delights in the ongoing reformation that occurs as we bring the gospel into engagement with culture in ever new ways. But I have been asked to respond to this ongoing demand for clarity and closure. I believe there are several reasons why Emergent should not have a "statement of faith" to which its members are asked (or required) to subscribe. Such a move would be unnecessary, inappropriate, and disastrous.

Why is such a move unnecessary? Jesus did not have a "statement of faith." He called others into faithful relation to God through life in the Spirit. As with the prophets of the Hebrew Bible, he was not concerned primarily with whether individuals gave cognitive assent to abstract propositions but with calling persons into trustworthy community through embodied and concrete acts of faithfulness. The writers of the New Testament were not obsessed with finding a final set of propositions the assent to which marks off true believers. Paul, Luke, and John all talked much more about the mission to which we should commit ourselves than they did about the propositions to which we should assent. The very idea of a "statement of faith" is mired in modernist assumptions and driven by modernist anxieties—and this brings us to the next point.

Such a move would be inappropriate. Various communities throughout church history have often developed new creeds and confessions in order to express the gospel in their cultural context, but the early modern use of linguistic formulations as "statements" that allegedly capture the truth about God with certainty for all cultures and contexts is deeply problematic for at least two reasons. First, such an approach presupposes a (Platonic or Cartesian) representationalist view of language, which has been undermined in late modernity by a variety of disciplines across the social and physical sciences (e.g., sociolinguistics and paleo-biology). Why would Emergent want to force the new wine of the Spirit's powerful transformation of communities into old modernist wineskins? Second, and more important from a theological perspective, this fixation with propositions can easily lead to the attempt to use the finite tool of language on an absolute Presence that transcends and embraces all finite reality. Languages are culturally constructed symbol systems that enable humans to communicate by designating one finite reality in distinction from another. The truly infinite God of Christian faith is beyond all our linguistic grasping, as all the great theologians from Irenaeus to Calvin have insisted, and so the struggle to capture God in our finite propositional structures is nothing short of linguistic idolatry.

Why would it be disastrous? Emergent aims to facilitate a conversation among persons committed to living out faithfully the call to participate in the reconciling mission of the biblical God. Whether it appears in the by-laws of a congregation or in the catalog of an educational institution, a "statement of faith" tends to stop conversation. Such statements can also easily become tools for manipulating or excluding people from the community. Too often they create an environment in which real conversation is avoided out of fear that critical reflection on one or more of the sacred propositions will lead to excommunication from the community. Emergent seeks to provide a milieu in which others are welcomed to join in the pursuit of life "in" the One who *is true* (1 John 5:20). Giving into the pressure to petrify the conversation in a "statement" would make Emergent easier to control; its critics could dissect it and then place it in a theological museum alongside other dead conceptual specimens the curators find opprobrious. But living, moving things do not belong in museums. Whatever else Emergent may be, it is a *movement* committed to encouraging the *lively* pursuit of God and to inviting others into a delightfully terrifying conversation along the way.

This does not mean, as some critics will assume, that Emergent does not care about belief or that there is no role at all for propositions. Any good conversation includes propositions, but they should serve the process of inquiry rather than shut it down. Emergent is *dynamic* rather than *static*, which means that its ongoing intentionality is (and may it ever be) shaped less by an anxiety about finalizing *state*-ments than it is by an eager attention to the *dynamism* of the Spirit's disturbing and comforting presence, which is always reforming us by calling us into an ever-intensifying participation in the Son's welcoming of others into the faithful embrace of God.

NOTES

CHAPTER ONE: Leaving the Old Country

1 Baylor Institute for Studies of Religion, *American Piety in the 21st Century: New Insights to the Depth and Complexity of Religion in the U.S.: Selected Findings from the Baylor Religion Survey* (Waco, Tex.: Baylor University, 2006), p. 8.

2 Federal Communications Commission, "Trends in Telephone Service: Industry Analysis and Technology Division Wireline Competition Bureau" (Washington, D.C.: FCC, Feb. 2007), pp. 7–11.

3 George Barna, *Revolution: Finding Vibrant Faith Beyond the Walls of the Sanctuary* (Carol Stream, Ill.: Tyndale, 2006).

4 Wikipedia lists one hundred different variations of Baptist, including some exotic flavors that you've probably never heard of before, like Sixth Principle Baptists and the New Testament Association of Independent Baptist Churches.

5 A great deal of research has been done on bureaucracies, resulting in "laws" like the Peter Principle, which states that employees in a bureaucracy will rise only to the level of their highest competence; the Abilene Paradox, which states that groups will decide on a course of action, even though the consensus of individuals in the group is for another course; and Parkinson's Law that work will expand to fill the time available. Each of these criticisms can be levied at modern denominations.

6 Patricia Mei Yin Chang, "Pulpit Supply: A Clergy Shortage?" *Christian Century*, Nov. 29, 2003, pp. 28–32. Seventy-one percent of American congregations have less than one hundred active adult members.

7 Lewis Center for Church Leadership, *Clergy Age Trends in the United Methodist Church, 1985–2005* (Washington, D.C.: Wesley Theological Seminary, 2006).

8 The Southern Baptist Convention, for instance, was founded as an association of proslavery churches. In 1995, the SBC apologized for its complicity with slavery.

9 Albert Schweitzer, *The Quest of the Historical Jesus* (London: Adam & Charles Black, 1954), pp. 370–371. Here's the whole paragraph:

> There is silence all around. The Baptist appears, and cries: "Repent, for the Kingdom of Heaven is at hand." Soon after that comes Jesus, and in the knowledge that He is the coming Son of Man lays hold of the wheel of the world to set it moving on that last revolution which is to bring all ordinary history to a close. It refuses to turn, and He throws Himself upon it. Then it does turn; and crushes Him. Instead of bringing in the eschatological conditions, He has destroyed them. The wheel rolls onward, and the mangled body of the one immeasurably great Man, who was strong enough to think of Himself as the spiritual ruler of mankind and to bend history to His purpose, is hanging upon it still. That is His victory and His reign.

10 California also witnessed a Pentecostal revival, but what started in 1906 on Azusa Street in Los Angeles took three-quarters of a century to truly infect all American evangelicals.

11 The one exception is the Partial Birth Abortion Ban Act of 2003, which affects 0.17 percent of the annual abortions in the United States.

12 I happen to agree with the rocker Ted Nugent, who thinks that every meat-eating American should have to kill and clean one chicken a year in order to be more appreciative of the food we eat.

13 See Christian Smith, *American Evangelicalism: Embattled and Thriving* (Chicago: University of Chicago, 1998), and Michael Emerson and Christian Smith, *Divided by Faith: Evangelical Religion and the Problem of Race in America* (New York: Oxford University Press, 2001).

14 You can find out more about Celestin and his African Leadership and Reconciliation Ministries at http://www.alarm-inc.org.

15 For more on this, see Nancey Murphy, *Beyond Fundamentalism and Liberalism: How Modern and Postmodern Philosophy Set the Theological Agenda* (Philadelphia: Trinity Press International, 1996).

16 Jonathan Klein, quoted in Bill Carter, "CNN Will Cancel 'Crossfire' and Cut Ties to Commentator," *New York Times*, Jan. 6, 2005.

17 Anthony Smith, "If I Could Pray to St. Martin . . . MLK Day," Jan. 15, 2007, http://postmodernegro.wordpress.com/2007/01/15/if-i-could-pray-to-st-martinmlk-day.

18 Anthony Smith, Feb. 3, 2007, http://postmodernegro.wordpress.com/2007/02/03.

19 The tongue-in-cheek article begins, " 'Crazy white people' are the words Curtis Glover used to sum up his experience at Spirit Depot, a church touting itself as 'a postmodern expression of Jesus apprentices' in Westchester, New York." *Holy Observer*, "Frightened Black Family Flees Emergent Church," May 2007, http://www.holyobserver.com/detail.php? isu=v02i08&art=black.

20 Anthony Smith, "Practicing Pentecost: Discovering the Kingdom of God amid Racial Fragmentation," in Doug Pagitt and Tony Jones, eds., *An Emergent Manifesto of Hope* (Grand Rapids, Mich.: Baker, 2007), pp. 279–290.

CHAPTER TWO: Dispatches from the Frontier of the American Church

1 Jean François Lyotard, *The Postmodern Condition: A Report on Knowledge, Theory, and History of Literature*, Vol. 10 (Minneapolis: University of Minnesota Press, 1984), p. xxiv.

2 "With the post–World War II decentering of Europe, the dwarfing of European populations, the demystifying of European cultural hegemony, the deconscruction of European philosophical systems, and, most important, the decolonization of the Third World, I came of age during the eclipse of one epoch and the emergence of another." Cornel West, *The Cornel West Reader* (New York: Basic Books, 1999), p. 4.

3 Jürgen Moltmann, *The Crucified God: The Cross of Christ as the Foundation and Criticism of Christian Theology* (Minneapolis, Minn.: Fortress, 1993), p. xi.

4 I am indebted to my friend Richard Osmer for this taxonomy. See Richard Osmer and Freidrich Schweitzer, *Religious Education Between Modernization and Globalization* (Grand Rapids, Mich.: Eerdmans, 2003), pp. 31ff.

5 For a sociologist's admission that he was "essentially wrong" about secularization, see Peter Berger, ed., *The Desecularization of the World: Resurgent Religion and World Politics* (Grand Rapids, Mich.: Eerdmans, 1999).

6 Tony Jones, "Introduction: Friendship, Faith, and Going Somewhere Together," in Doug Pagitt and Tony Jones, eds., *An Emergent Manifesto of Hope:* (Grand Rapids: Baker, 2007), p. 14.

7 Stanley J. Grenz and John R. Franke, *Beyond Foundationalism: Shaping Theology in a Postmodern Context* (Louisville, Ky.: Westminster/John Knox, 2001).

8 A hot topic in evangelical theology since the late 1990s, open theism posits that God is somehow bound to time and the future is unknowable, even to God. While this view allows human beings robust free will, it contradicts the classical view that God is immutable and impassible.

9 See Mike King, *Presence-Centered Youth Ministry* (Carol Stream, Ill.: InterVarsity Press, 2006), and Chris Folmsbee, *A New Kind of Youth Ministry* (El Cajon, Calif.: Youth Specialties, 2006). See also my own *Postmodern Youth Ministry* (El Cajon, Calif.: Youth Specialties, 2001) and *Soul Shaper* (El Cajon, Calif.: Youth Specialties, 2003).

10 He's referred to as "the Cussing Pastor" by Don Miller in his best-seller, *Blue like Jazz: Nonreligious Thoughts on Christian Spirituality* (Nashville, Tenn.: Nelson, 2003), p. 134.

11 Brian D. McLaren, *A New Kind of Christian: A Tale of Two Friends on a Spiritual Journey* (San Francisco: Jossey-Bass, 2001).

12 Ibid., pp. 12, 13.

13 Ibid., p. 52.

14 Ibid., p. 66. This comment by Neo provokes Pastor Dan to shout, "Damn you!" and that salty language got *A New Kind of Christian* temporarily banned from LifeWay, the bookstores of the Southern Baptist Convention.

15 Ibid., p. 92.

16 Ibid., p. 109.

17 Brian D. McLaren, *The Story We Find Ourselves In* (San Francisco: Jossey-Bass, 2003) and *The Last Word and the Word After That* (San Francisco: Jossey-Bass, 2005).

18 See, for instance, D. A. Carson, *Becoming Conversant with the Emerging Church: Understanding a Movement and Its Implications* (Grand Rapids, Mich.: Zondervan, 2005); R. Scott Smith, *Truth and the New Kind of Christian: The Emerging Effects of Postmodernism in the Church* (Wheaton, Ill.: Crossway Books, 2005); and John MacArthur, *The Truth War: Fighting for Certainty in an Age of Deception* (Nashville, Tenn.: Nelson, 2007).

19 Brian D. McLaren, *A Generous Orthodoxy* (Grand Rapids, Mich.: Zondervan, 2004).

20 Quoted in Peter J. Walker with Tyler Clark, "Missing the Point? The Absolute Truth Behind Postmodernism, Emergent, and the Emerging Church," *Relevant Magazine*, July-August 2006, p. 73.

21 You can experience their labyrinth digitally at http://www.labyrinth.org.uk.

22 Jonny Baker and Doug Gay, *Alternative Worship: Resources from and for the Emerging Church* (Grand Rapids, Mich.: Baker, 2004).

23 Rowan Williams, "Foreword," in *Mission Shaped Church: Church Planting and Fresh Expressions of Church in a Changing Context* (London: Church House, 2004), p. vii.

24 Visit their Web site at http://www.freshworship.org.

25 The Vineyard movement is an association of charismatic evangelical churches that began in 1982 under the leadership of John Wimber. A spinoff of the more conservative Calvary Chapel, the Vineyard emphasizes church planting and the activity of the Holy Spirit and of spiritual gifts bestowed upon believers. There are about 850 Vineyard churches worldwide.

26 Information is available at http://www.lareddelcamino.net/home/index.php?lang=eng.

27 For details, go to http://www.amahoro-africa.org.

28 The Web site is http://www.emerging.dk.

29 Eddie Gibbs and Ryan Bolger, *Emerging Churches: Creating Christian Community in Postmodern Cultures* (Grand Rapids, Mich.: Baker, 2006), p. 44.

30 Scot McKnight, "Bloglossary," *Jesus Creed*, Nov. 1, 2006, http://www.jesuscreed.org/?p=1691.

31 Quoted in Kirk Webb and Heather Webb, "Calling, Postmodernism, and Chastened Liberals: A Conversation with Os Guinness," *Mars Hill Review*, Summer 1997, pp. 69–87.

32 You think I'm kidding? Check out http://www.servantevangelism.com/matrix/public.htm#urinal.

33 That's not to say that one can't be "infected with the virus" and stay connected to a larger system. Recently, several online groups (Presbymergent, UMergent, and Anglimergent) have sprung up to explore the possibilities of bringing emergent thinking to bear on the legacy denominations.

34 This was no ordinary "Web guy." It was Tim Bednar, the founder of e-church.com and the author of an influential underground white paper titled "We Know More Than Our Pastors." He developed the Emergent Village Web site (http://emergentvillage.org).

35 Daniel Henderson, "A Life of Lasting Influence: Keys to a Fruitful Life," preached at Grace Church, Eden Prairie, Minnesota, Nov. 5, 2006, http://www.atgrace.com/_l/swf/grace-audio.swf?name=110506.

36 The writer is referring to the "Beatitudes" portion of Jesus' Sermon on the Mount, in which he says, "Blessed are those who are persecuted for righteousness' sake, for theirs is the kingdom of heaven. Blessed are you when others revile you and persecute you and utter all kinds of evil against you falsely on my account. Rejoice and be glad, for your reward is great in heaven, for so they persecuted the prophets who were before you" (Matthew 5:10–12).

CHAPTER THREE: Who Are the Emergent Christians?

1 A total of 2,020 surveys were completed and returned from the eight congregations. The mean age of all worshipers aged fifteen and older was 32.5. Being that these surveys come from eight handpicked congregations, the results are not generalizable across all emergent congregations. My research on these emergent congregations will be published in a more comprehensive fashion in a forthcoming book.

2 Cynthia Woolever and Deborah Bruce, *A Field Guide to U.S. Congregations: Who's Going Where and Why* (Louisville, Ky.: Westminster/John Knox, 2002), p. 13. Woolever and Bruce also note that the average American (aged fifteen and above) is forty-four.

3 Of the emergent congregations I surveyed, ninety-two percent of congregants were white on the Sunday in question. As to education, thirty-eight percent report a college degree as their highest level of education, seventeen percent hold a master's degree, and five percent have completed a Ph.D.

4 Miroslav Volf, *Exclusion and Embrace: A Theological Exploration of Identity, Openness, and Reconciliation* (Nashville, Tenn.: Abingdon Press, 1996).

5 Nineteen percent of Americans have read one or more of the books in the Left Behind series. Just over one percent have read Jim Wallis's *God's Politics*. Baylor Institute, *American Piety*, p. 19.

6 David Neff, "Testing a New Relationship," *Christianity Today*, June 2007, p. 8.

7 He's even hedged on whether his wife, an Anglican who "knows Jesus," is going to heaven. "There is no salvation for those outside the Church . . . , I believe it. . . . Put it this way. My wife is a saint. She's a much better person than I am. Honestly. She's, like, Episcopalian, Church of England. She prays,

she believes in God, she knows Jesus, she believes in that stuff. And it's just not fair if she doesn't make it, she's better than I am. But that is a pronouncement from the chair. I go with it." Jeanette Walls with Ashley Pearson, "Mel Gibson Says His Wife Could Be Going to Hell," MSNBC, Feb. 10, 2004, http://www.msnbc.msn.com/id/4224452.

8 In the Sermon on the Mount, Jesus preaches to his followers, "You are the salt of the earth. But if the salt loses its saltiness, how can it be made salty again? It is no longer good for anything, except to be thrown out and trampled underfoot" (Matthew 5:13). This is most often interpreted to mean that Jesus' followers are to be a preservative in the world, as salt was in Jesus' day.

9 Frederica Mathewes-Green, "Trinity and Transformation," paper presented at the Washington Arts Group Convocation, Washington, D.C., May 18, 2007.

10 A long and sophisticated theological debate has taken place around this very point. At the University of Chicago, the "Correlational School" of David Tracy and others has argued that culture asks the questions and theology is to provide the answers. Others have retorted that theology should set the agenda, not follow the agenda of culture. The best (postfoundationalist) response to these two poles comes from J. Wentzel van Huyssteen in *The Shaping of Rationality* (Grand Rapids, Mich.: Eerdmans, 1999), in which he proposes a method of "transversal rationality" that looks for the natural connections between theological reasoning and other rationalities and then promotes robust dialogue at those points of connection.

11 There are, of course, many brands of conservative Christian theology. This pastor's brand is called, alternatively, "Calvinism" or "Reformed." Tracing its roots to reformer John Calvin of sixteenth-century Geneva, Calvinism emphasizes God's sovereignty over all contingencies of history and also preaches the "total depravity," or complete sinfulness, of human beings.

12 Some definitions: the atonement is the Christian doctrine that attempts to explain how Jesus' death on the cross amends for human sin and reconciles human beings to God. This pastor's understanding of the atonement is called penal substitution or propitiation, which is the theory that God's hatred of human sin was imputed to Jesus Christ, who then atoned for that sin with his death. Theologians call it a "forensic theory" since its evolution was concomitant with the development of the Western legal mind. The theory, based primarily on Paul's letter to the Romans and the anonymous letter to the Hebrews, is based on the idea that God's perfect justice demands an atonement for the egregious insult of human sin. Jesus, being sinless, is able to atone

for the sins of humanity in his death, and that forgiveness is then available to any human being who accepts it. The first robust articulation of the penal substitution theory was *Cur Deus Homo?* (Why a God-Man?) by Anselm of Canterbury (1034–1109).

13 See note 12.

14 For Paul's exhortation to the church to be agents of reconciliation in the world, see 2 Corinthians 5:16–21:

> So from now on we regard no one from a worldly point of view. Though we once regarded Christ in this way, we do so no longer. Therefore, if anyone is in Christ, the new creation has come: The old has gone, the new is here! All this is from God, who reconciled us to himself through Christ and gave us the ministry of reconciliation: that God was reconciling the world to himself in Christ, not counting people's sins against them. And he has committed to us the message of reconciliation. We are therefore Christ's ambassadors, as though God were making his appeal through us. We implore you on Christ's behalf: Be reconciled to God. God made him who had no sin to be sin for us, so that in him we might become the righteousness of God.

15 "There are no such rights, and belief in them is one with belief in witches and unicorns. . . . Every attempt to give good reasons for believing that there are such rights has failed." Alasdair MacIntyre, *After Virtue* (Notre Dame, Ind.: University of Notre Dame Press, 1984), p. 69.

16 Walker and Clark, p. 73.

17 Jean Bethke Elshtain, "Christian Contrarian," *Time*, Sept. 17, 2001, http://www.time.com/time/magazine/article/0,9171,1000859,00.html.

18 Jeffrey Stout, *Democracy and Tradition* (Princeton, N.J.: Princeton University, 2004), pp. 183ff.

19 This purloined copy of the memo was leaked to me by an anonymous source. It appears here, unedited, in all its Schrutian glory.

20 Eugene H. Peterson, *The Message: The Bible in Contemporary Language* (Colorado Springs, Colo.: Navpress, 2002), Matthew 18:15–17; italics added.

CHAPTER FOUR: The Theology, Stupid

1 Bill Bright, the founder of Crusade, wrote, "It is our prayerful objective to help take the gospel to over six billion by the year 2000 with at least one billion receiving Christ and one million churches being planted." SeekGod.ca, http://www.seekgod.ca/fuller1.htm#bright.

2 The working assumption among many conservative evangelicals is that Roman Catholics put their faith in the priests and the sacraments, not in Jesus Christ alone. Various permutations of this formula also apply to Orthodox, Anabaptists, and mainline Protestants.

3 See, for instance, R. T. France, *The Gospel of Matthew: New International Commentary on the New Testament* (Grand Rapids, Mich.: Eerdmans, 2007). Robert Gundry refers to Jesus' statements in this passage as "noneschatological characteristics of the church age." See Robert H. Gundy, *Matthew: A Commentary on His Handbook for a Mixed Church Under Persecution* (Grand Rapids, Mich.: Eerdmans, 1994), pp. 479–481.

4 My thanks to Scot McKnight for helping me decipher this passage.

5 For more on this notion, see three works by Alvin Plantinga: *Does God Have a Nature?* (Milwaukee, Minn.: Marquette University Press, 1980), *God, Freedom, and Evil* (New York: HarperCollins, 1974), and *The Nature of Necessity* (Oxford: Clarendon Press, 1974).

6 A local and independent fraternity, Heorot is named after the mead hall in the epic poem *Beowulf*, the spot where warriors gather to drink, carouse, and regale each other with tales of battle.

7 *Unteachable* is a made-up Christian word, and when paired with *spirit* makes for an irrefutable condemnation.

8 The writer is referring to the Sinner's Prayer, also known as the Prayer of Salvation. That's what many evangelicals instruct new believers to pray to inaugurate their personal relationship with Jesus.

9 For more information on this research, see Commission on Children at Risk, *Hardwired to Connect* (New York: Institute for American Values, 2003).

10 Rick Warren, speaking on the *Charlie Rose Show*, Public Broadcasting System, Aug. 17, 2006.

11 1 Corinthians 1:23.

12 Caputo, *Deconstruction in a Nutshell*, p. 31.

13 I am not here espousing a strong version of rational actor theory at the expense of structuralism. In fact, when it comes to an understanding of human activity,

I am drawn to what I consider the postmodern—or "third way"—of Pierre Bourdieu. See, for instance, Pierre Bourdieu, *The Logic of Practice* (Stanford, Calif.: Stanford University Press, 1980).

14 Proverbs 27:17.

15 Acts 17:26.

16 *revolve: The Complete New Testament* (Nashville, Tenn.: Nelson, 2002).

17 Ibid., p. 310.

18 Ibid., p. vii.

19 Linda J. Sattgast, *The Rhyme Bible Storybook* (Grand Rapids, Mich.: Zonderkidz, 2000), pp, 128–130.

20 Joshua 6:20–21 (TNIV).

21 To this end, the philosopher of religion Jeffrey Stout, in *Democracy and Tradition*, p. 269, quotes Ralph Waldo Emerson:

> "Where do we find ourselves?" writes Emerson. "In a series of which we do not know the extremes, and believe that it has none. We wake and find ourselves on a stair; there are stairs below us, which we seem to have ascended; there are stairs above us, many a one, which go upward and out of sight." The stair I am on is higher than the one below me. It affords a better view. This view excels the other. I declare it excellent – but not perfect, for I can imagine a better one. Does this judgment depend, for its objectivity, on whether the uppermost actual stair affords a perfect view? If I cannot yet see to the top, don't I still know what I'm talking about when I assert the excellence of the view I now enjoy?

22 Colossians 3:11.

23 *Egalitarian* and *complementarian* are the current euphemisms in evangelicalism for stances on women's roles. The former accepts women as pastors and leaders, while the latter argues that women "complement" men in subordinate roles.

24 1 Corinthians 11:6.

25 C. S. Lewis, *The Weight of Glory and Other Addresses* (San Francisco: Harper-SanFrancisco, 2001), pp. 84–85. Originally published 1942.

26 Consultation on Common Texts, Revised Common Lectionary (1992).

27 Luke 22:38.

CHAPTER FIVE: After Objectivity: Beautiful Truth

1 Daniel Henderson, "A Life of Lasting Influence: Keys to a Fruitful Life," preached at Grace Church, Eden Prairie, Minnesota, Nov. 5, 2006.

2 Lesslie Newbigin, *Proper Confidence: Faith, Doubt, and Certainty in Christian Discipleship* (Grand Rapids, Mich.: Eerdmans, 1995).

3 Genesis 9:20–27.

4 Today, various scholarly explanations attempt to make sense of the curse of Canaan, the most popular being that that phrase "saw his father's nakedness" is a biblical euphemism for incest, implying that Canaan was the product of Ham's intercourse with his own mother.

5 Let me again emphasize that this is not the case in the academy. Seminaries, divinity schools, and Christian colleges regularly expose their students to these biblical passages. But that practice has not filtered down to the church.

6 We are not the first Christians to confront this unpleasant story. As John Thompson points out in his excellent book, this passage has been troubled over by theological minds from Origen (185–254) to Peter Abelard (1079–1142) to Martin Luther (1483–1546). See John L. Thompson, *Reading the Bible with the Dead: What You Can Learn from the History of Exegesis That You Can't Learn from Exegesis Alone* (Grand Rapids, Mich.: Eerdmans, 2007), pp. 33–47. The most famous modern explication of this story is Phyllis Trible, *Texts of Terror: Literary-Feminist Readings of Biblical Narratives* (Saint Paul, Minn.: Augsburg Fortress, 1984), pp. 93–118. She writes:

> [Here] the savior figure has spoken on his own, for neither Yahweh nor the people of Gilead require the vow.... [He asks] for divine help that ironically is already Jephthah's through the spirit of Yahweh. The making of the vow is an act of unfaithfulness. Jephthah desires to bind God rather than embrace the gift of the spirit. What comes to him freely, he seeks to earn and manipulate. The meaning of his words is doubt, not faith; it is control, not courage. To such a vow the deity makes no reply.... A vow led to victory; victory produced a victim; the victim died by violence; violence has, in turn, fulfilled the vow [pp. 97, 105].

7 That friend is Ivy Beckwith, author of *Postmodern Children's Ministry: Ministry to Children in the 21st Century* (Grand Rapids, Mich.: Zondervan, 2004).

8 My answer is no, I don't think that humans can make deals with God. I came to this conclusion in 1992. I was in graduate school in Southern California, and I took a friend's advice to get my hair cut by a guy who was giving deals. Maybe it was my fourth or fifth time getting my hair cut there when I asked him why he gave such good prices to seminary students. "Well, I've made a deal with God," he told me, scissors in his hand. "If I cut the hair of seminary students for half price, he lets me hate Jews." Needless to say, I never went back.

9 Elie Wiesel, *Night* (New York: Hill and Wang, 2006), p. 65. Originally published 1956. Wiesel also said, "Always question those who are certain of what they are saying."

10 Moltmann, p. 278.

11 In this understanding of the cross, many emergents have been influenced by the writings of the theologians Jürgen Moltmann and Miroslav Volf, as well as many of the liberation theologians of the late twentieth century.

12 Quoted in Nick Paumgarten, "Dept. of Super Slo-Mo: No Flag on the Play," *New Yorker*, Jan. 20, 2003, p. 32.

13 In the entire corpus of the ante-Nicene, Nicene, and post-Nicene church fathers, *truth* with a qualifier ("absolute Truth") occurs only once, in Origen's commentary on Matthew.

14 John Piper, "Putting My Daughter to Bed Two Hours After the Bridge Collapsed," Desiring God, Aug. 1, 2007, http://www.desiringgod.org/Blog/745_putting_my_daughter_to_bed_two_hours_after_the_bridge_collapsed.

15 Barack Obama, "'Call to Renewal' Keynote Address," June 28, 2006, http://obama.senate.gov/speech/060628-call_to_renewal_keynote_address/index.html.

16 John 14:6.

17 *Oxford Dictionary of the Christian Church* (Oxford: Oxford University Press, 1997), p. 1641.

18 Matthew 28:19.

19 Some feminist theologians point out that Wisdom is also personified in the Old Testament, in places like Ecclesiastes 7 and Proverbs 8, as a kind of female deity, leading some to posit a "Quadrinity."

20 Actually, it was used about twenty years earlier by Theophilus of Antioch (who died around 185), but he was referring to "God, his Word, and his Wisdom."

Tertullian was the first to use the Latin term *trinitas* to refer to "the Father, the Son, and the Holy Spirit."

21 Augustine of Hippo, *De Trinitate*, in John Burnaby, ed. and trans., *Augustine: Later Works* (Philadelphia: Westminster Press, 1955), p. 58.

22 John 3:8.

23 F. LeRon Shults, *Reforming the Doctrine of God* (Grand Rapids, Mich.: Eerdmans, 2005), p. 165.

24 John 14:11.

25 Hilary of Poitiers, *On the Trinity*, bk. 3, sec. 1. In Philip Schaff and Henry Wace, *A Select Library of Nicene and Post-Nicene Fathers of the Christian Church: Second Series* (New York: Christian Literature Co., 1899), p. 62.

26 Mark 14:60–62; John 4:25–26.

27 John 10:30, 14:9.

28 By the first one hundred years of the church, I refer to both canonical (Gospel of John, c. A.D. 100) and noncanonical (I Clement, A.D. 96; Ignatius of Antioch, A.D. 113; Shepherd of Hermas, c. A.D. 140) sources. Before 150, there was little debate about the nature of Jesus (as far as we know); the Pauline explanation carried the day.

29 The heirs of this branch of the church are still active, known as the Assyrian Church of the East or the Nestorian Church.

CHAPTER SIX: Inside the Emergent Church

1 Peter Steinfels, "John H. Yoder, Notre Dame Theologian, Is Dead at 70," *New York Times*, Jan. 7, 1998, p. A17.

2 Leon Trotsky, *The Revolution Betrayed*, trans. Max Eastman (New York: Doubleday, 1937), p. 41.

3 As is often the case with Wikipedia, this line was in the article, "Wikipedia," Wikipedia, http://en.wikipedia.org/wiki/Wikipedia#Editing, in June 2007, but two months later, it had been edited out.

4 Jim Giles, "Internet Encyclopedias Go Head to Head," *Nature*, Dec. 14, 2005, http://www.nature.com/news/2005/051212/full/438900a.html.

5 Stanley Fish, *Is There a Text in This Class? The Authority of Interpretive Communities* (Cambridge, Mass.: Harvard University Press, 1980).

6 Max Weber, *Economy and Society* (Berkeley: University of California Press, 1978), pp. 46ff.

7 Your purchase of this book may be a sign of the very routinization that emergents would like to avoid.

8 Willard Van Orman Quine, *From a Logical Point of View* (Cambridge, Mass.: Harvard University Press, 1953), p. 42.

9 In his version of the tale of the elephant, the poet John Godfrey Saxe (1816–1887) concludes:

> So oft in theologic wars,
> The disputants, I ween,
> Rail on in utter ignorance
> Of what each other mean,
> And prate about an Elephant
> Not one of them has seen!

Paul Galdone, *The Blind Men and the Elephant: John Godfrey Saxe's Version of the Famous Indian Legend* (London: Egmont Children's Books, 1979).

10 Gro Harlem Brundtland (ed.), *Our Common Future: The World Commission on Environment and Development* (Oxford: Oxford University Press, 1987), p. 19.

11 Matthew 18:20.

12 In 2006, Journey moved to Northway Baptist Church; in 2007, it moved again.

13 Robert D. Putnam, *Bowling Alone: The Collapse and Revival of American Community* (New York: Simon & Schuster, 2000).

14 Yes, the people at Watermark™ have trademarked their name. Their Web site states that they're concerned that churches in other states might use the name before they have the opportunity to plant a new church there.

15 See Acts 1:4–6.

16 I am, of course, disregarding the televised sermons of the Word of Faith preachers. Their pneumatology (doctrine of the Holy Spirit) is patently unorthodox. The popular multimillionaire preacher-healer Benny Hinn, for instance, has been accused of believing in four persons (the Quadrinity) rather than three, and he's been quoted preaching that the Father is a Trinity within himself and the Holy Spirit is a being with a distinct body and soul from the Father and the Son. Other TV preachers who are negligibly Pentecostal put forth similarly unorthodox teachings on the Spirit.

17 Parker J. Palmer, *Let Your Life Speak: Listening for the Voice of Vocation* (San Francisco: Jossey-Bass, 1999), p. 88.

18 Matthew 21:11–13; Mark 11:11–13; Luke 19:44–46.

19 Driscoll's newspaper column was dropped in 2006 after he implied on his blog that Ted Haggard's wife was somewhat responsible for Haggard's affair with a male prostitute. Driscoll later apologized.

20 "God of Rage" by Corey Carlson. Reprinted by permission of Corey Carlson.

21 See Doug Pagitt and Kathryn Prill, *Body Prayer* (Colorado Springs, Colo.: Waterbrook, 2005).

Epilogue: Feral Christians

1 "Feral Camel," *Farmnote 122/2000* (Perth: Department of Agriculture of Western Australia, 2005), p. 2.

Appendix A: "Emergent Village Values and Practices"

1 Tim Keel, *Intuitive Leadership: Embracing a Paradigm of Narrative, Metaphor, and Chaos* (Grand Rapids, Mich.: Baker, 2007).

Appendix B: "A Response to Our Critics"

1 D. A. Carson, *Becoming Conversant with the Emerging Church: Understanding a Movement and Its Implications* (Grand Rapids, Mich.: Zondervan, 2005).

2 For example, see sidebar comments and multiple perspectives in *The Church in Emerging Culture*, *The Post-Evangelical*, *Postmodern Youth Ministry*, and *The Emerging Church*. We hope that our critics will consider this or similar approaches to encourage and model respectful Christian dialogue.

3 Dr. David Mills, professor at Cedarville College, has responded helpfully to one recent critique. His response is available at http://people.cedarville.edu/employee/millsd/mills_staley_response.pdf.

Appendix C: "Disastrous Statements"

1 LeRon Shults is a professor of theology at Adgar University in Norway, and he previously held that position at Bethel Seminary in St. Paul, Minnesota. He's the author of many books, including *Reforming the Doctrine of God* (Grand Rapids, Mich.: Eerdmans, 2004), and *Transforming Spirituality: Integrating Theology and Psychology*, with Steven J. Sandage (Grand Rapids, Mich.: Baker, 2006).

⤚⫷ ACKNOWLEDGMENTS ⫸⤙

Five midwives share responsibility for helping me birth this book.

The first is my spouse, Julie McMahon Jones. It is not easy to be partnered with someone, like me, who spends much of his time on the road and much of the rest of it locked in a cabin in the north woods. As many authors have said before, without my spouse, this book wouldn't have been written. With utmost sincerity, I echo that claim.

Several years ago, a renowned author told me, "Sheryl Fullerton is the best editor I've ever worked with." That's another claim that I echo. She's tough *and* gentle (like all good midwives), and she cares about her authors. She also exhibits the patience of Job, even on fourth drafts.

The third midwife, Kathy Helmers, has just the right mix of cheeriness and cynicism to be the perfect literary agent. She knows the business, she loves books, and she pastors self-doubting authors. I'm blessed to work with her.

The fourth midwife is Doug Pagitt (that may provoke strange images). Many of the ideas in this book were shaped (and chastened) over 49er Flapjacks and bacon on Monday mornings at the Original Pancake House. I simply could not ask for a better friend.

And the fifth is Brian McLaren, who has been a mentor, pastor, and friend to me over the past decade. His comments on an early draft of this book improved it immeasurably.

Thanks also to my mother, Sarah Jones, who faithfully proofread the manuscript with her keen eye.

The writing of this book has not been a solitary enterprise—I've had myriad phone calls, e-mails, blog comments, Facebook wall posts, and most important, face-to-face conversations over the last ten years, and many of those have shaped me and my ideas. Emergent Village is truly a network of friends—a "growing, generative friendship." And if a person's wealth is measured by his friends, then I am rich indeed. Honestly, the names are too many to mention, but here's an incomplete list: Chad Allen, Time and Cammy Baer, Dean Barnes, Carla and Jim Barnhill, Ivy Beckwith, Paul Bertelson, Nate Bettger, Troy Bronsink, Diana Butler-Bass, Bob Carlton, Brad Cecil, Steve and Eve Clark, Julie and Mike Clawson, Adam Walker Cleaveland, Tim Conder, Kenda Dean, Jan Edmiston, Chris Enstad, Chris Folmsbee, Chaim Goldberger, Jon Good, Julianna Gustafson, Tim and Saranell Hartman, Andrea and Shane Hipps, Andrew and Beth Jones, Danielle Jones, Doug and Sarah Jones, Scott Jones, Kurt Kalland, Tim Keel, Dan Kimball, Mike King, Dixon Kinser, Heather Kirk-Davidoff, Sivin Kit, Steve Knight, Jeff Kursonis, John Kutsko, Shawn Landres, Lilly Lewin, Jeff Lindsay, Charlie McGlynn, Scot and Kris McKnight, Grace McLaren, the entire McMahon Clan, James Mills, Luke Miller, Jason Mitchell, Habeeb Nacol, John Neal, Jim Newberry, Mark Oestreicher, Thom Olson, Rick Osmer, Rich Phenow, John Potts, John Raymond, David Robertson, Andy Root, Sara and Ted Sampsell-Jones, Lisa and Will Samson, Nanette Sawyer, Mark Scandrette, Laci Scott, Chris Seay, Samir Selmanovic, Holly and Ryan Sharp, Dave Sheldon, Danielle Shroyer, Anthony Smith, Paul Soupiset, Mike and Stacy Stavlund, Mark Van Steenwyk, Karen Ward, Brett Watson, and Tim West.

Thanks to all of you who've opened your lives and your emergent faith to me over the past decade. I pray that this book captures, at least in part, what you've been experiencing.

And finally, to Tanner, Lily, and Aidan: my simple prayer is that I will hand on to you a Christian faith that is beautiful.

⪻ THE AUTHOR ⪼

Tony Jones is the national coordinator of Emergent Village (http://www. emergentvillage.org) and among the founders of the emergent Christian movement. A keen observer of the church in postmodern times, he holds degrees from Dartmouth College and Fuller Theological Seminary and is a doctoral fellow and senior research fellow at Princeton Theological Seminary. In addition to his academic specialty in practical theology, he was a pastor for more than ten years and is conducting an in-depth case study of emerging churches around the United States. Tony has written, edited, and coedited many books, including *The Sacred Way: Spiritual Practices for Everyday Life* (2005) and *An Emergent Manifesto of Hope* (2007), and he regularly speaks and lectures around the United States and the world. He lives with his wife, Julie, and three children in Edina, Minnesota, his hometown, where he serves as a volunteer police chaplain and a Cub Scout den leader and is active in the PTA.

You can follow the conversation about this book, correspond with Tony, and see where he's appearing at www.tonyj.net.

◈ INDEX ◈

A

Abigail Church allegory, 31–35
Accountability, and Wikipedia, 185–187
Adolescents, and theology, 107–108
"Aesop's fablization of Bible," 146
Africa, 54
Age, of emergent Christians, 68
Agility, and Wikipedia, 187–188
Albert Molher radio show, 115–116
The Allegory of Peace and War (Rubens),
  105
Alternative Worship (Baker and Gay), 53
alt.worship, 52–54
Amahoro Africa, 54
American Idol (program), 75–76
Anglicanism, 5, 52–53, 134–137
Anselm of Canterbury, 77
Anti-statement of faith, 233–235
Apostle James, 231
Apostle Paul, 166–167, 231
Aquinas, Thomas, 36
Atheism, functional, 202–203
Atonement, doctrine of, 77–78, 116
Augustine of Hippo, 36, 75, 105, 112,
  164–165, 183

B

Baker, J., 52, 53
Barna, G., 6
Barth, C., 117
Baseball, and umpiring, 148–152
Beauty, and truth, 157–162
*Becoming Conversant with the Emerging
  Church* (Carson), 227
Begala, P., 22
Benedictine monastics, 210
"Between Sundays" (blog of R. Floyd),
  17–18
Bible: interpretation of, 123–129,
  140–143, 151–152; and reading
  entirety of, 143–148; selective
  approach to, 130–132; translations of,
  117–122; and Trinity, 164; versions
  of, 91; views of, 43–46, 49–50
Biblical scholarship, 12
Biblicist, definition of, 124
Billy Graham Evangelistic Association, 73
Binitarians, 201–203
Bishop, E., 118–119
Body prayer, 216
Bolger, R., 56

Bonhoeffer, D., 112, 142

Borg, M., 154

Bowling Alone (Putnam), 195

Bright, B., 97

Bronsink, T., 157

The Brothers Karamazov (Dostoyevsky), 105

Bruegemann, W., 40

Brundtland, G. H., 191

Buford, B., 48

Bureaucracy, 9–10, 180, 191–192

C

Calvin, J., 36

Calvinism, 186

Campus Crusade for Christ, 96–104

Canaan, curse of, 143–144

Capitalism, 186

Caputo, J. D., xxi, 38, 41, 110

Caravaggio, M., 159

Carlson, C., 213

Carlson, T., 22

Carlton, B., 189

Carrasco, R., xvii

Carson, D. A., 227

Carville, J., 95

Cecil, B., xvii, 41–43, 44–45, 48, 203

Chalke, S., 77

Christian Booksellers Association, 50

The Christian Century (periodical), 9

Christian Coalition, 82

Christian Right, 82

Christianity: disappointment with, 70–71; and emergent Christianity, 57–59; as exclusive truth, 50; and liberal vs. conservative, 18–21; and paradoxes, 162–169

Christianity Today (periodical), 72–73

Church affiliation, 3, 6–7

Church growth, concept of, 190–191

Church of England. *See* Anglicanism

Church of the Apostles (COTA), 203–208

City of God (Augustine), 105

Cizik, R., 6

Clark, J., 54

Clergy, 204, 209–210

Colbert, S., 22

Collins, S., 53

Complementarianism, 125

Conder, T., xvii, 41

Connectivity, and Wikipedia, 188–190

Conservative Christianity, 18–21

Consumerism, 37, 80

Conversation, 112–113, 141–143, 234–235

Council of Chalcedon, 167–168

Creationism, 124

Critiques, of emergent Christianity, 55–57, 227–232

Cross of Christ, 148

Crossfire (TV program), 22

Crowder, D., 42

Crucifixion, of Jesus Christ, 78–79

Culture, and emergent Christianity, 72–76

D

Dafur, genocide in, 18

Daniel, L., 9–10

Dartmouth College, 96–104

Day, D., 142

Decentralization, 181–182

Deconstruction, 40, 110

Deep ecclesiology, 223–224

Democracy, 80–81, 83

Denominationalism, 6, 8–10

Depression, epidemic of, 17–18

Derrida, J., 35, 40, 41

Descartes, R., 112–113

The Devil Came on Horseback
(film), 18

Dialogue, and emergent Christianity,
141–143, 155–157

Dispensational view, of end-time,
99–100

Dobson, J., 6, 17

Doctrine, emphasis on, 79

Dostoyevsky, F., 105

Driscoll, M., 41–45, 48, 207

E

Eastern Orthodox, 166

Egalitarianism, 125

Eli and Samuel, story of, 157

Emergent Christianity: characteristics of,
68–72, 176; and concept of story,
142–143; critiques of, 55–57; and
culture, 72–76; and decentralization,
181–182; definition of, xix–xx; and
dialogue, 141–143, 155–157; essence
of, 37–40; and friendship, 76–79; and
hierarchy, 180; and humility,
115–122, 139–141; origins of, 41–43;
and politics, 80–84; and seminary,
209–210; theology of, 96, 105,
111–115

Emergent Gathering, 171–172

An Emergent Manifesto of Hope (Pagitt
and Jones), 27

Emergent Village, 27, 222–226

Emergent Village Theological
Conversation, 71

The Emerging Church (Kimball), 59

Emerging Churches (Gibbs and Bolger),
56

Empiricism, 43

End-time, 97–100

England, 52–55

Enlightened mysticism, 43

The Enlightenment, 38, 79

Episcopal Church. *See* Anglicanism

Eschatological hope, 72, 176

Ethnocentrism, 39

Evan Almighty (film), 72–73

Evangelical Protestantism, 11–13, 17

Evangelism, 50, 100–101, 109

Exclusion and Embrace (Volf), 71

F

Faith, vs. reason, 154–155

FaithfulDemocrats.org, 82

Falwell, J., 17, 18

"Feeling of utter dependence," 20

Feral Christians, definition of,
219

Fideism, 154–155

Fish, S., 35, 150, 185

Five Fundamentals, of Christian belief,
12

Floyd, R., 16, 17–18

Foundationalism, 18–21, 103

Four Spiritual Laws tract, 101

Francis of Assisi, 36, 101, 142

Franke, J., 42, 59

Freud, S., 20

Friendship, 76–79, 101

Fuller, C., 12

Functional atheism, 202–203

Fundamentalism, 12–13, 39

G

Gaston Oaks Baptist Church, 192–193

Gay, D., 53

Gay, lesbian, bisexual, transgender (GLBT) community, 69–70, 71, 118

Generous orthodoxy, 223

A Generous Orthodoxy (McLaren), 51

GenXers, 67, 68

George and Henrietta Church allegory, 31–35

Gibbs, E., 56

Gibson, M., 73

Giles, J. L., 26–27

The Giving Tree (Silverstein), 81

Globalization, 39

God: in Bible accounts, 120–122; nature of, 99–100, 148; and Trinity, 163–166; and truth, 152–155. *See also* Jesus of Nazareth

"God of Rage" (Carlson), 213–215

Gornto, S., 193, 195

Gospel, definition of, 35–37, 110

Graham, B., 12

Great Britain, 52–55

Great Commandment, 222

Grenz, S., 42, 59

Group of Twenty, 49

Guinness, O., 57

H

Hauerwas, S., 27, 83

Henderson, D., 61

Henry, C., 12

Heorot House, 101

Hermeneutics, 139–143

Hierarchy, 180, 191–192

Hilary of Poitiers, 166

The Holy Observer (periodical), 25

Holy reading (*lectio divina*), 91

Holy Spirit, belief in, 201–203

Home groups, 6

Homosexuality, 69–70, 71, 118

Hope-filled eschatology, 72, 176

House churches, 6

Humility, 115–122, 139–141

Hunter, T., xvii

I

Incarnation, of Jesus Christ, 161–162

Inclusion, desire for, 71–72

Individual rights, concept of, 80–81

Individualism, 13, 36–37, 166

Infanticide, 147

Infinite regression, 18–21

Internet, 55, 180–192

Interpretation, of Bible, 123–129, 140–143, 151–152

Intuitive Leadership (Keel), 222

Iowa Beef and Pork Company, 13–18

J

Jacob's Well Church, 175–179

Jefferson, T., 80

Jephthah, story of, 144–148

JESUS film, 97, 99

The Jesus God (McKnight), 59

Jesus of Nazareth: cross of, 148; crucifixion of, 78–79; and Evangelicalism, 17; and Holy Spirit, 202; incarnation of, 161–162; in Matthew 24, 97–98; nature of, 166–169; and politics, 83; resurrection of, 124, 154; views of, 12, 35–37, 229; virgin birth of, 160. *See also* God; Trinity

Jews, 79, 155–157

Jones, A., 41, 44, 45–46, 59

"Joshua 1–6: The Walls Fall Down" (rhyme), 120–122

Journey (emergent church), 192–200

Jude 24–25, 217

K

Keel, M., 177

Keel, T., xvii, 41, 157, 176–179, 222

Kimball, D., 42, 59

Kingdom of God, nature of, 114–115

Kit, S., 189

Klem, B., 150

Knight, S., 27

Koukl, G., 114

L

Laity, concept of, 204

Landres, S., 156

Language, view of, 234

The Late Great Planet Earth (Lindsey), 99

Latin America, 54

Lazarus, raising of, 159–160

Leadership Network, 42, 48, 49, 67

Lectio divina (holy reading), 91

Lectionary, in mainline churches, 130–132

Left Behind novels, 99

Left vs. right confrontation, 18–22

Levinas, E., 38

Lewis, C. S., 27, 130

Liberal Christianity, 18–21

Liberal democracy, 80–81

Liberation theology, 53

Lindsay, J., 102

Lindsey, H., 99

Linux Kernel, 181–182

Liturgy, 136, 208

Localness, of theology, 112

Locke, J., 80

Luther, M., 36, 75, 79, 112, 142

Lyotard, F., 38

M

MacIntyre, A., 80

Mainline Protestantism, 7–11

Manning, B., 81

Mars Hill Fellowship, 207

Martin Luther King Day, 24–28

Marx, K., 20

Mathewes-Green, F., 74

The Matrix (film), 58–59

Matthew, Gospel of, 97–98, 164

McClendon, J., 42, 103

McKnight, S., 56, 59

McLaren, B.: books by, 49–51; and origin of emergent Christianity, xvii, xxii, 27, 54, 77; and paradoxes, 168; political writings of, 82; and response to critics, 227

Megachurches, 11, 46–47

Mere Christianity (Lewis), 27

The Message (Peterson translation of Bible), 91

Messiah, Jesus as, 166–167

Messiness, and Wikipedia, 190–192

Michelangelo, 105

Middle Ages, 42

Milton, J., 105

Mission Shaped Church (report to Church of England), 53

Mitchell, J., xvii, 48

Modern era, definition of, 4

Mohler, A., 6

Molher, A., 115–116

Moltmann, J., 38, 147–148

Monastic model, for seminaries, 209–210

Moore, R., 115–116

Moral Majority, 82

Morgenthaler, S., xvii

Murphy, N., 42, 103

Musekura, C., 18

"Mysterious Ways" (song), 105

Mysticism, 42

N

National Association of Evangelicals (NAE), 6

Neff, D., 72–73

New Century Version, of Bible, 118–119

A New Kind of Christian (McLaren), 49–51

Newbigin, L., 141

Nietzsche, F., 2–3, 20

Nine o'Clock Service (NOS), 53

Noah, story of, 143–144

O

Obama, B., 156

Ockenga, H., 12

Open access, and Wikipedia, 182–183

Open-source software, 181–182

Orthodox Christianity, 36

Osteen, J., 73

The Other, definition of, 38

Oxford Dictionary of the Christian Church, 163

P

Pacifism, 130

Pagitt, D., xvii, 41–46, 48, 77

Pagitt, S., 48, 159

Palmer, P., 202–203

Paradise Lost (Milton), 105

Paradoxes, and Christianity, 162–169

The Passion of the Christ (film), 73

Pastors, women as, 123, 125

Patterson, P., 6

Paul, Apostle. See Apostle Paul

Pentecostalism, 5–6

Peterson, E., 91

Pietà (Michelangelo), 105

Pietism, definition of, 198

Piper, J., 155

Plato, and Trinity, 164

Pluralism, 39

Politics, 80–84

Pontius Pilate, 154

The Post-Evangelical (Tomlinson), 117

Postmodernism: definition of, xxii, 35, 38–39, 43; theology of, 102–103; views of, 57

Progressivism, 197–198

"Proper confidence," 141

Protestantism, 5–6, 7–13, 17, 36, 39

Psalm 104:24–35, 130–132

The Purpose-Driven Life (Warren), 37, 50, 73, 108–109

Putnam, R., 195

Q

Quest for the Historical Jesus (Schweitzer), 12

Quine, W.V.O., 188–189

R

The Raising of Lazarus (Caravaggio), 159–160

Rave worship, 52, 53

Reason, faith vs., 154–155

Reconciliation, 76–79

Red Del Camino, 54

Relationality, 46, 56–57, 165–166, 222–226

Relativism, 117–118

Relevant (magazine), 82

Republican Party, 82

Resurrection, of Jesus, 124, 154

revolve: The Complete New Testament, 118–120

The Rhyme Bible Storybook (Sattgast), 120–122

Rice, W., 46

Right vs. left confrontation, 18–22

Robbins, D., 117

Robertson, P., 18

Roman Catholicism, 36, 73

Rorty, R., 41

Rose, C., 108–109

"Routinization of the charisma," 187

Roxburgh, A., xvii

Rubens, P. P., 105

Rule of Saint Benedict, 210

S

Sacred Scripture. *See* Bible

"Sacred-secular divide," 75

Salvation, nature of, 50

Samuel and Eli, story of, 157

Sanger, L., 182

Sattgast, L., 120–122

Scale-free network, 180–181

Scandrette, M., 42

Schleiermacher, F., 20

Schori, K. J., 135

Schuller, R., 109

Schutzwohl, F., 86–92

Schweitzer, A., 12

Science, and truth, 157–159

Scripture. *See* Bible

Seacrest, R., 76

Seay, C., xvii, 42, 43, 44, 46

Second Vatican Council, 73

Secularism, 2–3

Secularization, 39

Seeker-sensitive church movement, 109

Seminary, and emergent Christianity, 209–210

Shroyer, D., xvii, 42, 71–72, 193–200

Shults, L., 59, 165–166, 233–235

Silverstein, S., 81

Simons, M., 36

Slippery slope, concept of, 115–122

Smith, A., 26–28, 49

Sojourners/Call to Renewal, 51, 82, 198

Solomon's Porch, 86, 210–218

Solomon's Temple, 98

Soul Survivor, 54

Southern Baptist Convention (SBC), 5–6

Statement of faith, 233–235

Stations of the Cross, 178–179

Stewart, J., 22

Story, interest in, 142–143

Stout, J., 83

Sustainability movement, 191

Sweet, L., 51, 82

Synagogue 3000, 156

T

"Tall Skinny Kiwi" blogger, 59
Teenagers, and theology, 107–108
Temporality, of theology, 114
Tertullian, and Trinity, 164
Theology: definition of, 104–106; of
    emergent Christians, 96, 105,
    111–115; interest in, 106–110;
    questioning of, 47–48
Thomas Aquinas, 36
Tickle, P., 50, 160
Tikkun (magazine), 82
Tomlinson, D., 117
Torvalds, L., 181–182
Translations, of Bible, 117–122
Trinity, 163–166, 201–203
Trotsky, L., 180
Trucker Frank story, 86–92
Trust, and Wikipedia, 183–185
Truth, 75, 152–155, 157–162, 229
24–7 prayer movement, 54
Tyson Foods, 13–18

U

Uganda, 54
Umpiring, and baseball, 148–152
Underwood, C., 73
United Church of Christ, 6
United Kingdom, 52–55
United Methodist Church, 10–11
Unteachable spirit, 101

V

"Values and Practices," of Emergent
    Village, 222–226
Van Impe, J., 151

Ventura, J. "The Body," 80
Virgin birth of Jesus, 160
Virginia Tech shooting, 17–18
Volf, M., 42, 71, 103, 193
Voters' guide, 80–84

W

Waddington, M., 53
Wales, J., 182, 186
Wallis, J., 51, 198
Ward, K., 41, 203–208
Warren, R., 37, 50, 73, 108–109
Watson, B., 170–172
Weber, M., 186
West, C., 38
Wiesel, E., 147
Wiki, definition of, 182
Wikichurch, 180–192
Wikipedia, 182–191
Williams, R., 53
Women, as pastors, 123, 125
Worldwide Pictures, Inc., 73

Y

Yaconelli, M., 46
Yoder, J. H., 177–178
Young Leaders Network, 48
Young Life, 46
Your Best Life Now (Osteen), 73
Youth for Christ, 46
Youth ministry, 46

Z

Zondervan, 51
Zwingli, U., 36